Theory and Measurement
of
Economic Externalities

ECONOMIC THEORY AND MATHEMATICAL ECONOMICS

Consulting Editor: Karl Shell

UNIVERSITY OF PENNSYLVANIA
PHILADELPHIA, PENNSYLVANIA

Theory and Measurement
of
Economic Externalities

EDITED BY

Steven A. Y. Lin

Department of Economics
Southern Illinois University
Edwardsville, Illinois

ACADEMIC PRESS   New York   San Francisco   London

A Subsidiary of Harcourt Brace Jovanovich, Publishers

ACADEMIC PRESS, INC.
111 Fifth Avenue, New York, New York 10003

United Kingdom Edition published by
ACADEMIC PRESS, INC. (LONDON) LTD.
24/28 Oval Road, London NW1

Library of Congress Cataloging in Publication Data

Main entry under title:

Theory and measurement of economic externalities.

(Economic theory and mathematical economics)
"This volume is the direct result of a conference
on externalities held at Southern Illinois Univer-
sity at Edwardsville, April 19–20, 1974."
Includes bibliographies and index.
1.   Externalities (Economics)–Congresses.
I.   Lin, Steven A. Y.,   Date   II.   Southern
Illinois University, Edwardsville.
HB199.T48   1976   330'.01   75-32030
ISBN 0–12–450450–7

Contents

List of Contributors

Numbers in parentheses indicate the pages on which the authors' contributions begin.

Gerald E. Auten (37), Department of Economics, University of Missouri, Columbia, Missouri

Theodore C. Bergstrom (111), Department of Economics, The University of Michigan, Ann Arbor, Michigan

David F. Bradford (201), Department of Economics, Princeton University, Princeton, New Jersey

Charles J. Cicchetti (183), Department of Economics and Environmental Studies, University of Wisconsin, Madison, Wisconsin

Arthur S. De Vany (205), Department of Economics, Texas A & M University, College Station, Texas

Theodore Groves (65), Graduate School of Management, Nathaniel Leverone Hall, Northwestern University, Evanston, Illinois

Donald R. Haurin (217), Department of Economics, Ohio State University, Columbus, Ohio

David F. Heathfield (215), University of Southampton, England, and Department of Economics, Washington University, St. Louis, Missouri

Walter P. Heller (9), Department of Economics, University of California at San Diego, La Jolla, California

Arye Leo Hillman (103), Department of Economics, Tel-Aviv University, Ramat-Aviv, Tel-Aviv, Israel

John O. Ledyard (23), Department of Economics, Northwestern University, Evanston, Illinois

Steven A. Y. Lin (45), Department of Economics, Southern Illinois University, Edwardsville, Illinois

James T. Little (61,85), Department of Economics, Washington University, St. Louis, Missouri

Edna T. Loehman (87), Department of Food and Resource Economics, University of Florida, Gainesville, Florida

Hugh O. Nourse (243), Department of Economics, University of Missouri, St. Louis, Missouri

J. Trout Rader, III (135), Department of Economics, Washington University, St. Louis, Missouri

Robert W. Rosenthal (177), Department of Industrial Engineering and Management Science, Northwestern University, Evanston, Illinois

Lloyd S. Shapley (155), The Rand Corporation, Santa Monica, California

V. Kerry Smith (183), Department of Economics, State University of New York, Binghamton, New York

Charles G. Stalon (259), Department of Economics, Southern Illinois University, Carbondale, Illinois

David A. Starrett (9,133,153), Department of Economics, Stanford University, Palo Alto, California

Ephraim F. Sudit (247), Trust Division, The Chase Manhattan Bank, New York, New York

George S. Tolley (217), Department of Economics, University of Chicago, Chicago, Illinois

Andrew B. Whinston (87), Graduate School of Industrial Administration, Purdue University, West Lafayette, Indiana

David K. Whitcomb (45), Graduate School of Business Administration, Rutgers University, New Brunswick, New Jersey, and Salomon Brothers Center for the Study of Financial Institutions, New York University, New York

Richard O. Zerbe (29), Program in the Social Management of Technology and Department of Economics, The University of Washington, Seattle, Washington, and Department of Economics, Northwestern University, Evanston, Illinois

Preface

Externalities (or sometimes, "third-party effects" or "spillover effects") arise whenever the value of a production function or a consumption function depends directly upon the activity of others. Interest in this notion of externality as a phenomenon in the context of partial equilibrium analysis has grown steadily and picked up momentum in the postwar period; many economists will now agree that externalities should be a new field of specialization within the broader terrain of welfare economics.

Despite its popularity, the field of externalities remains one of the relatively underdeveloped areas of economics, an exception to "the principles" of price and welfare theory rather than a part of them. Clearly, it would be desirable to integrate externalities into the core of modern economic theory, and this volume is but one of the major efforts in this direction.

Basically, economists are serving the function of turning out consumers' goods in the form of applications of existing knowledge to current problems, and of turning out producers' goods in the form of better knowledge, analytical formulations, and approaches for application to current problems. The latter function is stressed in this book. The objective of the book is to provide cross references and opportunity for give-and-take discussion on some recent analytical and empirical developments in the field of externalities.

This volume is the direct result of a Conference on Externalities held at Southern Illinois University at Edwardsville, April 19–20, 1974. Support for the conference was provided by the University's School of Business.

A large number of people cooperated to make the conference and this book possible. I would especially like to thank Professors Paul Sultan, William Vickrey, Louis Drake, and Trout Rader for chairing the four sessions, and Professors Ted Bergstrom and J. F. Schwier for their editorial advice. Dean Paul Sultan's interest and encouragement is also greatly appreciated. In addition, I would like to thank Ms. Mary Lelik for her excellent typing. My greatest debt is to all the conference participants, especially those contributing to this volume. Frankly, I had not foreseen the depth of their cooperative spirit and patience. The participants' experience, good judgement, and friendliness made it all possible.

I

Introduction

Generally, effects on persons not directly privy to the decision leading to an activity are termed *externalities* or *third-party effects* (or sometimes "spillover effects"). Externalities arise whenever the value of an objective function, for example the profits of a firm or the happiness of an individual, depends upon the unintended or incidental by-products of some activity of others (Bergstrom [2, 3], Buchanan and Stubblebine [5], Cheung [6], Coase [7], Demsetz [9, 10], Freeman *et al.* [12], Mishan [15], Starrett [19]). For instance, when a paper mill produces pulp for newsprint, more people are affected than its suppliers, employees, and customers. Its emissions into the air may annoy people who live nearby and may make nearby resort areas less attractive thus reducing tourist revenues which local motel operators and boat renters can expect; its effluent discharged into the water may hurt the fishing, and thus fishermen who ply the waters in the vicinity. All these are examples of external diseconomies; but, of course, there are external *economies* as well.

The notion of externalities is especially interesting in connection with analyses of economic welfare. When externalities exist, benefits or costs seen by private individuals differ from the true social cost consequences of their actions. Consequently, decentralized decision making and Lerner's "rule" may fail, in the

1

presence of externalities, to produce an optimal allocation of resources for the society.

In Pigou's celebrated *Economics of Welfare* [17], externalities appear as one of the chief causes of divergence between "private net product" and "social net product." Pigou's welfare criterion is that the national dividend will be maximized when the values of marginal social net products are equal in all uses. That criterion is met if marginal social net products and marginal private net products are the same because the values of marginal private net products are equal in all uses and the values of marginal social net products are computed without regard to whom they accrue.

Pigou recognized that marginal social and marginal private products may diverge even under perfect competition. He mentioned two cases. In the first case, there are uncompensated services or disservices to the general public arising from the production of a good or service. In the second, a competitive industry has an increasing or decreasing long-run supply price as industry output increases. Pigou, of course, was also aware of the inconsistency between increasing returns to a firm and competitive equilibrium.

When the "new welfare economics" appeared in the early 1940s utilizing Pareto optimality (Pareto [16]) as the strongest welfare criterion, externalities were also shown to lead in an otherwise perfectly competitive system to an equilibrium that violated the conditions of Pareto optimality. Rigorous proof of this is to be found in such standard price theory texts as Henderson and Quandt [13].

What, if anything, can be done about the welfare effects of externalities? Pigou believed that he could see a modified invisible hand: a system of taxes and bounties. He was convinced that a *determinate* scheme of taxes and bounties exists that would equate marginal social and private products and, hence, that would induce profit maximizing firms which are generating externalities to move to the ideal output level; that is, the one at which the national dividend is maximized. However, he was unable to specify the means by which such taxes and bounties could be computed.

Recently, a rather different school of thought has emerged. It is primarily concerned with ways of achieving optimal allocation under externalities. The prescriptions of this school contrast with centralized tax and bounty schemes, and it may be classified under the general heading of decentralized approaches to the externality problem. One wing of this school is the "private bargaining approach" advanced by Coase [7] and endorsed by Buchanan [4]. Because, as Coase pointed out, the socially optimal outputs are those that maximize the combined profits of the firms affected by externalities, this approach holds that the firms themselves have incentive to agree to produce the optimal outputs, kinds and quantities of commodities, and then distribute the total profit such that each firm's profit is greater than, or equal to, the profit that it could earn by maximizing profit individually without bargaining. Thus, state intervention by means of taxes and subsidies is not always needed in order to achieve a social optimum.

Relative legal rights are of more than incidental concern in considerations of the achievement of an accommodation among the parties whose objective functions are involved in an externality. Neither property nor personal rights are always clear and negotiation often is difficult. Of course, the legal rights of the affected parties may be defined or clarified by the legislature or by the courts, thereby enabling the parties to negotiate a settlement of their own differences and, presumably, a solution of the social optimization problem more readily. Furthermore, a "merger" is often an alternative. For example, suppose the occupants of a boarding house next door bother us with loud noises. We may "merge" by buying the house next door, thus "internalizing" the externality because the newly formed "organization" would take all costs into account. But merger is not always an option. No single party owns a river, or, as a practical matter, can acquire all the property rights by buying the land on both sides of a river. Thus factories as well as fishermen and others may seek to use the river and exercise the rights to its use; and the fishermen, and the others, may have difficulties merging with the factories. In addition, the transaction costs of bargaining can be very great and information about other peoples' preferences is quite difficult to obtain, hence very costly. This would be the case when the parties are so numerous that there is no way that they can sit down and talk with one another — for example, a great number of people using contaminated water from a certain river.

Coase has also brought to the analysis of externalities an emphasis on opportunity costs which prevail in price theory. In addition to considering the social product of the firms as the amount of the externality varies, he insists that we must also take into account the social product that would be forthcoming if some of the firms move into another line of business. In particular, in Pigou's example of the damage done to crops by the sparks from a passing train, the unavoidable damage will *not* be the total value of the crops destroyed — *if* the farmer can grow crops elsewhere or switch to a strain of spark-resistant crops (Coase [7], Mishan [15]).

Coase argued that once property rights were clearly defined it was in the interests of the rancher and of the farmer whose crops were being damaged by roaming cattle to negotiate a solution. It can be pointed out, of course, that such would be true even if the property rights were not clearly defined. Indeed, the *less* clear the relative rights, the better it may be for the farmer to negotiate an agreement that settles the question.

However, even if property rights are well enough defined that an agreement might be negotiated, motivation may remain for defections from the agreement by the parties unless some clear responsibility for harm can be invoked to discipline the decision makers. Consider an example of competitive landlords who are deciding whether to invest in improvements in their properties. Davis and Whinston [8] made a plausible case in which two property owners may be led to allow their properties to deteriorate, thus contributing to urban blight.

But Coase also argued that an optimal allocation of resources results from negotiation whether or not the malfeasor (damage creator) is liable for the damages caused — at least as long as transaction costs are zero. Apparently, Dolbear has conceded this as far as externalities on producers are concerned; but, in what he regards as a consumer case, he has concluded that the "amount of externality which will tend to emerge depends on the extent of legal responsibility" [11].

All of that is part and parcel of an issue that concerns the status quo (starting point): the initial "extent" of externality and relative legal rights. Here, a difficulty in reaching socially optimal solutions by bargaining where externalities exist can be traced to the fact that a party may choose some particular status quo which he deems to be to his advantage in his effort to negotiate an agreement with other parties, or to achieve certain legal rights in the courts or the legislature. For example, if the degree of pollution caused by a paper mill will affect the ultimate outcome of the bargaining, the paper mill owner may prefer to begin at a very high level of pollution in order to make his "concessions" appear greater than if he started with a lower level of pollution. In the dynamic context of the bargaining, the paper mill owner is in somewhat the same position as a monopolist who must estimate the possible effect of his initial position, "status quo point," on the ultimate outcome of the bargaining. Thus, a choice of the extent of the externality as a bargaining strategy may lead to different negotiated settlements, hence to a different distribution of incomes and different solutions of the allocation problem — even different efficient solutions — rather than the unique solution.

Governmentally imposed tax or subsidy schemes may be useful for achieving efficient resource allocation, especially where decentralized bargaining is expensive or impossible. There are some difficult problems involved in the imposition of such schemes. The income redistribution effects, for example, could make such schemes politically more unpopular than the bargaining approach. In addition, we may not be able to obtain an efficient tax—subsidy solution because we do not know enough about individuals' preferences. Other difficulties are discussed by Arrow [1], Buchanan and Stubblebine [5], Davis and Whinston [8], Dolbear [11], Kneese [14], Rothenberg [18], and Walters [20]. Nevertheless, approximately ideal taxes or subsidies, occasionally readjusted, may accomplish a great deal in controlling pollution and other external effects. There are several other methods proposed for correcting outputs for external diseconomies. For example, outright prohibition, regulation, and auctions of rights to pollute have received attention.

Papers at the conference dealt with the nature of externalities and alternative resource allocation schemes under collective and decentralized circumstances — those by Heller and Starrett, Groves, Loehman and Whinston, Lin and Whitcomb, and Zerbe. In those papers, a considerable amount of attention was directed to a variety of schemes utilizing levies and bounties as means of achieving efficient resource allocation in the presence of externalities. This may be centrally (government) administered or nongovernmentally (trade association) administered. Much attention was also directed to the problem of securing truthful information from consumers and firms concerning their preferences and profits. However, discussions were not confined to analyses within the partial equilibrium framework as is usually the case in the consideration of externalities. For example, the general equilibrium approach is utilized by Bergstrom, Rader, and Shapley.

Finally, there are the very difficult problems of measurement of external effects which were discussed in detail at the conference. In particular, Cicchetti and Smith presented a general method of accommodating and measuring congestion costs related to quality deterioration in wilderness recreation; DeVany proposed a means of measuring the reaction of individuals to airport noise; Haurin and Tolley discussed the fiscal externalities and welfare costs in a city—suburban model; and Sudit and Whitcomb presented a general framework for the estimation of externality production functions.

The book is divided into four sections: the nature of externalities, externalities in collective and decentralized decision making, externalities in general equilibrium, and measurements of externalities. The logic of this arrangement will be amplified in the introductory synopses provided for each section.

REFERENCES

1. Arrow, K. J., "Political and Economic Evaluation of Social Effects and Externalities," in M. D. Intriligator, ed., *Frontiers of Quantitative Economics*, Amsterdam: North-Holland Publ., 1971, 3–25.
2. Bergstrom, T., "The Use of Markets to Control Pollution," *Recherches Economique de Louvain*, December 1973.
3. Bergstrom, T., "Regulation of Externalities," *Journal of Public Economics*, forthcoming.
4. Buchanan, J., "Joint Supply, Externality and Optimality," *Economica*, N.S., November 1966, 33, 404–415
5. Buchanan, J., and C. Stubblebine, "Externality," *Economica*, N.S., November 1962, 29, 371–384.
6. Cheung, S., "Transaction Costs, Risk Aversion and the Choice of Contractual Arrangements," *Journal of Law and Economics*, April 1969, 12, 23–42.
7. Coase, R., "The Problem of Social Cost," *Journal of Law and Economics*, October 1960, 3, 1–44.

8. Davis, O. A., and A. B. Whinston, "Externalities, Welfare and the Theory of Games," *Journal of Political Economy*, June 1962, 70, 241–262.
9. Demsetz, H., "The Exchange and Enforcement of Property Rights," *Journal of Law and Economics*, October 1964, 7, 11–26.
10. Demsetz, H., "Some Aspects of Property Rights," *Journal of Law and Economics*, October 1966, 9, 61–70.
11. Dolbear, F. T., Jr., "On the Theory of Optimal Externality," *American Economic Review*, March 1967, 57, 90–103.
12. Freeman, A. M., III, R. H. Haveman, and A. V. Kneese, *The Economics of Environmental Policy*, New York: Wiley. 1973.
13. Henderson J. M., and R. E. Quandt, *Micro-economic Theory – A Mathematical Approach*, New York: McGraw-Hill, 1958.
14. Kneese, A. V., *The Economics of Regional Water Quality Management*, Baltimore, Maryland: Johns Hopkins Univ. Press, 1964.
15. Mishan. E. J., "Reflections on Recent Developments in the Concept of External Effects," *Canadian Journal of Political Economy*, February 1965, 31, 3–34.
16. Pareto, V., *Manual of Political Economy*, English translation by Ann S. Schwier, New York: Kelley, 1971.
17. Pigou, A. C., *The Economics of Welfare*, 4th ed., New York: Macmillan, 1932, reprinted 1952.
18. Rothenberg, J., "The Economics of Congestion and Pollution: An Integrated Essay," *American Economic Review*, May 1970, 60, 114–121.
19. Starrett, D., "Fundamental Nonconvexities in the Theory of Externalities," *Journal of Economic Theory*, April 1972, 4, 180–199.
20. Walters, A. A., *The Economics of Road User Charges*, Baltimore, Maryland: Johns Hopkins Univ. Press, 1968.

II

The Nature
of Externalities

An externality is frequently defined to occur whenever a decision variable of one economic agent enters into the production or utility function of some other agent. Heller and Starrett argue that this is not a very useful definition, at least until the institutional framework is given. They define an externality to occur whenever the private economy does not offer sufficient incentives to create a potential market. They argue that their definition is not only general enough to include both pecuniary and nonpecuniary externalities, but also provides a key to determining what types of economic situations are likely to lead to externalities. They demonstrate that one can identify roughly that nonpecuniary externalities occur in situations where it is either costly or impossible to define private property, whereas pecuniary externalities occur when setup costs rule out the operation of competitive market.

Heller and Starrett also discuss the relationship between publicness and external diseconomies when either production or consumption or decision sets are nonconvex due to a high degree of externalities. If one considers solving the "public externality" problem by excluding at a cost, the problem reduces to one of handling nonconvexities in the transactions technologies (which they have identified with pecuniary externalities). Public externalities and returns to scale are also discussed.

7

In discussing various ways of correcting for externalities, they stress the importance of institutional costs in determining the optimal public policy. For example, if a piece of land is treated as a common, it is generally believed that it will be overgrazed in the absence of any interference. Two possible remedies are proposed. One involves assigning private property rights on the common, while the other involves taxing users at the rate of the marginal congestion damages caused by their sheep. Aside from institutional costs (such as fences or tax administrators' salaries) it turns out that either of these schemes will work. Which scheme is to be preferred will depend entirely on the relative administration costs.

Zerbe reconsiders the "Coase theorem," the optimal liability rule, and transactions costs and the incidence of the law. He argues that the greatest mischief has been the adoption by some of the view that Coase was advocating bargaining as a universal solution to externality problems. The Coase theorem strictly applies only to a zero transactions cost world of perfect competition.

More clearly defined property rights and other legal rules, taxes, administrative systems, and bargaining narrowly conceived are legitimate tools for correcting externalities. Which of these solutions or combination of solutions are relevant depends on the circumstances. In an important sense the question of which legal and administrative structures are most appropriate depends on transaction costs. The contribution of the Coase article, according to Zerbe, is that it highlights the importance of transactions costs in a bargaining context, in a market context, and in a political and legal context.

On the Nature
of Externalities

WALTER P. HELLER

University of California, San Diego
La Jolla

DAVID A. STARRETT

Stanford University

I. INTRODUCTION

Although the literature on externalities is voluminous,[1] much of the underpinnings of the subject have never been written down in a systematic way. Probably this is because those working in the subject feel that the foundations are "well known" and thus not worth further exposition. Thus, a proposition such as "all externalities are in the nature of public goods or bads" is commonly accepted, occasionally argued in vague terms, but never rigorously justified. In this paper, we propose to explore the nature of externalities from a rigorous, analytic viewpoint. Part of the result is simply a justification of commonly held beliefs, but we believe that we can also provide some additional insights into when the problems are likely to arise, and what remedies are most likely to work.

An externality is frequently defined to occur whenever a decision variable of

The authors would like to thank K. J. Arrow for helpful discussions. The research for this paper was supported in part by National Science Foundation Grants GS-33958 and GS-40104 at the Institute for Mathematical Studies in the Social Sciences, Stanford University and by NSF GS-41494.

[1] For a good survey and excellent bibliography, see Mishan [1].

one economic agent enters into the utility function (or production function) of some other agent. We shall argue first that this is not a very useful definition, at least until the institutional framework is given.[2]

Suppose, for example, that we are in a barter economy in which no prices are ever quoted. Then, if I am trading with you, my welfare is going to depend on how much you are willing to give up in exchange. Hence, by the above definition, there is an externality; yet we would not ordinarily think of this as an externality-producing situation.

Of course, the introduction of competitive markets eliminates the externality. Indeed, one of the prime attributes of the market system is that it isolates one individual from the influence of others' behavior (assuming, of course, that prices are taken by everyone as given). Hence, perhaps we should modify our definition to encompass only situations in which interdependences exist *even* in the framework of the market system.

But then it should be clear that the definition of externalities will depend on which markets exist. At one extreme is the barter situation in which everything is an "externality." At the other extreme is the situation discussed by Arrow [1]. He shows that for any situation in which externalities appear to occur, there exists a sufficiently rich set of markets so that the externalities are "eliminated." The idea is roughly that of Meade [10] who set up a market for "nectar" to solve the bees and honey problem; in the general case, one needs a market for each external effect.[3]

Viewed in this light, one can think of externalities as nearly synonymous with nonexistence of markets. We define an externality to be a situation in which the private economy lacks sufficient incentives to create a potential market in some good and the nonexistence of this market results in losses in Pareto efficiency. It is general enough to include both pecuniary and nonpecuniary externalities (more on this later), and it provides a key to determining what types of economic situations are likely to lead to externalities.

We shall argue (roughly) that situations usually identified with "externality" have more fundamental explanations in terms of (1) difficulties in defining private property, (2) noncompetitive behavior, (3) absence of relevant economic information, or (4) nonconvexities in transactions sets.

II. EXTERNALITY AS ABSENCE OF MARKETS

When are there appropriate incentives for private markets? We shall explore this question with an example. Suppose that individuals consume commodities and absorb garbage. We let c^i be a vector of consumption of goods by i and

---

[2] This point was certainly recognized implicitly at least as early as Scitovsky [13].

[3] See Starrett [15] for a rigorous formulation of the Arrow model.

$(z^i, z_g{}^i)$ his exogenous holdings of goods and garbage respectively. At the outset, we assume that there are competitive markets for goods, but no market (or other institutional arrangements) for garbage. In the absence of such arrangements, individuals dump their garbage on each other; let $d_j{}^i$ stand for the garbage dumped by j on i. In this situation, i's utility function will take the form

$$U^i = U^i(c^i, d_1{}^i, \ldots, d_n{}^i).$$

Given prices p in the existing markets, individual i faces the problem

$$\max_{c^i, d^i} U^i(c^i, d^i) \qquad \text{subject to} \qquad p \cdot c^i \leqslant p \cdot z^i.$$

Clearly there are externalities relative to that set of markets. On the other hand, if one establishes a property right (effectively forcing each person to be responsible for his own garbage) and sets up a market for garbage, the externality disappears: letting p_g be the price of garbage, and g^i the net amount sold by i, i's problem may now be stated as

$$\max_{c^i, c_g{}^i} U^i(c^i, c_g{}^i) \qquad \text{subject to} \qquad p \cdot c^i + p_g \cdot c_g{}^i \leqslant p \cdot z^i + p_g \cdot z_g{}^i.$$

where $c_g{}^i = z_g{}^i - g^i$.

Except for the fact that the price of garbage will be negative, the model is classical in form and there are no externalities. Will the market for garbage be set up? We argue that *if the first market equilibrium is inefficient*, then there is surely a private incentive to operate the garbage market. If there is inefficiency in the initial equilibrium, then there must be a man somewhere who would pay s (in terms of some numeraire) to get rid of a unit of garbage and another who would absorb a unit of garbage upon payment of t, where $t < s$. Hence, the potential marketeer could expect to collect some part of the difference $s - t$ from them for the transaction service he provides.

Several things may go wrong with this story. First, it may be too expensive to run this market; specifically, the cost of making transactions may exceed $s - t$. If this is true, no garbage is exchanged and the market is inactive. In this situation, everybody *must* be absorbing his own garbage, and there appears to be no externality. Furthermore, as long as the transactions technology is convex, Foley [6] has shown that there is no market failure[4] either; the easiest way to see this is to think of the transactions technology as a way of producing retail goods from wholesale. Then the model is completely classical in form, so the competitive outcome when there are convex transaction costs will be efficient relative to that transaction technology.

On the other hand, we know that transactions technologies tend to involve substantial setup costs, and therefore are not convex. If transactions costs are

---

[4] Market failure in the sense of a failure to attain efficiency, rather than nonexistence of markets.

purely setup, then competitive operation of the market is impossible since the competitive manager is certain to lose money. However, it is easy to give examples (we give one later) in which it is desirable to subsidize the market. So in the absence of government intervention, there can be market failure even when it is possible to set up a property right and the implied market is inactive. We shall return to an analysis of nonconvexity as a cause of market failure below.

Of course, there are other classical reasons why the garbage market could fail to work properly. Perhaps there is no one well enough informed to realize that a profit potential exists. Or the market may be operated in a noncompetitive way. We shall comment later on whether or not these types of market failure should be called "externality."

The other thing that can go wrong with our example above is that we could have difficulty defining the property right that is a precondition for a market. Of course, there is also the problem of enforcing the property right, but this is true in any market; if there were no sanctions against theft, the market system would clearly break down immediately.[5] "Externality-producing" situations may involve particularly severe enforcement problems, but this is an issue of degree and not of kind.

The property right will be difficult to define whenever exclusion is costly or impossible, that is whenever there is no "commodity" that is being traded in such a way that whatever you get, I do not get. Such exclusion is certainly costly in situations where there is air, water, or noise pollution or congestion. Exclusion in the above sense is impossible by definition when we are dealing with commodities such as national defense, open rangeland, or public parks.[6]

Whenever exclusion is undesirable, we clearly should not establish a market by assigning property rights to any physical commodity. We defer for the moment the question of whether this vitiates the possibility of private operation of externality markets as, for example, by having everyone contract for all of a public good. First, we would like to forge a stronger link between the concepts of "nonpecuniary externality" and "public good or bad."

III. PUBLICNESS OF EXTERNAL DISECONOMIES

We can make a strong argument that all diseconomies must be inherently public in nature. The argument derives from the "fundamental nonconvexity" discussed in Starrett [15]. As in that paper, we discuss first the case of production externalities.

---

[5] For detailed discussion of the property right issue, see Demsetz [5] or Furubotn and Pejovich [8].

[6] The relevance of exclusion in the theory of externalities has been explored by many authors, among them Davis and Whinston [4] and Turvey [17].

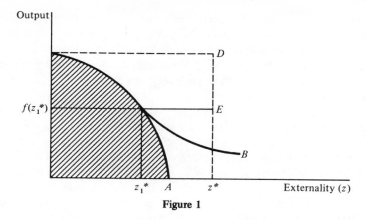

Figure 1

Briefly, the nonconvexity can be explained as follows: the presence of an external diseconomy in production (as, for example, air pollution affecting worker productivity) must mean that if all inputs of the firm are held at fixed levels, then increases in the level of the externality must cause output to fall. Thus, the corresponding section of the production set looks as shown in Figure 1. Two cases are possible. Either output is eventually forced to zero (A), or it remains forever above zero (B). In either case, the production surface exhibits a nonconvexity since output cannot be forced below zero, while the externality can (in principle) be increased without bound.

Such a nonconvexity must naturally imply that the production set violates one of the more primitive postulates: additivity or divisibility. Which of our primitive economic postulates is violated? It may be possible in some cases to argue that both are violated, but it is always possible to argue that at least one is violated.

Suppose that we try to accept divisibility, so in particular the external variable z is divisible. Now, let the firm divide z^* into two equal parts ($z_1{}^*$ and $z^* - z_1{}^*$). If additivity holds, the firm should be able to run two separate operations, one using the other's inputs to produce $f(z_1{}^*)$, and the other using no other inputs and producing nothing. Adding the two activities together, we wind up at the point E. But if there is a real diseconomy, points like E cannot be possible, so one of the postulates must fail. Actually, if the postulates held, the firm could do better than E. By dividing z^* into one very large part with which it puts no complementary inputs and one small part that it uses with its essential operations, the point D can be approached; clearly the apparent nonconvexity vanishes, as would the apparent externality.

The breakdown of primitive postulates can be interpreted in this situation to mean that it is impossible to exclude (without cost) z^* from any part of your operations since to do so would imply the feasibility of points like D. It is but a short step from here to argue that z must have the property of a public bad. For it makes no sense to say that some firms can costlessly exclude while others cannot (of course, some firms may be unaffected by z, but that is beside the point). In the standard theory of economic equilibrium, there is nothing to prevent firms from diversifying. So if firms with label A can costlessly exclude while firms of type B cannot, the externality can be avoided by having firms of type A move into type B operations.

Of course, not all firms face the same z since z may vary with location, for example. Indeed, a firm may avoid the pollution by moving far enough away; but then it is not the same firm since it will incur transport costs that it did not incur before. Location is a defining characteristic of the firm all too frequently ignored. The above statements should be modified to read that firms at the same general location cannot costlessly exclude. If it were possible for any firm to exclude, then it would be desirable for all other firms to be transformed immediately into inessential "garbage absorbing" operations, so as to effectively eliminate the externality.

IV. EXCLUSION AT A COST

Naturally, none of this is to argue that all external diseconomies are pure public bads: exclusion may be possible at a cost. For example, in the air pollution case, one could exclude (at admittedly a prohibitive cost) by erecting barriers around individual pieces of property. One could effectively exclude from buildings by air conditioning (again at a cost). In Coase's [2] example of the farmer and the cowman, one can exclude cows from farmland by building fences. For the case of congestion, one needs a system for monitoring the use of particular lanes at particular times of day with sanctions against those who use them without the "permission" of the owner of the property right.

The costs of exclusion should be thought of as fixed costs associated with setting up a market for private property. Viewed in this way, we can see the reasons for nonexistence of an externality market become blurred. If we consider solving the public externality problem by excluding at a cost, the problem reduces to one of handling nonconvexities in the transactions technologies. On the other hand, if we fail to exclude so that there is no market for private property, active or inactive, then we have a public externality.

Since there are setup costs associated with establishing all types of markets, we can argue that the problem of whether to exclude is no different in principle from the problem of whether or not to set up any given market. However, there are certainly differences in degree. Ordinarily we argue (implicitly at least) that the setup costs of operating a market are so small relative to the overall surplus to be gained from its use that the costs are surely justified. But in general, naturally, we cannot determine the socially optimal policy without a comparison of costs with total surplus generated. And, certainly for the case of erecting air pollution barriers, the costs would not be justified. Other cases are less obvious.

For example, in the farmer and cowman example it is certainly possible to exclude by building fences and establishing private property; a market for grazing rights will then be expected to emerge. There now appear to be no externalities, and the problem is "solved." However, suppose that there is a collection of small farmers scattered throughout otherwise open rangeland. Then it is quite possible that the costs of fence building are not justified by the social benefits to be derived. In that case, it is simply not desirable to exclude and set up private property rights. Chances are that the likely outcome will and should be that farmers find their operations unprofitable and the land becomes open rangeland. And, this is not the outcome that will arise if we subsidize fence building.

The problem, in a broader perspective, is one of choosing an optimal set of institutions. Since institutions are inherently indivisible, marginal analysis will not work; this leaves us with a difficult cost—benefit problem. Furthermore, we cannot argue that the nonconvexities are small relative to the size of the market (so as to make use of the results of Starr [14] and Heller [9]) since the nonconvexities are associated with the market itself. We shall return to the choice-of-institutions problem in the section on remedies.

One further point should be made here. Sometimes it may be possible to exclude and assign property rights, but still undesirable because it changes the nature of the commodity. For example, it would be possible to divide national parkland up into private plots, but clearly what is left is not the same commodity as "open parkland." Similarly, we could provide each person in a country with his own personal protection, but this is not at all the same thing as national defense. In these cases, the commodity in question is by its very nature public, and we have no choice of how to consider it.

The logical link between nonpecuniary diseconomies and publicness is not as strong for the case of consumption externalities. We can still argue that a diseconomy implies a nonconvexity in consumer indifference surfaces, as long as the consumer has some option for escaping the diseconomy at some finite sacrifice (as, for example, by moving away from or ceasing to swim in a polluted lake).[7] However, since households are inherently indivisible (and therefore cannot costlessly divide themselves into various independent lives), the arguments generated above break down. On the other hand, most externalities in consumption seem to generate externalities in production since consumers work in firms. And it is hard to see how an externality that is public to firms could fail to be public to households.

The only possible private consumption externalities will be those that can

[7] See Starrett and Zeckhauser [16] for a general discussion of this point.

(and are) avoided in production. The best example that we can think of involves personal jealousies: one person may dislike another because of a personality clash. This will be a perfectly private externality involving only the two of them. But this externality is completely avoidable in production since if having the two of them working together would lower productivity over what it otherwise would have been, efficient worker allocation will adjust so that they do not work together. Most consumption externalities (such as pollution and congestion) are unavoidable in production and therefore public in nature.

V. PECUNIARY EXTERNALITIES

We ask now whether there are instances of "externality" that cannot be fit into the framework developed above. Most potential examples in the literature fall under the rubric of "pecuniary externalities."

Pecuniary externalities were first discussed by Marshall and were named by Viner. *Pecuniary* is supposed to convey the idea that the externality occurs via the market mechanism insofar as the actions of one agent affect the prices faced by another agent. This, of course, brings to mind oligopoly rather than externality. We all know about the market failure brought on by noncompetitive behavior. The question is, Are there instances in which agents take price as given (competitive behavior) and yet there is market failure due to unforseen interdependencies?

Clearly, this cannot happen in a perfectly competitive environment since we know that equilibrium exists and is efficient in that instance. Indeed, in these environments, it is good that agents do *not* take into account the effect of their behavior on the opportunities of others. However, we may be able to salvage the concept of pecuniary externality in situations where some of the usual competitive assumptions fail to hold. When Scitovsky [13] discusses pecuniary externalities, he seems to have in mind a situation in which there are nonconvexities (increasing returns to scale) in production technology sets. It is well known that the presence of nonconvexities may lead to nonexistence of equilibrium, but this is a type of market failure in itself and not something that we would like to call "externality."

On the other hand, if equilibrium exists, there is certainly no market failure due to nonconvexity since equilibrium is efficient with or without convexity. Again, it appears that market failure reduces to either nonconvexity or noncompetitive behavior, neither of which we want to call externality.

Of course, firms may behave myopically by maximizing short-run profit and ignoring the possibility of lowering costs by adopting larger plants. Such myopia may lead to a market failure since the (myopic) necessary conditions of efficiency are not sufficient in the presence of nonconvexities. For example, if there were a steel industry that possessed an increasing returns to scale technology and which failed to take into account the possibility of expanding its size and thus lowering costs to (say) a railroad industry, then there is a market failure in that the true competitive equilibrium is not reached. However, again it does not seem that we should call this "externality." The failure does not occur because the steel industry fails to take into account some external effect, but rather because it fails to take into account its own increased profit potential from expansion.

Thus, if pecuniary externalities are to be salvaged as a separate concept, it is crucial to find an instance of market failure characterized by inadequate signalling of economic interdependencies by the price system, even when there is convexity in production and the possibility of exclusion. The following example (inspired by Arrow's claim[8] that the absence of a futures market was responsible for Scitovsky's "pecuniary externality") would appear to provide such an instance.

Suppose that neither the steel nor the rail industries are yet in operation. Entrepreneurs in each industry are deciding whether or not to start operations. Neither finds it profitable to go it alone; the steel industry figures that without the rail industry around to transport its outputs and provide part of the demand for its outputs, its costs will be too high and selling price too low to justify operations. Similarly, the rail industry figures that without the steel industry to provide some of its inputs cheaply and bolster its demand then it (the rail industry) cannot turn a profit. Thus, if the system is decentralized without coordination of plans, neither industry will grow. On the other hand, it may well be that both together would be profitable.

Let us analyze the situation described in Figure 2. We will abstract for the moment from any other inputs into either of the industries (though this is inessential) and plot the production functions of steel from rail and rail from steel respectively. We have drawn the production functions purposely so that the pair of industries is jointly productive and can provide positive net value; this means that the two industries together are jointly desirable.

Now let us look at the prices that the two industries must be expecting in isolation. The steel industry must be expecting a price line such as p_1 in which the price of rail in terms of steel is sufficiently high so that he cannot expect to make a profit. The rail industry must be expecting a price like p_2 in which the ratio is correspondingly low. Note in particular that it is impossible that they both expect the same price ratio since if they did and neither found that he could make a profit by himself, then they could not make a profit jointly either. Note also that the difficulty has nothing to do with nonconvexities in the industry production sets since both are convex above.

[8] See footnote 16 in Scitovsky [13].

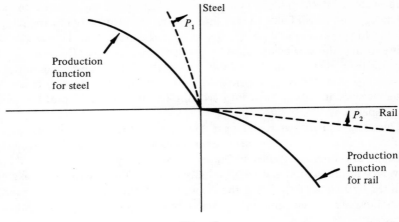

Figure 2

But the difficulty clearly depends on the absence of effective futures markets since if a futures price were in effect, the two industries could not be expecting different prices to prevail. Furthermore, in the situation described above, there is a strong private incentive for someone to run futures markets in both industries. As it stands, such a person could expect to buy "rail" for "steel" from the rail industry at prices slightly less favorable than p_2, and sell the "rail" to get "steel" back at prices slightly less favorable than p_1. Clearly he makes a profit in the process.

Thus, the example reduces to the absence of a market, in this case the futures market. And the incentive to establish such a market is exactly the same as it was for the case of garbage. Hence, we must still explain why the market fails to exist. We can argue (just as in Section II) that as long as transaction technologies are convex and there is a broker who will operate a market whenever it is profitable, then the market will come into existence whenever it should and there is no market failure. In fact, we can argue that the reasons we may not find an efficient equilibrium in the missing market must be attributable to types of market failure we have already discussed.

For example, it may be that there are setup costs to the operation of a market and that as a consequence, no marketeer can turn a profit; this would be an instance of nonexistence due to a nonconvexity in the transactions technology set. Or it could be that no one perceives the profit opportunity presented; this would be a case of extreme myopia. Alternatively, the absence of a market may be explained by more subtle combinations of the causes we have already discussed.

Suppose (as suggested by many authors) that the demand for futures contracts is low because they are perceived as risky. (One may not wish to make a long-term commitment to a particular grade of steel when technological change

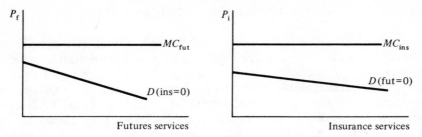

Figure 3

may make that grade obsolete.) Then, the inactivity on the futures markets may be explained by the nonexistence of a complementary market, in this case the insurance against these technological risks. The insurance marketeer fails to open operations because he perceives no current demand from the inactive futures market.

The situation described is very similar in form to our original example of the steel and rail industries. And one can easily find similar explanations of this market failure in terms of nonconvexities and/or noncompetitive behavior of the marketeers. However, there is a more interesting explanation having to do with a certain type of myopia. Let both marketeers act as perfect competitors and have constant marginal costs of providing services. Further, let each perceive his demand as a function of his own price and the other's *quantity*. Then, if the situation is as described in Figure 3, both markets will be inactive under marginal cost pricing. However, this "equilibrium" is not the full competitive equilibrium since it is based on individual assumptions that are mutually inconsistent over some ranges of parameters. And the equilibrium will surely be inefficient if the two markets are able to generate positive net surplus jointly. Such a surplus is likely to be generated if, as each comes into operation he stimulates the demand for the other; so we wind up with a true competitive equilibrium as depicted in Figure 4. Clearly, the markets generate net surplus at this equilibrium.

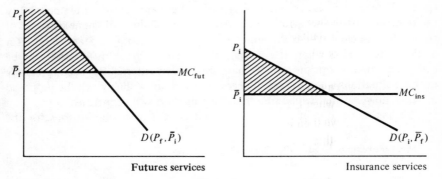

Figure 4

VI. THE DEFINITION OF EXTERNALITIES

What should we mean by externality? We have argued that instances of externality can always be associated with the failure of some potential market to operate properly. Therefore, all externality problems can be traced to some more fundamental problem having to do with market failure. Therefore, one might take the position that the concept of externality should be dropped altogether. Our taxonomy of market failure might then consist of (1) nonexclusiveness of commodities, (2) nonconvexities, (3) noncompetitive behavior, and (4) imperfect or incomplete information.

However, we might still like to put the label "externality" on market failure due to interdependencies not properly taken into account by price-taking agents. One might be tempted to identify these situations with item 1 above. However, as we have shown above, the distinctions are not so clear-cut. The absence of a market for pollution may be attributable to either nonexclusiveness or to nonconvexities in the technology of setting up property rights. Furthermore, some instances of myopic behavior (such as the failure of a futures market maker to take into account correctly the insurance marketeer's effect on demand for futures market services) should be included in this concept of externalities, while other instances (such as failure to take advantage of scale economies) should not. It seems to us that the intuitive concept of externality must remain somewhat imprecise.

VII. REMEDIES

Many authors have discussed various ways of correcting for externalities. Therefore, rather than give an extensive discussion here, we confine ourselves to a few implications that can be derived from the previous discussion.

A number of suggested remedies operationally amount to setting up markets for externality rights.[9] It is well known that operation of such markets (particularly in the case of public externalities) is complicated by the possibility of noncompetitive behavior and even the possibility of nonexistence of equilibrium in cases where the nonconvexity is important (see Starrett [15] for a discussion and further references). But even if these difficulties can be overcome, there is a prior issue. We have shown that externalities occur precisely in those situations when the private economy will not willingly run the proposed markets; how can we then be sure that these markets will be justified?

The answer to this question will depend on the particular reasons for the

[9] See, for example, Meade [10], Coase [2], and Foley [7].

private economy's reluctance. Suppose that the private economy does not act because the necessary property right has not been legally established; this is very frequently the case with public externalities where the property right cannot be defined as involving ownership of some physical commodity, but must involve ownership of some fictitious "externality right." Suppose that once the right is established private brokers will willingly take up the function of marketeer. In this case, public policy is clear. Assuming that the costs of establishing property rights are relatively small, the market should be encouraged to operate.

But if the costs of establishing property rights are large, or the private economy would still not be willing to run the market, then the issue is not so clear; a nonconvex choice must be made among institutions; and, as we know, the right choice will depend on a comparison of costs and benefits. Note, in particular, that in this case *we cannot ignore the costs of institutions* in making the social decisions since these costs are now the primary reason the externality is there in the first place. Indeed, once this point is recognized, it is clear that rule of thumb procedures may in fact be optimal. A policy of setting pollution standards at "reasonable" levels may do best at maximizing the difference between the net surplus gain in "pollution variables" and the institutional costs of correction.

The importance of institutional costs suggests that taxation schemes might generally be preferred to market type schemes since the government can tax that side of the market with the fewest participants (generally externality producers) and minimize the number of transactions.[10] However, as is well known, the administrative costs of computing the correct tax rates may be very large and clearly should not be ignored.

We give one final example to illustrate the importance of institutional costs in determining the optimal public policy. Suppose that we are allocating some facility among symmetric users. For concreteness, assume that we have a fixed piece of land to allocate among shepherds. If the land is treated as a common, it is well known that it will be overgrazed in the absence of any interference.

Two possible remedies are proposed. One involves assigning private property rights on the common, while the other involves taxing users at the rate of the marginal congestion damages caused by their sheep. Aside from institutional costs (such as fences or tax administrators' salaries) it turns out that both of these schemes will work. Which is to be preferred will depend entirely on the relative administrative costs. Of course, both of these schemes are second best compared to the alternative of turning the common over to a single owner, *assuming* that he could be expected to operate in a competitive way.

---

[10] The correction-by-taxation method has a long literature. See Pigou [12], Coase [2], Davis and Whinston [3], and Mishan [11].

REFERENCES

1. Arrow, K. J., "The Organization of Economic Activity: Issues Pertinent to the Choice of Market versus Non-Market Allocation," in Joint Economic Committee, *The Analysis and Evaluation of Public Expenditures: The PPB System*, Washington, D.C.: Govt. Printing Office, 1969, 47–64.
2. Coase, R., "The Problem of Social Costs," *Journal of Law and Economics*, October 1960, 3, 1–44.
3. Davis, O., and A. Whinston, "Externalities, Welfare and the Theory of Games," *Journal of Political Economy*, June 1962, 70, 241–262.
4. Davis, O., and A. Whinston, "On the Distinction Between Public and Private Goods," *American Economic Review*, May 1967, 57, 360–373.
5. Demsetz, H., "Toward a Theory of Property Rights," *American Economic Review*, May 1967, 57, 347–359.
6. Foley, D., "Economic Equilibrium with Costly Marketing," *Journal of Economic Theory*, September 1970, 2, 276–291.
7. Foley, D., "Lindahl's Solution and the Core of an Economy with Public Goods," *Econometrica*, January 1970, 38, 66–72.
8. Furubotn, E., and S. Pejovich, "Property Rights and Economic Theory: A Survey of Recent Literature," *Journal of Economic Literature*, December 1972, 10, 1137–1162.
9. Heller, W. P., "Transactions with Setup Costs," *Journal of Economic Theory*, June 1972, 4, 465–478.
10. Meade, J., "External Economies and Diseconomies in a Competitive Situation," in A. Arrow and T. Scitovsky, eds., *Readings in Welfare Economics*, Homewood, Illinois: Irwin, 1969, 185–198.
11. Mishan E., "The Postwar Literature on Externalities," *Journal of Economic Literature*, March 1971, 9, 1–28.
12. Pigou, A., *The Economics of Welfare*, New York: Macmillan, 1932, reprinted 1952.
13. Scitovsky, T., "Two Concepts of External Economies," *Journal of Political Economy*, April 1954, 62, 70–82.
14. Starr, R., "Quasi-Equilibria in Markets with Non-Convex Preferences," *Econometrica*, January 1969, 37, 25–38.
15. Starrett, D., "Fundamental Nonconvexities in the Theory of Externalities," *Journal of Economic Theory*, April 1972, 4, 180–199.
16. Starrett, D., and R. Zeckhauser, "Treating External Diseconomies Markets or Taxes?" Discussion Paper No. 3, John F. Kennedy School of Govt., Harvard Univ., Cambridge, Massachusetts, 1971.
17. Turvey, R., "On Divergences Between Social Cost and Private Cost," *Economica*, August 1963, 30, 309–313.

Discussion

JOHN O. LEDYARD

Northwestern University

In this stimulating paper, a definition of *externality* is presented, three theoretical observations are made concerning externalities, and a discussion of remedies for the nonoptimality of market systems in the presence of externalities, is carried out. As Heller and Starrett point out, "part of the result is just a justification of commonly held beliefs." However, they do accomplish, in part, their other goal which is to "provide some additional insights into when the problems are likely to arise, and what remedies are likely to work." Most of the insights they provide are valuable and deserve emphasizing even if they have been previously recognized; however, some of their remarks are debatable. A discussion of these issues can, it is hoped, lead to a better understanding of the nature of externalities.

I. WHAT ARE EXTERNALITIES?

Heller and Starrett provide us with the following "somewhat imprecise" definition: "externalities [are] nearly synonymous with nonexistence of markets." I find this a useful definition. Their garbage disposal example gives emphasis to its validity. Standard general equilibrium and welfare theory tells us that if enough markets exist and if consumers are locally nonsatiated (i.e., they desire to spend all their wealth), then a market equilibrium with price-taking agents will be Pareto optimal. Thus (taking the second assumption as holding) nonoptimality of competitive market systems arises only when potential markets do not exist. Since "externalities" are of interest only because they lead to a nonoptimal allocation of resources, a theory of externalities must encompass a theory of the existence or nonexistence of markets. Heller and Starrett's definition correctly emphasizes this fact.

Three primary sources of problems are identified which might operate to hinder the establishment of a potential market: transaction setup costs, property rights setup costs, and the absence of relevant information. There is another source of market failure which was hinted at but not really confronted at all in Heller and Starrett's paper: the failure of an equilibrium price to exist even if the market is in operation. Without dwelling on this well-known problem at this time, let me just mention that the results contained in Section III of the paper (that external economies may imply increasing returns to scale) indicate that even if we establish enough property rights, pay the appropriate transactions costs, informed markets may still lead to a nonoptimal allocation of resources because of a failure of the existence of equilibrium. This is especially important to recognize when considering remedies for externalities.

Finally, I should note one possible drawback to the externality definition that they propose. It depends on an equilibrium concept and is not institution free. That is, to identify whether an externality exists (or not) we must calculate whether, *in equilibrium*, a potential market will operate or not. This in turn may depend on such things as the distribution of initial endowments, etc. Clearly it would be more desirable if one did not have to compute an equilibrium before recognizing where the problems will occur.

II. SOME THEORETICAL OBSERVATIONS

Heller and Starrett make two theoretical observations in their paper. One, contained in Section V, is that in the absence of returns to scale a type of externality considered by Scitovsky can be attributed to the lack of effective futures markets. This is a valid and important observation with obvious implications for, among other things, development economics.

A second observation, contained in Section III, is an extension of an argument contained in Starrett [4]. The argument is basically that external diseconomies create a "fundamental nonconvexity" in the aggregate production possibility set. This insight is important for its implications for the existence of tax—subsidy schemes to counteract the nonoptimality property of externalities.[1]

[1] In particular, if the production possibility set is nonconvex, one may not be able to "support" Pareto-optimal allocations with a tax-subsidy scheme.

Heller and Starrett seem to say that the existence of this nonconvexity implies that "all diseconomies must be inherently public in nature." Apparently they have their argument backward. That is, it is the public nature of the externality that creates the nonconvexity, not the converse. To see this let us consider a formal argument that provides conditions under which the nonconvexity exists. To make things simple we consider only two firms (imaginatively called A and B) each producing a single output with a single input and one firm's output produces an external diseconomy for the other. (The argument is easily generalized to many firms and many commodities.) We let Y be the feasible set of pairs of input output plans (x^A, y^A, x^B, y^B) where x is an output and y is an input. We let

$$Y^A(\bar{x}^B, y^B) = \{(x^A, y^A) \mid (x^A, y^A, \bar{x}^B, y^B) \in Y\}.$$

Heller and Starrett's argument seems to be that if $\bar{x}^B > x^{*B}$ implies $Y^A(\bar{x}^B, y^B) \subset Y^A(x^{*B}, y^{*B})$ (i.e., x^B creates an external diseconomy), then Y cannot be convex. This is in fact not true. For example, let

$$Y = \{(x^A, y^A, x^B, y^B) \mid x^A + y^A + x^B \leqslant 0,$$
$$x^B + y^B \leqslant 0, x^A \geqslant 0, x^B \geqslant 0, y^A \geqslant 0, y^B \geqslant 0\}.$$

Then x^B creates an external diseconomy, but Y is convex as is $Y^A(\bar{x}^B, \bar{y}^B)$ for all $(\bar{x}^B, \bar{y}^B)$. An additional condition is needed. The firm must be allowed to escape the impact of the diseconomy through inaction. More precisely we mean that $(0, 0) \in Y^A(\bar{x}^B, \bar{y}^B)$ for all $\bar{x}^B > 0$. Taking these together we have

Proposition The following three conditions cannot hold simultaneously:

(1) Y is convex.
(2) $(0, 0) \in Y^A(\bar{x}^B)$ for all $\bar{x}^B \geqslant 0$.
(3) There is an efficient allocation (x^A, y^A) in $Y^A(\bar{x}^B)$ such that

$$\{(x^A, y^A, \bar{x}^B)\} + \Omega \cap Z = \{(x^A, y^A, \bar{x}^B)\}$$

where Ω is the nonnegative orthant of three-dimensional space and

$$Z = \{(x^A, y^A, \bar{x}^B) \mid (x^A, y^A) \in Y^A(\bar{x}^B)\}.$$

((3) simply states there is at least one efficient point at which an external diseconomy occurs.)

Proof (1) implies Z is convex. Let $s = (x^A, y^A, \bar{x}^B)$ be the allocation whose existence is guaranteed by (3), $s \in$ Boundary Z. Hence, there exists a supporting hyperplane to Z through s. That is, there is a vector $\pi = (\pi_1, \pi_2, \pi_3)$ such that $\pi \cdot r \leqslant \pi \cdot s$ for all $r \in Z$. Furthermore, by (3), π can be chosen such that $\pi_i > 0$ for $i = 1, 2, 3$. Now condition (2) implies, therefore, that $\pi(0, 0, x^{*B}) \leqslant \pi \cdot s$ for all $x^* \geqslant 0$ since $(0, 0, x^{*B}) \in Z$. Choose $x^{*B} > \pi \cdot s / \pi_1$. Then we have a contradiction. q.e.d.

Several relationships can be highlighted by this proposition. First, any two of the conditions taken alone are not inconsistent. Second if (1) were changed to requiring that $0 \in Y^A(x^B)$ for all $x^B \in Y_{xB}$ (the projection of Y on x^B), it is possible that the conclusion need not follow. This is indeed true if $Y_{xB} \subseteq [0,K]$ for some finite bound K. This can be illustrated by Heller and Starrett's example of a common green for grazing sheep. Clearly there is an upper bound on the number of sheep the other person can have grazing. Therefore, it is perfectly possible to have convexity in the production possibilities set even if inaction is usually possible.

Finally, the propostion indicates that one should make a distinction between exclusion of an externality and *escape* from one. By perfect exclusion I mean that (at zero cost) $Y^A(x^B) = \overline{Y}^A$ for all x^B. By perfect escape I mean that $0 \in Y^A(x^B)$ for all x^B. No escape and no exclusion would mean that condition (2) of our propostion need not hold and, therefore, that the "fundamental nonconvexity" need not exist.[2] One is tempted, at this point, to enter into a metaphysical discussion about the similarity and differences between escape being possible and allowing $Y^A(x^B) = \phi$ (the empty set). Rather than dwell on the distinction I have in mind, let me illustrate with an example proposed by Stanley Reiter. Suppose a government is willing to subsidize farmers who do not grow poppies. How do they distinguish between those who are currently choosing inaction (the zero input—output vector) and those who were not producers in the first place since with reasonable capital markets anyone could potentially be a poppy grower? The dilemma is one not allowed for by our models of production.

III. A DISCUSSION OF REMEDIES

Heller and Starrett's main point, and one that I heartily agree with, is that in discussing remedies for correcting the nonoptimality created by externalities one "cannot ignore the costs of the institutions in making social decisions." In fact, this is always a relevant consideration in any choice of institutional arrangements for the allocation of resources. For example, it must be considered when choosing between a centrally planned economy and a market system.[3] That is, one should be interested in *net* optimality, the level of social satisfaction attained after institutional costs are netted out. Heller and Starrett make these points; however, they do not carry them to their logical conclusion. In particular, let us look at their final example, in Section VI. The problem is to allocate a fixed piece of land among shepherds. They state, without proof, that

---

[2] Another problem arises, however, for market equilibrium since it is now possible, but not necessary unless Y is a cone, that losses will be sustained by firm A in equilibirum.

[3] See Hurwicz [2] for a fuller elaboration of these ideas.

"of course, both of these schemes (taxes or property rights) are second best compared to the alternative of turning the common over to a single owner." In saying this they ignore the costs to the single owner of operating the common as a competitive firm. If there were no costs of administering such a firm, one might argue that, even with externalities, the best organization of production for all economies is that in which one firm carries out all the productive activity of the world. Empirical evidence seems to contradict such a conclusion. Thus, before accepting single ownership as an optimal one, one must also weigh the costs of that institution. In particular, it may not be desirable to internalize all externalities if there is a cheaper way to solve the problem.

IV. CONCLUSION

I find much of interest in Heller and Starrett's paper. It should be required reading for anyone interested in externalities. However, one must be careful to distinguish those conclusions grounded on solid theoretical analysis from those that are supported only by example. The latter, in many cases, raise more questions than they answer. For example, we need more research on models into which are incorporated the costs of assigning property rights and the costs of exclusion.

A good paper should not only provide answers but should also lead to provocative questions. Therefore, Heller and Starrett's is a good paper.

REFERENCES

1. Debreu, G., *Theory of Value*, New York: Wiley, 1959.
2. Hurwicz, L., "On Informationally Decentralized Systems," in C. B. McGuire and R. Radner, eds., *Decision and Organization*, Amsterdam: North-Holland Publ., 1972.
3. Scitovsky, T., "Two Concepts of External Economies," *Journal of Political Economy*, April 1954, **62**, 70–82.
4. Starrett, D., "Fundamental Nonconvexities in the Theory of Externalities," *Journal of Economic Theory*, April 1972, **4**, 180–199.

The Problem of Social Cost:
Fifteen Years Later

RICHARD O. ZERBE

The University of Washington
and
Northwestern University

I. INTRODUCTION

Coase's seminal work on social cost has rightly had an enormous impact on work in the profession [2]. Unfortunately confusion or controversy still shrouds many of the issues raised. The aim here is to consider again some of the important issues raised by Coase.[1]

II. THE COASE THEOREM

The Coase theorem, without violence to common usage, may be expressed as:

In a world of perfect competition, perfect information, and zero transactions costs, the allocation of resources will be efficient and invariant with respect to legal rules of liability.

This paper is part of a work supported by a grant from the General Electric Corporation to the Program in the Social Management of Technology, University of Washington, Seattle.

[1] The interpretations of Coase's work given here are based on what seems the most useful view of this work, not necessarily on what Coase himself meant. This can be determined only by Coase himself.

This question of the theorem's validity is ultimately an existential one since the theorem does not constitute a testable hypothesis, but the theorem itself is a useful benchmark.

Two claims are made by the theorem, an efficiency claim and an invariance claim. The correctness of the invariance claim may be understood by realizing that the externality will persist only if the rents of both externality generator and receptor exceed the costs of adjusting to the externality plus the residual damage.

Otherwise, if the rents of one party are less than this, this party will adjust so as to eliminate the externality when liable, and will be bribed to similarly adjust when not liable. Thus, the liability change simply transfers rents and does not affect the distribution of resources. Regan's [11] lengthy criticism of the invariance claim is voided once this point is appreciated.

Marchand and Russell [6] criticize Gifford and Stone's [4, 5] mathematical demonstration of the invariance (and efficiency) claim on two grounds: (1) that the firms being modeled are cast in a situation of bilateral monopoly so that costless bargaining is unrealistic, and (2) that the gains from trade should not be split but should all go to the party holding the property right.

These criticisms cannot be supported. It is trivial to convert the Gifford–Stone bilateral monopoly formulation into a competitive one, of course costless transactions is an unrealistic assumption whether the situation is bilateral monopoly or competition. The point is whether or not the assumption is useful.

The argument about gains from trade is puzzling. Gains from trade are determined by the assignment of property rights, the production functions, and the utility functions. If one party owned *all* property, there would be no trade. Otherwise, the typical result has both parties gaining from trade. For one party to capture all the gains would be both a special and an unusual case.

One criticism of the efficiency claim of the theorem (Shoup [12], Regan [11], Mumey [8], and Wellisz [13]. pp. 352–353]) is that it is a questionable proposition in the theory of games that "reaches a conclusion about the result of individuals' economic behavior without any model of how individuals behave" (Regan [11], p. 438]). The theorem is then seen as unestablished either (1) because rationality is not defined within a bargaining context or (2) because within this context resources will be inefficiently devoted to threat.

This criticism is vitiated when the theorem is seen as a proposition in perfect competition. Bargaining in the game theory sense is, then, no longer the context of the theorem. The proper context of the theorem is one in which the market setting is pervasive. This is true for transactions involving marauding cattle, fire-setting trains, or clean air The context of the theorem is one in which there is a market for externalities or, since this is a contradiction in terms, there are no externalities. Certainly Coase's bargaining examples can be easily reproduced with similar results, in the context of perfect competition, by letting the number of farmers and ranchers increase without limit and by defining a market.

The inevitable example of misallocations in a Coase theorem world is that of resources devoted to threat (Shoup [9], Mumey [8], Regan [8, pp. 429–431]; and Wellisz [10 p. 353]). Devotion of resources to threat, however, clearly violates the assumption of zero transactions costs since threat is a part of the transaction process. Moreover, perfect competition eliminates resources devoted to threat since price is forced to marginal cost and, as Demsetz [3] points out, the production of nuisances imposes an unnecessary cost so that the price of such unnecessary nuisances falls to zero.

Actually, the formulation of the theorem presented here is too narrow. Perfect competition is best seen not as an assumption of the theorem, but as a result of zero transactions costs. Zero transactions costs are equivalent to a guarantee of an optimal set of institutions. If there is any method at all by which a joint maximization process, e.g , perfect competition, could be brought about, it would be discoverable and accessible with zero transactions costs. This view of the Coase theorem draws attention to those elements of transactions costs that produced different types of legal and institutional arrangements. Monopoly may thus be seen as a product of defects in the institutional structure arising from transactions costs. Its customers would pay enough to eliminate it but do not because of high transactions costs. With zero transactions costs bargaining with a monopolist could lead to a Pareto improvement by converting the monopolist into a perfectly discriminating one. More importantly, monopoly would be incompatible with the institutions that would grow out of such a world. In this context, optimal antitrust laws and the like may be seen as the product of a zero transactions cost world.

III. TRANSACTIONS COSTS AND THE DEFINITION OF EXTERNALITY

The understanding of the relationship between externalities and transactions costs casts doubts on the importance and the meaning of externalities as a phenomenological category.[2] The usual definition of an externality, as a situation in which a decision variable of one economic agent enters into the production or utility function of another agent, is unsatisfactory not only since it defines all transactions in a barter economy as externalities, but because it fails to capture the accidental nature of externalities [Heller and Starrett, this

---

[2] The Coase article never mentions the word *externality*. This seems eminently appropriate in an article that emphasizes the importance of transactions costs

volume]. The usual notation fails to distinguish between accidents and deliberate actions, as Mishan notes [4, p. 2].

Externalities as a concept are devoid absolutely of any policy implications per se. They exist because of costs. The case in which a divergence between private and social costs may be said to exist is when one knows some method by which improvements could be brought about. Thus much of the traditional literature is logically forced into defining externalities as goods not produced (or bads produced) by reason of high transaction costs, for which a worthwhile method, now known but as yet unapplied, nevertheless exists for their production (or elimination). Such a category is neither logical nor useful. The proper approach is to explain the nature and form of various categories of transactions costs. Transactions costs are an appropriate and useful phenomenological category. Externalities are not.

Externalities may, however, profitably be viewed as accidents that arise because of the magnitude of subcategories of transactions costs. Pricing or transactions costs are a convenient sobriquet for a multifarious category of costs which include (1) information costs, (2) negotiating costs (3) exclusion costs, and (4) revenue collection costs. The bulk of externality examples arise from situations in which exclusion costs are high. In Meade's bees—apple case too few apples are produced because no account is taken of their effect on honey production. This problem disappears if bees can be costlessly excluded from the benefits of apple production. Even in the ubiquitous pollution case the externality arises because large exclusion costs prevent the operation of a market for clean air.

A difficulty with the usual definition of externality is the lack of clarity concerning which costs give rise to the phenomenon. Exclusion costs may give rise to a traditional externality. Information costs that have the same effect make a less clear case by some previous treatments. This difficulty disappears when externality is defined as synonymous with the nonexistence of markets, regardless of which costs give rise to this nonexistence. There would then arise some externalities that might not have been previously considered externalities, and vice versa. For example, the public good aspects of goods do not per se create a problem any more than does the public good aspect of movies.

IV. OPTIMAL LIABILITY

The principal example used by Coase to illustrate the effects of transactions costs is that of the fire-setting railroad The essential result of this example is that with positive transactions cost the distribution of liability does make a difference. Coase's figures, except for the last column which he did not consider, are given in Table 1.

In Coase's analysis the optimal solution is for one train to run with crops worth $60 destroyed. If the railroad is not liable, two trains will run with net

TABLE 1

Trains	Total revenue	Total costs	Total crop damage when RR not liable	Total crop damage when RR liable	Foregone rent on land unplanted when RR not liable
1	150	50	60	120	10
2	250	100	120	240	20

social benefits of $30. Coase notes that with railroad liability no trains would run since total costs would exceed revenues. Coase then argues that Pigou's conclusion that the railroad should necessarily be liable is wrong. Coase's analysis is incorrect.

Actually it would be surprising if Coase's conclusion was not wrong since his example involves no transactions costs, and should, therefore, by the Coase theorem itself involve no misallocation. The conclusion he draws is wrong because the liability rule he considers is not optimal. An optimal rule would be that (1) the damage generator is liable for damages plus adjustments costs of the externality receptors where the adjustments are determined to be the efficient adjustments.[3] An equivalent and symmetrical liability rule is that (2) the receptor be allowed to collect damages when the adjustments of the externality generator are not optimal. With zero costs of collecting damages these rules are equivalent.

Consider the Coase example in the context of a liability rule that allowed suit for net damages, with the additional information that the rent on the land unplanted when the railroad is not liable is $10 in the case of one train and $20 in the case of two trains. With the first optimal liability rule, the farmers could sue for their efficient adjustments costs plus residual damages. With one train direct damages are $60, with adjustments costs equal to the land rent foregone or $10. When two trains run, damages would be $120 plus rents foregone of $20. The net gain to the railroad is $30 with one train and $10 with two trains. One train would run even though the railroad is liable, and the optimal result would be obtained.

The second liability rule would hold that the farmers bear the damages as long as the railroad is acting optimally; in this case, running one train. If, however, two trains were run, the farmers would be able to collect damages.

Actually, without considering the adjustment cost of both externality generators and the receptors, no conclusion at all can be drawn from Coase's figures as to how many trains should run. Suppose simply that the rent on the land that would be left unplanted when the railroad is not liable is $50 regardless of how many trains ran. If one train were to run, total social costs would be $160, and no trains should run.

[3] If there are no discontinuities in externality control, adjustment costs should not be included in damages.

The example presented by Coase suffers from a peculiar defect in that, although it explicitly assumes pricing costs exist, it implicitly assumes that damages may be costlessly collected. This is, of course very peculiar. The distinction presented by this example is not between the cases in which transactions costs do and do not exist, as Coase suggests, but rather between the cases of optimal and nonoptimal liability rules.

V. TRANSACTIONS COSTS AND THE INCIDENCE OF LIABILITY

Because of transactions costs, the first liability rule of the preceding section may be less efficient than a strict liability rule. As long as the damages that may be collected are real damages, and as long as there is less than perfect chance of winning damage suits, then those damaged could be expected to perform efficient adjustments [11, 12]. Now, when the requirement of collecting only damages net of efficient adjustments by the plaintiff is dropped, the first liability rule becomes a rule of strict liability, which says simply that one is liable for damages caused. Why not, then, make the damage generator always liable? Is not a system of strict liability preferable?

On an a priori basis, it is difficult to make a choice between the strict liability rule and the second rule above, a negligence rule under which a basis for a suit can be established only when it can be shown that efficient adjustments were not performed by the damage generator. Under strict liability more suits would be brought since the damage generator would be liable under a broader range of conditions and since the generally noncollectable legal costs to the plaintiff would be lower, as less lawyer time would be required However, the costs per suit would be lower since no inquiry need take place as to whether or not the adjustments of the damage generator were efficient.

However, if an initial judgment can be made concerning the optimal outcome, then a choice among liability rules may be made. Suppose in the case of the fire-setting train that the number of trains the railroad would run if they were not liable at all was in fact close to the optimum. In this case, the efficient liability rule might be to make the railroad not liable, or liable only under negligence. In this case few transactions costs in the form of suits or bargains would likely be incurred. If the trains were liable, under a rule of strict liability, suits or other transactions costs might occur that were avoided with the negligence rule.

A quite different argument for strict liability has been presented by Mishan [4, p. 23] and Randall [6, p. 178] who have argued that liability or prohibitions should be imposed on the party for whom transactions costs are least. They maintain that in the case where there are many receptors of the external bad or few producers of the bad (which Mishan and Randall see as the common case) liability or prohibitions should be placed on the externality generator. This argument appears incorrect. If negotiations are profitable, they will be organized by the most efficient organizer. Consider the case of prohibitions. The polluter who is prohibited from polluting will, say, offer sum M (if there were no transactions costs) to be allowed to pollute to the optimal level Q. This sum will be accepted if it exceeds the damages, say D, associated with the pollution beyond Q. Let transactions cost be T_1 and T_2 for the externality generator and receptor, respectively. Thus the agreement will be made if M minus transactions costs for the polluter (T_1) exceeds D plus T_2. On the other hand if the polluter has freedom to pollute he can organize negotiations to accept a new sum D', minus T_2 from the receptors in exchange for reducing his pollution to level Q. He will organize such negotiations as long as D' minus T_2 exceeds his new control costs M' plus T_1. These conditions are certainly affected by transactions costs, but the *difference* between the first and second condition are invariant with respect to the transactions costs.

The contribution of the Coase article is that it highlights the importance of transactions costs in a bargaining context in a market context, and in a political and legal context. The implications of Coase's article have been profound. If these implications receive the attention they deserve, their influence will continue to be positive.

REFERENCES

1. Calabresi, G., "Transactions Costs, Resource Allocation, and Liability Rules — A Comment," *Journal of Law and Economics*, April 1968 **11**, 67–73
2. Coase R. H., "The Problem of Social Cost," *Journal of Law and Economics*, October 1960, **3**, 1–44.
3. Demsetz, H., "Theoretical Efficiency in Pollution Control: Comment on Comments," *Western Economic Journal*, December 1971, **4**, 444–446.
4. Gifford, A., and Stone, C. C., "Externalities, Liability and the Coase Theorem: A Mathematical Analysis," *Western Economic Journal*, September 1973, **11**, 260–269.
5. Gifford, A., and Stone, C. C., "Externalities, Liability, Separability, and Resources Allocation: Comment," *American Economic Review*, September 1975, **65**, 724–727.
6. Marchand, J. R., and Russell, K. P., "Externalities, Liability, Separability and Resource Allocation: Reply," *American Economic Review*, September 1975, **65**, 730–732.
7. Mishan, E. J., "The Post War Literature on Externalities; An Interpretive Essay," *Journal of Economic Literature*, March 1971, **9**, 1–28.
8. Mumey, G. A., "The 'Coase Theorem': A Re-examination," *Quarterly Journal of Economics*, November 1971, **85**, 718–723.
9. Randall, A., "Market Solutions to Externality Problems: Theory and Practice," *American Journal of Agricultural Economics*, May 1972, **54**, 175–183.
10. Rausser, G. S., and R. O. Zerbe, "Taxes as Solutions to Externalities," Urban Econ. Paper, Univ. of Chicago, April 1974.
11. Regan D. H., "The Problem of Social Cost Revisited," *Journal of Law and Economics*, October 1972, **15**, 427–438.

12. Shoup, D.C., "Theoretical Efficiency in Pollution Control: A Comment," *Western Economic Journal*, November 1964, 9, 310–313.
13. Wellisz, S., "On External Economies and the Government Assisted Invisible Hand," *Economica*, November 1964, 31, 345–362.
14. Zerbe, R. O., "Theoretical Efficiency in Pollution Control," *Western Economic Journal*, December 1970, 8, 364–376.
15. Zerbe R. O., "Theoretical Efficiency in Pollution Control: Reply " *Western Economic Journal*, September 1971, 9, 314–317.

Discussion

GERALD E. AUTEN

University of Missouri
Columbia

In the first part of my comments on Zerbe's paper I would like to suggest several clarifications of his clarification of Coase [1]. First, it should be noted that the theorem applies only to Pareto relevant externalities. Therefore it would exclude a class of externalities for which it might not be possible to arrange Pareto improvements, such as the case where the income distribution is such that one party is unable to make a large enough payment to induce a change in the behavior of the other. The Coase theorem thus excludes a potentially significant externalities class which might be relevant under another social welfare criterion such as that proposed by Rawls [5].

A second point that deserves emphasis is that the Coase theorem does not imply an invariant allocation of resources, only that the allocation will be efficient whatever it turns out to be. A theorem stating that results will be efficient but may change as the assignment of liability and property rights changes is much less powerful than one proclaiming invariant results. Even more extreme Pigouvians are not likely to take offense at this weakened version of the theorem.

One example of the possibility of varying results may be found in the case of externalities in consumption. If the income elasticity of demand for clean air by the receptor is not zero then the equilibrium level of abatement will be greater when liability is assigned to the polluter than when assigned to the receptor. The additional assumption of zero income elasticity of demand for clean air is required in order to obtain an invariant allocation.

Another example can occur when the distribution of income is an argument in individual preference functions. When this is the case the assignment of liability to one party may be a Pareto inferior solution to assignment to the other. With sufficiently low transactions costs, voluntary redistribution and thus changes in resource allocation could occur.[1] A third possibility for varying results arises when the product and the associated externality are not joint products in fixed proportions as they are assumed to be in Coase's examples.[2] In this case the possibility for substitution in production exists, and bribery and compensation may not bring about the same results.

In Coase's examples the results will also vary with liability depending on the Ricardian rents of polluters and receptors.[3] If both pollutor and receptor operate on marginal land the polluter must cease operations in the long run if liable, and the receptor will be driven out if liable. On land where economic rent is received the polluter or receptor will continue operating as long as the necessary tax or bribe does not exceed rent.

In order for the Coase theorem to imply invariant allocation, therefore, a number of additional assumptions are required including: zero income elasticity of demand, the distribution of income does not affect utility functions, products and externalities are joint products in fixed proportions, and rents must exceed any required payments.

The problem with this weakened theorem is that it borders on being tautological and therefore of little interest to either the theoretician or the policymaker. The Coase theorem like Pareto optimality is based on the concept of taking maximum advantage of all gains from trade. Thus both the existence and the absence of transactions are viewed as evidence of optimality even though uncompensated externalities may exist. This clearly borders on the philosophy that Professor Pangloss passed on to his famous pupil Candide, to the effect that whatever happens, it must be the best of all possible worlds.

In the third section of the paper Zerbe argues that externalities should be dropped as a phenomenological category in favor of transactions costs. Although this may be a useful approach for some purposes, it leads to peculiar implications. For example nothing could be said about the situation where the income distribution does not allow receptors of pollution damage to bribe polluters to reduce pollution when no transactions costs exist. Therefore, it

[1] By focusing on largest total value of products the theorem ignores all aspects of the distribution question including both allocative and equity aspects. For a discussion of Pareto optimal redistribution of income see Hochman and Rogers [2]

[2] This point was discussed by Tybout [6].

[3] The first to note that Coase assumed the existence of Ricardian rents was Wellisz [7].

would appear to be preferable to emphasize the relationship between externalities and transactions costs rather than attempting to do away with the externality concept.

In the fourth section of the paper Zerbe proposes two optimal liability rules which are said to be equivalent and symmetrical with zero transactions costs. The first rule provides for liability of the pollution generator equal to the net damages which are defined as damages plus adjustment costs of the receptors where the adjustments are efficient. The second rule provides for liability of the receptor provided the pollutor is operating optimally.

Zerbe's first rule appears to be substantially correct. However, it should be noted that this rule gives the same allocative results as the usual Pigouvian single tax rule except in one unusual case: when the receptor's adjustment costs are less than the cost of the pollution control device, but the sum of the receptor adjustment costs and residual pollution damages after efficient adjustments by the receptor exceed the cost of the pollution control device. Before this liability rule can be considered preferable to the usual Pigouvian rule, the significance of this case will have to be clarified.

The case for the first rule seems stronger on equity criteria since the pollutor is liable for full damages including efficient adjustment costs of the receptor. However, the case for the rule is weakened relative to his own standards if it must be made on equity grounds.

One problem in this section is that the example of the fire-setting railroad is not a good illustration of the rule. In the example damages are given as direct damages plus net rent which equals total rent. The net rent does not arise from crops because the land is unplanted. If it comes from an alternative use of the land then it should not be included in damages. The problem is thus to find an interpretation for the residual net rent. The example also suffers in that it involves extortion, the production of crops for the purpose of collecting damages, which violates Coase's assumption of no transactions costs.

With respect to the argument that the two liability rules are symmetric and equivalent, the comments made earlier pertain here as well. Pollution will be greater if the pollutor is not liable even with zero transactions costs unless several additional assumptions are made. The rules are symmetric, however, in the sense that some Pareto optimal outcome will occur in either case. The only difference in the rules will be in the distribution of income.

In the final section of the paper Zerbe examines the question of whether a strict liability rule or a negligence rule would be preferable when transactions costs exist. He argues that the choice between strict liability and negligence should be made only after the optimal outcome is determined. This is an interesting suggestion but it is doubtful that the optimal outcome could often be determined in advance in an adversary setting. Thus we are likely to have to make our choice on the basis of an assessment of the probable transactions and legal costs as Mishan and Randall have done.

Gerald E. Auten

REFERENCES

1. Coase R. H., "The Problem of Social Cost," *Journal of Law and Economics*, October 1960, **3**, 1–44.
2. Hochman, H. M., and J. D. Rodgers, "Pareto Optimal Redistribution," *American Economic Review*, September 1969, **59**, 542–557.
3. Mishan E. J., "The Post War Literature on Externalities: An Interpretive Essay," *Journal of Economic Literature*, March 1971, **9**, 1–28.
4. Randall, A., "Coase Externality Theory in a Policy Context," *Natural Resources Journal*, January 1974, **14**, 35–54.
5. Rawls, J., *A Theory of Justice*, Cambridge Massachusetts: Harvard Univ. Press, 1971.
6. Tybout, R., "Pricing Pollution and Other Negative Externalities," *Bell Journal of Economics and Management Science*, Spring 1972, **3**, 252–266.
7. Wellisz, S., "On External Diseconomies and the Government-Assisted Invisible Hand," *Economica, N.S.*, November 1964, **31**, 345–362.

III

Externalities in Collective and Decentralized Decision Making

Until recent years there have been few notable attempts to prove or disprove Pigou's theory that taxes and/or subsidies can give firms experiencing externalities incentives to produce the socially optimal outputs. The Coase work provides the first attack on the blind application of the Pigouvian approach. Another line of attack on the Pigouvian scheme is the contention that it is difficult and/or very costly to get information on the profit functions of firms. An even more serious attack is the assertion that even with perfect, costless information available to the "center," tax–subsidy schemes cannot always enforce Pareto optimal output levels.

Lin and Whitcomb's paper develops rigorously a tax–subsidy algorithm that is valid under very general conditions (convex production functions or decision sets). The algorithm allows for many products and firms and permits externalities to be varied independently of salable commodity levels.

A major part of their paper aims at disproving the following prevailing pessimistic conclusions concerning tax–subsidy schemes in the literature:

(1) If the proceeds of taxes on external diseconomies are not paid to the injured party, bargaining opportunities will be set up which may result in moving away from optimal externality production.

(2) When externalities are "nonseparable," taxes and subsidies cannot enforce Pareto optimal externally levels.

Lin and Whitcomb show that the externality tax need not be paid to the injured party in the cases that are most likely to result in administration cost exceeding welfare improvement; a unit tax on physical quantities of nonseparable externalities works perfectly well. The implications with respect to the control of environmental externalities are also briefly explored.

The coordination of decisions having external effects is a central issue in the theory of externalities. In Grove's paper an n-firm model is formulated in which some decisions of the firms have an external effect on other firms. In the absence of coordination the firms collectively will make inefficient decisions or decisions that do not maximize joint profits. The coordination of these decisions (or the internalization of the externalities) is accomplished by another agent, called the center. The center is interpreted either as an agent hired by the n firms in the case of voluntary coordination or a governmental body in the case of imposed coordination. The center's task is to choose the level of the external decisions that will maximize the firms' joint profits. The center is, however, dependent on information it receives from the firms, which introduces the problem of incentives. In order for the center to make the optimal decision, the firms must send truthful information, yet it may not be in their interest to do so. In order to induce the firms to send truthful information, the center may levy charges against the firms or make payments to the firms. Groves formulates an explicit mechanism in his paper that respects the informational limitations of the center and yet provides the firms with appropriate incentives to communicate truthful information to the center.

Loehman and Whinston derive a general cost allocation formula based on game theoretic and linear algebra concepts. The form of the cost allocation is shown to depend on both the choice of basic subgames and the choice of weights on users in these subgames. Using this general formulation, cost allocation schemes different from the Shapely value are obtained by: (1) using a definition of basic subgames different from Shapely's while using the Shapely axioms that define equal weights; (2) changing the axioms that define weights while using the Shapley basis; (3) changing both weights and basic subgames. By allowing these changes in the basic subgames and weights, it is possible to develop cost allocations schemes for nonsubadditive game situations and situations where not all combinations of users are possible. By making these alternations, although it is possible theoretically to obtain many different cost allocations schemes that will cover costs in a given situation, only some schemes will be "acceptable." *Acceptable* means that the charge scheme gives the proper incentives for coalition formulation to build a common facility when there are economies of scale and that the scheme is compatible both with costs of meeting demands and with bargaining power of members of a coalition.

Some alternative definitions of basic subgames and weights are considered in this paper. It is shown by means of an example that probabilistic definitions result in a charge scheme based on expected incremental cost. This expected incremental cost scheme is acceptable in the above sense since it covers costs and takes into account both the incremental cost and relative bargaining power of potential users of a common facility.

Externality Taxes and Subsidies

STEVEN A. Y. LIN
Southern Illinois University
Edwardsville

DAVID K. WHITCOMB
Rutgers University
and
New York University

Most economists consider taxes on externalities a feasible means of control when outright prohibition would result in excessive reduction of desirable activities (such as electricity production which jointly supplies various pollutants). However, the literature lacks a rigorous and general externality tax model.[1] The main purpose of this paper is to develop rigorously a tax—subsidy algorithm that is valid under very general conditions (convex production

The authors wish to thank Enrique Arzac, William Baumol, Sadik Gokturk, Kelvin Lancaster, James Little, Robert Schwartz, Ephraim Sudit, and Stanislaw Wellisz for their suggestions and comments on earlier drafts. We are indebted to the Ford Foundation and the New York University Schools of Business Research Fund for financial assistance to the second author.

[1] Pigou [14] suggested no precise means of calculating the optimal tax which would equate marginal social with marginal private product. The first precise scheme, that of Meade [11], applies to the special case of a production function homogeneous of degree one. Fairly similar schemes have been proposed (or at least introduced for purposes of discussion) by Henderson and Quandt [10], Davis and Whinston [8 and 9], and Mishan [13]. In all of these a tax is placed on the salable joint product equal to the difference between social and private marginal cost at the optimal output level. All assume strict joint production, and hence set a tax that is probably higher than is needed to achieve optimality, given the true production possibilities. Such a tax will bring excessive reductions in desirable outputs and in externalities.

functions allowing for many products and firms and permitting externalities to be varied independently of salable commodity levels).[2]

The secondary purpose of this paper is to show that the following prevailing pessimistic conclusions concerning tax—subsidy schemes are wrong:

(A) If the proceeds of taxes on external diseconomies are not paid to the injured party, bargaining opportunities will be set up which may result in moving away from optimal externality production.[3] The pessimistic implication of this conclusion has not been pointed out: if the ten cents damage the owner of a small taxi fleet does me each year by his exhaust emissions *is* paid to me, the administration cost may well exceed the welfare improvement.

(B) According to the widely accepted conclusion of Davis and Whinston [8], when externalities are "mutual and nonseparable," that is, when the externality level set by one firm in maximizing its profit depends on the externality level set by another, and vice versa, taxes and subsidies cannot enforce Pareto optimal externality levels.[4] Since this type of output interdependency is reasonably likely to occur, Davis and Whinston's conclusion is a serious challenge to the Pigouvian approach. This paper shows that the externality tax need not be paid to the injured party in the cases that are most likely to result in adminstration

---

[2] The argument is still valid as long as the feasible decision sets are convex for the firms involved. This is a weaker assumption because the feasible decision sets of the firms may be convex even though the production functions are not. For the feasibility of convex decision sets with nonconvex production functions arising from externalities, see the excellent discussion by Starrett [18]. However our tax—subsidy rule does not survive all forms of nonconvexity. In the spirit of our model, the presence of a sufficiently strong detrimental externality (see Baumol and Bradford [4]), for example, can be expected to produce a violation of the convexity conditions, in whose absence one finds a multiplicity of local optima.

[3] This conclusion was first suggested by Coase [7] and developed more fully by Buchanan and Stubblebine [6] and Turvey [19]. The reasoning of these authors has been questioned by Mishan [13], who observes that, if the producer and recipient(s) of an externality can reach voluntary agreement *after* a tax is imposed, they can as well reach agreement before the tax is imposed, thereby optimally "internalizing" the externality. Mishan fails to note that government intervention and taxation may change the relative bargaining strength or willingness of the participants to bargain. This possibility must be considered in devising a general tax scheme.

[4] This conclusion has been accepted by Turvey [19] and Buchanan [5]. Baumol [3] even went so far as to define externalities as consisting only of the nonseparable case. Surprisingly, Mishan [13] does not cite the Davis—Whinston conclusion although their article appears in his near-exhaustive bibliography. Wellisz [20] developed a nonlinear tax scheme to eliminate the uncertainty arising from nonseparability and enforce optimal externality levels. Davis and Whinston [9] noted that his scheme requires solving differential equations for which general solution methods do not exist. No other attack on the Davis—Whinston conclusion appears to have been made and no one has challenged their notion that per unit taxes (such as a tax per pound of pollutant, frequently discussed in the press) are ineffective under nonseparability.

cost exceeding welfare improvement, and that a unit tax on physical quantities of mutual, nonseparable externalities works perfectly well.

Following some preliminary material, two conditions for optimal externality taxes will be stated. Then, an externality tax—subsidy algorithm for a competitive economy of many firms and many interdependent externalities will be developed and given a graphical interpretation. Finally, several theorems on taxes and subsidies will be proved and their implications for conclusions (A) and (B) above and for the control of environmental externalities will be briefly explored.

I. THE MODEL

Following much of the externalities literature, the goal of the analysis is taken to be production sector efficiency in a perfectly competitive economy where only firms are directly affected by externalities. The assumption that consumers are not affected by externalities except in the form of altered prices (pecuniary externalities) limits us to such cases as pollutant damage to the surfaces of commercial buildings, to the productivity of fisheries and to the economist's inevitable outdoor laundry. Unfortunately the valuation problems in determining optimal levels of externalities affecting consumers (well surveyed by Mishan [13]) make it desirable to limit the scope of this attempt to rehabilitate the tax—subsidy approach. It is hoped that much of the approach to be developed here can be carried over to externalities affecting consumers.

It is commonly assumed in the literature that externality and salable commodity levels that maximize the combined profit of the set of firms affected are Pareto efficient. This can be proved rigorously,[5] so we shall take maximization of combined profit as our optimization rule.

The externalities cost function used throughout is derived from a "generalized joint supply" production function.[6] It permits externalities to be varied

---

[5] See Whitcomb [21, Chapter 3] for a derivation of Pareto efficiency conditions for a production sector externalities model and a proof that the rule "maximize combined profit" meets them. Note that to apply the rule with given commodity prices (see Eq. (2), for example) is to assume that a partial equilibrium analysis is appropriate

[6] Whitcomb [21] argues that externalities are produced only as by products of the production of salable commodities. Since the levels of relevant externalities are not zero in laissez faire equilibrium, the single equation implicit production function $F(q, x, v_1, v_2) = 0$ (where q is a salable commodity, x an externality and v_1 and v_2 inputs) cannot be used. It implies a transformation function for q and x, with x free to assume zero values. Then, given that x has zero "market price," profit maximization implies that x will always be set to 0. Nor can the "strict joint supply" model, $F(q, v_1, v_2) = 0$, $x = g(q)$, be used, though it is implied by most of the externality literature. This model makes it impossible to vary the externality "output" for a given level of salable commodity output, whereas in reality it is

(continued)

independently of the level of salable outputs by varying the input mix, tracing out the least cost feasible locus of externality and salable output levels. In cost function (1) we assume each firm produces several salable commodities, and several externalities, and is affected by externalities produced by $R - 1$ other firms:

$$c_i = c_i(q_i, X_i) \qquad (i = 1, \dots, R) \tag{1}$$

where

$$q_i = (q_{i1}, \dots, q_{il}, \dots, q_{iL}),$$

a vector of salable commodities produced by firm i, and

$$X_i = (x_i{}^m, x_j{}^m)_{j,m} \qquad (j = 1, \dots, R \neq i, \quad m = 1, \dots, M),$$

an R by M matrix. $x_i{}^m$ is an externality of type m produced by firm i and "given" to all other firms as a "public" or "collective" good.[7] $x_j{}^m$ is an externality of type m produced by firm j ($\neq i$) and received by i along with other firms.[8]

II. AN OPTIMAL TAX–SUBSIDY ALGORITHM

The purpose of setting taxes or subsidies is to enforce particular (already determined) efficient externality levels without promulgating output directives. Thus, before taxes and subsidies can be found, it is necessary to find Pareto efficient outputs $q_i{}^*$ and $X_i{}^*$ satisfying

$$\max \sum_{i=1}^{R} \pi_i = \sum_{i=1}^{R} pq_i{}' - \sum_{i=1}^{R} c_i(q_i, X_i), \tag{2}$$

---

usually efficient to reduce pollutant levels (for example) by varying the input mix rather than reducing salable output precipitously. A generalized joint supply production function, $F_1(q, v_{11}, v_2) = 0, F_2(x, v_{12}, v_2) = 0$, introduces "joint inputs" (v_2 – an example is fuel oil used by electrical utilities) which explain positive externality levels in laissez faire equilibrium and, in conjunction with ordinary inputs like v_{12} allocated to F_2, make it possible to alter the externality level efficiently. By constrained cost minimization subject to strictly convex F_1 and F_2, we can derive the cost function $c(q, x)$ and with M externalities produced and received by the firm, the more general cost function (Eq. (1)).

[7] The treatment of externalities as collective goods has been around at least since Bator [2] and is developed most rigorously by Mishan [12]. Although there may be private good cases, the environmental externalities of current interest seem to be collective goods. If the damage declines with distance from the source, this can be reflected in the recipient's cost function with the public good character not diminished.

[8] Some elements of q_i and X_i may be zero to reflect an output not produced or not received by firm i.

where π is a vector of profits and p is a vector of salable commodity prices. We then set shadow prices so that firms having strictly convex cost functions of the type of Eq. (1)[9] and maximizing individual profit will be led (1) to produce Pareto efficient externality levels and (2) to desire producers of externalities affecting them to produce efficient levels.

For the method to make intuitive sense, it helps to conceive of an *externality control authority* setting the shadow prices in the following informationally centralized manner: Find the (Pareto efficient) externality levels that maximize combined profit (i.e. satisfy Eq. (2)). Modify each firm's profit function by assigning a matrix of unknown shadow prices. Form the first order conditions for a maximum of each modified profit function, with both externality levels and shadow prices still unknown variables. Finally, substitute the Pareto efficient externality levels in these first order conditions and solve for the optimal shadow prices.

Some new notation must be defined:

$$s_i = (s_i{}^m \cdot s_{ji}^m)_{j,m} \qquad (j = 1, \ldots, R, \neq i; \quad m = 1, \ldots, M),$$

an R by M matrix of shadow prices.

$s_i{}^m$ is the total price received by i from all other firms for 1 unit of $x_i{}^m$ produced by i. $s_i{}^m$ will be positive or negative as the externality is an economy or a diseconomy.

s_{ji}^m is the price paid by i to j for 1 unit of $x_j{}^m$. If $x_j{}^m$ is an external diseconomy, $s_{ji}^m > 0$, indicating positive tax revenue to i.

$$D_i = (s_i{}^m \cdot x_i{}^m, s_{ji}^m \cdot x_j{}^m)_{j,m} \qquad (j = 1, \ldots, R, \neq i; \quad m = 1, \ldots, M),$$

an R by M matrix in which each element is the product of element in s_i and the corresponding element in X_i.

The externality control authority first modifies each firm's profit function by adding to it the net revenue from the firm's "purchase" and "sale" of externalities at the (unknown) shadow prices:

$$E_i = pq_i{}' - c_i(q_i, X_i) + kD_i t' \qquad (i = 1, \ldots, R), \qquad (3)$$

where k and t are sum vectors, $k, t = (1, 1, \ldots, 1)$, having as many elements as D_i has rows and columns respectively.[10]

---

[9] Strict convexity of c_i is implied by strict convexity of each function of the production set from which c_i is derived. This may be interpreted as requiring strictly diminishing returns to all inputs. See Whitcomb [21, Chapter 2.2] for derivation of c_i from the production set $F_{i1}, F_{i2}, \ldots$ and discussion of the special meaning of diminishing returns in externality production or reduction. The shapes of the cost curves shown in Figures 1 and 2 are implied by these assumptions.

[10] $kD_i t'$ is a scalar, giving the sum of the elements in D_i which is i's net receipts from shadow prices on all externalities affecting it.

The necessary conditions for a maximum to E_i are:

$$\frac{\partial E_i}{\partial q_i} = p - \frac{\partial c_i(q_i, X_i)}{\partial q_i} = 0 \qquad (i = 1, \ldots, R); \qquad (4)$$

$$\frac{\partial E_i}{\partial X_i} = - \frac{\partial c_i(q_i, X_i)}{\partial X_i} + s_i = 0 \qquad (i = 1, \ldots, R). \qquad (5)$$

The optimal values of the elements of s_i may be found by evaluating Eq. (5) at the Pereto efficient (P.E.) values q_i^*, X_i^*:

$$s_i^{*m} = \frac{\partial c_i(q_i^*, X_i^*)}{\partial x_i^m} \qquad (m = 1, \ldots, M); \qquad (6)$$

$$s_{ji}^{*m} = \frac{\partial c_i(q_i^*, X_i^*)}{\partial x_j^m} \qquad (j = 1, \ldots, R, \neq i; \quad m = 1, \ldots, M).$$

The straightforward interpretation is that the "price" received by i for the externality it produces must equal its marginal cost of increasing the externality above the P.E. level. In the case of an external diseconomy this marginal cost will generally be negative (i would save money by producing more) so s_i^{*m} will be negative — a tax. The marginal cost of an incremental increase in an external economy will generally be positive, hence a positive subsidy. The "price" paid by i for the externality it consumes must also equal the marginal cost resulting from an increase in the externality above the P.E. level.[11]

The optimal shadow prices may also be interpreted graphically for an externality producer and any number of recipient firms, although we shall assume a single recipient for simplicity.

The upper panel of Figure 1 represents a two-dimensional slice of firm 1's *total* cost hypersurface, with the level of the external economy it produces (x_1^1)

---

[11]The values of the q_i and the X_i should of course be constrained to the nonnegative orthant. Given this constraint, a corner solution, $x_j^m = 0$, may occasionally be optimal for an external diseconomy. For such a corner solution to be enforced, we need only set the shadow prices such that

$$s_{ji}^{*m} \leqslant \frac{\partial c_i(q_i^*, X_i^*)}{\partial x_j^m} \qquad (i = 1, \ldots, R \neq j),$$

and

$$\sum_{i=1}^{R \neq j} \frac{\partial c_i(q_i^*, X_i^*)}{\partial x_j^m} \geqslant \sum_{i=1}^{R \neq j} s_{ji}^{*m} \geqslant \frac{-\partial c_j(q_j^*, X_j^*)}{\partial x_j^m}.$$

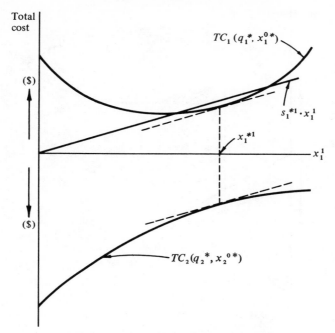

Figure 1.   Subsidy for external economy.

free to vary and all other variables fixed at their Pareto efficient levels (hence the notation $q_1{}^*, X_1^0{}^*$). Note that total cost (TC) falls to a minimum at some positive level of $x_1{}^1$, which is the level firm 1 would set in laissez-faire equilibrium. This is how an external economy differs from a Bowen—Lindahl—Samuelson public good (Samuelson [16]). The lower panel maps the same slice of (the recipient) firm 2's cost function on an inverted scale. Note that firm 2's total cost of producing given levels of its outputs falls with increases in the external economy level. Clearly, with all other variables affecting the two firms at their P.E. levels, combined total cost is minimized (and, by duality, combined profit is maximized) where the distance between the two curves is smallest, or equivalently where their slopes are equal. Thus, x_1^{*1} is the P.E. value of the externality which a shadow price is now set to enforce.

Since the shadow price received by firm 1 equals its marginal cost (MC) at x_1^{*1}, the revenue from the "sale" of $x_1{}^1$ can be represented by a ray from the origin whose slope equals the slope of TC at x_1^{*1}. The same ray represents the recipient's cost of "purchasing" $x_1{}^1$ if we treat the upper panel as negative revenue for firm 2. Each firm will choose that level of $x_1{}^1$ where its "externality

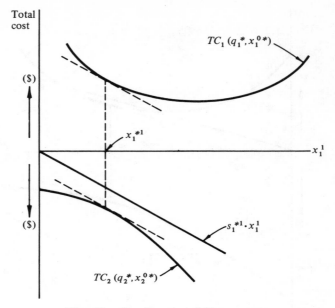

Figure 2.   Tax for external diseconomy.

revenue" (all other revenue is fixed) minus total cost is algebraically greatest. Firm 1 will produce, and firm 2 will want 1 to produce, x_1^{*1}.[12]

Figure 2 depicts the case of firm 1 producing and firm 2 receiving an external diseconomy. Here, because firm 2's total cost of producing given levels of its outputs rises with increases in the external diseconomy, the P.E. level is less than what 1 would set in laissez-faire equilibrium. Again, the optimal shadow price produces an "externality revenue" (now negative for 1 and positive for 2) which enforces efficient externality levels.

Note that the tax paid to the party injured by an external diseconomy bears no necessary relation to the damage done him (unless "damage" is taken to mean "marginal damage" evaluated at the optimal externality level). When the profit maximizing level of q_2 does not depend on the level of x_1^1, we can demonstrate this point using Figure 2 because in this case total damage can be

---

[12] If there are several recipient firms j $(j = 2, \ldots, R)$, we can represent variations of each firm's cost as the externality varies (with all their other variables set equal to their P.E. values) as a curve in the lower panel of Figure 1. Combined total cost is the vertical sum of these curves. We can represent the subsidy each pays by a (negative) revenue line $(s_{1j}^1 \cdot x_1^1)$ having the same slope as firm j's TC curves at x_1^{*1}. The vertical sum of these revenue lines must equal the subsidy revenue line of firm 1. This point will be proved rigorously in **Theorem 2.**

measured by the cost of the extra resources required by 2 to produce its output when the externality level goes from zero to the laissez-faire level.[13] This is measured by the difference in height of the total cost curve, and is generally different from the height of the tax revenue line at x_1^{*1}. Even the conceptually best approaches to damage measurement in the real world (e.g., Ridker's [15] use of real estate price differences) tend to measure the total damage resulting from a large change in pollutant levels.

III. THEOREMS ON TAXES AND SUBSIDIES

Before one can have much confidence in the tax—subsidy algorithm just developed, it is necessary to prove that it makes firms wish to produce *and receive* P.E. externality levels. Next it is proved that the total "price" s_i^{*m} received by firm i per unit of its production of externality m must equal the *sum* of the prices s_{ij}^{*m} paid by firms $j = 1, \ldots, R, \neq i$. A corollary is that a different price is generally paid by each recipient firm. Finally, we return to the pessimistic conclusions in the literature, cited at the beginning of the paper, and disprove them.

Theorem 1 *Externality shadow prices s_i^* will cause the firms, maximizing individually, to prefer P.E. output levels.*[14]

Having been assigned the prices s_i^*, firm i's modified profit function is

$$E_i = pq_i' - c_i(q_i, X_i) + kD_i^*t' \qquad (i = 1, \ldots, R), \qquad (7)$$

where D_i^* is understood to mean the matrix where each element is the product of an element of s_i^* and the corresponding element of X_i.

The necessary conditions for a maximum of (7) are

$$\frac{\partial E_i}{\partial q_i} = p - \frac{\partial c_i(q_i, X_i)}{\partial q_i} = 0 \qquad (i = 1, \ldots, R), \qquad (8)$$

and

$$\frac{\partial E_i}{\partial X_i} = -\frac{\partial c_i(q_i, X_i)}{\partial X_i} + s_i^* = 0 \qquad (i = 1, \ldots, R). \qquad (9)^{15}$$

[13] In the general case, where q_2 depends on the level of x_1^1, the seemingly most appropriate measure of damage to 2 is its loss of profit when x_1^1 goes from 0 to $\hat{x}_1^1$ and q_2 is optimally adjusted. This can only be measured on a three-dimensional diagram where variations in q_2 and in revenue from its sale are represented in addition to cost and x_1^1. Damage will still not generally equal tax revenue.

[14] Important elements of this proof were suggested by Enrique Arzac.

[15] Firm i, in maximizing its profit, would normally only take the derivatives of (8) with respect to x_i^m ($m = 1, \ldots, M$), the externalities under its control, accepting whichever

Designate the maximum $\hat{q}_i, \hat{X}_i$. Equations (9) state, for each i, the equality of two matrices, so the corresponding elements of each matrix must be equal. Substituting (6) for the elements of s_1^*, we get

$$\frac{\partial c_i(\hat{q}_i, \hat{X}_i)}{\partial x_j^m} = \frac{\partial c_i(q_i^*, X_i^*)}{\partial x_j^m} \qquad (i, j = 1, \ldots, R; \quad m = 1, \ldots, M). \quad (10)$$

Now if the cost functions c_i are strictly convex, their first partial derivatives are monotonic. Since monotonic functions are one-to-one functions, we can make use of the definition: if a function F is one-to-one, then $F(x) = F(y)$ implies $x = y$.[16] Thus in (10), $\hat{q}_i = q_i^*$ and $\hat{X}_i = X_i^*$ for all i, j.

Thus it is proved that the s_i^* modify each firm's profit function such that it will, by maximizing its individual profits, choose unique externality output levels that are equal to the P.E. levels, and will also want other firms to set externalities under their control at P.E. levels. The latter is because some of the elements of X_i^* are externality levels of firms other than i.

Theorem 2   *The total price received by firm i per unit of its production of an externality must equal the sum of the prices paid per unit by all the firms receiving the externality:*

$$s_j^{*m} = - \sum_{i=1}^{R \neq j} s_{ji}^m .$$

The total shadow price received by j per unit of the externality it produces (x_j^m) is computed using j's cost function. The shadow price paid by each firm i $(\neq j)$ is computed using i's cost function. If the amount j expects to receive from all the other firms $s_j^{*m} \cdot x_j^m$ is to equal the sum of the payments each firm expects to make to j, $-\Sigma_{i=1}^{R \neq j} s_{ji}^{*m} \cdot x_j^m$, then $s_j^{*m} = -\Sigma_{i=1}^{R \neq j} s_{ji}^{*m}$. But will the equality hold? We must prove it.

The P.E. value of x_j^m is that value at which

$$\frac{\partial \Sigma P_i}{\partial x_j^m} = - \frac{\partial(\Sigma c_i(q_i, X_i))}{\partial x_j^m} = - \sum_{i=1}^{R} \frac{\partial c_i(q_i, X_i)}{\partial x_j^m} = 0. \quad (11)$$

Rearranging the terms of the expression in parentheses, the following must

---

values of the x_j^m (over j, m) that are set by the other firms. In this proof, however, we take the derivatives with respect to all elements of X_i, because we wish to prove that the prices s_i^* remove all conflict among the firms about output levels, i.e., we wish to find out what levels of the x_j^m firm i *wants*.

[16]Apostol [1, Definition 2–7, p. 29]. This definition can be applied in a very broad sense so x and y can be vectors. If x and y are vectors, $x = y \Rightarrow$ all elements in x equal the corresponding elements in y. Thus x is $(\hat{q}_i, \hat{X}_i)$ and y is (q_i^*, X_i^*); and if $x = y$, then $\hat{q}_i = q_i^*$ and $\hat{X}_i = X_i^*$.

hold when the derivatives are evaluated at P.E. values of the relevant variables:

$$\frac{\partial c_j(q_j^*, X_j^*)}{\partial x_j^m} = - \sum_{i=1}^{R \neq j} \frac{\partial c_i(q_i^*, X_i^*)}{\partial x_j^m} \tag{12}$$

From (6) we have

$$s_j^{*m} = \frac{\partial c_j(q_j^*, X_j^*)}{\partial x_j^m}, \tag{13}$$

and

$$s_{ji}^{*m} = \frac{\partial c_i(q_i^*, X_i^*)}{\partial x_j^m} \qquad (i = 1, \ldots, R, \neq j). \tag{14}$$

Substituting (13) and (14) into (12) we get

$$s_j^{*m} = - \sum_{i=1}^{R \neq i} s_{ji}^{*m}. \tag{15}$$

An obvious corollary is that there is no requirement that the price charged for externality x_j^m be equal for each of the firms $i = 1, \ldots, R, \neq j$. In general, it will not be since each firm's marginal cost evaluated at P.E. variable levels is different.

This theorem guarantees that a tax—subsidy scheme based on this algorithm is self-sufficient: the "center" need not expend its own resources except on administration. The shadow price algorithm and this theorem can be applied to Bowen—Lindahl—Samuelson public goods supplied as intermediate factors of production (weather forecasting, rainmaking, some R&D, etc.) with this proviso: if the entity producing a public good of this sort has a downward sloping *MC* curve, this pricing scheme may lead to negative profit. The government may have to subsidize the activity or alter the pricing scheme so as to pass some of the recipient's increased profit on to the producer.[17]

Theorem 3 *When the number of firms receiving an externality is large, none of them need pay a subsidy or receive a tax in order for a stable optimum to be enforced.*

Theorem 1 shows that shadow prices s_i^* make recipients want producers to set P.E. externality levels. But we have not fully explained when this property is necessary and when it is not. In its absence, firm i will not want other firms to produce efficient levels of externalities affecting i. For example, as Coase [7]

---

[17] This contingency is much less likely when the good is an externality. An externality is always produced as a by-product. Given charges s_i^*, the firm's choice is between producing P.E. levels of all variables or shutting down the joint activity altogether.

first pointed out, when the tax on (diseconomy) x_j^m is not paid to firm i, it still wants x_j^m set equal to zero. With such a tax, firm j will set $x_j^m = x_j^{*m}$, but it may be persuaded by a payment from i to reduce x_j^m, below the optimum. When the tax s_{ji}^{*m} is paid to firm 1, there is no incentive to offer such a payment.

The unfortunate implication of requiring that the tax be paid to the injured party is that if there are many parties injured by x_j^m and the tax paid to each is small, the cost of paying it may exceed the benefit of reducing the externality. Happily, in this situation it is not really necessary that the tax be paid to the injured party. Each injured party receives a very small benefit from further reducing x_j^m below x_j^{*m}. It would take a very large coalition of firms to be able to offer j enough to reduce x_j^m by more than an infinitesimal amount. Since the externality is a public good, it is in the interest of each firm to encourage others to join the coalition and refuse to do so itself, or, joining it, to offer too small a contribution. (Note that the benefit to each firm from a reduction of x_j^m is, in general, different from that of every other firm, so each could not be expected to make the same contribution.) The fact that threat strategies employed by j and/or the coalition might break down bargaining is superfluous.

A successful coalition, though so unlikely as to be nearly impossible, cannot be ruled out as forcefully as it can be in the model of perfect competition without externalities.[18] Thus it may be reassuring to add that the action of a successful coalition would be visible enough to be prevented by law.

Theorem 4   *Even if $c_i(q_i, X_i^0, x_j^m)$ cannot be written as $c_{i1}(q_i, X_i^0) + c_{i2}(x_j^m)$ for any or all $i, j \in R$, $i \neq j$, profit maximizing firms assigned the shadow prices s_i^* will still produce P.E. externality levels.*

Davis and Whinston [8], defining nonseparable externalities in a manner similar to the above, claimed to have proved that no set of externality taxes and subsidies can enforce the P.E. solution when two firms each produce an externality that is nonseparable in the other's cost function. The heart of their argument is the fact that when profit maximizing levels of i's decision variables depend on the level of a variable under j's control and vice versa, *and* when i knoweth not what j doeth, neither can be sure its decisions are correct. In the language of noncooperative non-zero-sum game theory chosen by Davis and Whinston, neither firm has a dominant strategy (an output level that maximizes profit regardless of the other firm's choice of output level). Imposition of taxes and subsidies supposedly makes no difference.

---

[18] The conclusion that coalitions large enough to restrict price effectively cannot be formed underlies the perfectly competitive model. What makes the conclusion stronger than in the externalities case is that the refusal of nonmembers to restrict output at the coalition price actively injures the coalition (by producing excess supply) rather than simply limiting its financial resources. A more rigorous proof of the existence of the core and Lindahl equilibrium is currently underway. Please see also Shapley and Shubik [17].

Davis and Whinston's error is their failure to recognize that optimal taxes and subsidies make one strategy dominant for each firm by giving each a certain and correct predictor of the other's strategy. Consider firm i, a recipient of the external diseconomy x_j^m. If i will simply calculate the optimal strategy it *wants* firm j to play, given the optimal tax it receives (s_{ji}^m), that will serve as a prediction of the strategy j *will* play. Firm i wants j to set $x_j^m = x_j^{*m}$ and knows j will, so long as j believes i will set $x_i^m = x_j^{*m}$. So long as all firms are rational and believe all other firms are rational, the circle of indeterminacy is broken by the information contained in optimal taxes and subsidies.

Straightforward application of Theorem 1 provides a rigorous proof of this for convex cost functions. If firm i treats all elements of X_i (its own externalities and those of other firms affecting it) as decision variables and seeks optimal values given the s_i^*, Theorem 1 tells us that it will choose $\hat{X}_i = X_i^*$. Since firm j, by the same reasoning, will set $\hat{X}_j = X_j^*$, each firm has a perfectly accurate predictor of the other firm's externality output decision. Knowledge that this is so is the only additional ingredient required.

If i, for whatever reason, incorrectly predicts that j will set $x_j^m \neq x_j^{*m}$, i may set $x_i^m \neq x_i^{*m}$. If j will just play, and continue to play, the strategy x_j^{*m}, i will get new, correct information and change its strategy to the efficient one.

What if one firm engages in extortion? It can only do this by demanding payment for setting its externality at the P.E. level. Successful extortion will result only in a transfer of wealth, and efficient outputs will still be produced. If the extorter plays a threat strategy unsuccessfully, he loses part of the profits from efficient operation as well as the extortion payment. Presumably, for this reason, such threat strategies (which result in non-P.E. outputs) would not often be carried out. In any case, such extortion could be pretty effectively banned by law since one of the active parties is being injured and has every incentive to report the offense. Such offenses as collusion in restraint of trade, illegal consumption, etc. are harder to prevent because no party directly involved is injured.

If the number of firms affected by a nonseparable externality is large and the tax paid to each would be small, then the tax need not actually be paid. Each firm needs to know only what the tax would be to predict correctly the producer's activity level. Alternatively, the producer would have incentive to announce its prospective output levels and no incentive to withhold the information (since extortion payments would be smaller than the costs of demanding them).

IV. CONCLUSIONS

The central conclusion of this paper is of course that unit taxes and subsidies on physical quantities of externalities among firms can, in theory, be calculated, and they will enforce Pareto efficiency. Let us briefly examine the implications of this for such real world problems as pollution control. First, since most forms of pollution probably affect individuals more profoundly than firms, it would be hoped that a tax—subsidy scheme could be proved to work in an economy with externalities affecting consumers. The main problem in extending these results to such an economy would seem to be that of finding a unique Pareto optimum.[19] Once a set of externality levels are accepted as being optimal, it seems intuitively plausible that taxes and subsidies can be found to enforce them.

It was assumed in setting forth the tax—subsidy algorithm that a central authority calculates taxes and subsidies. Once they are assigned, decision making is decentralized (compared with the alternatives of externality quotas or nationalization). In this approach, it is unrealistically assumed that firms possess perfect information that they are capable of transmitting to the center at zero cost and that they will transmit honest information. With these assumptions relaxed, centrally computed taxes and subsidies are only approximations to optimality. There can be no assurance that they will not bring about a welfare reduction. We can only rely on the same intuition that justifies attempts in other areas to restore "workable competition": carefully (perhaps conservatively) calculated taxes and subsidies should result in improvement more often than not. Any attempt at a decentralized *tâtonnement* shadow pricing scheme would seem to founder on the parties' incentive to misstate information transmitted to the center and might produce poorer results than those flowing from the center's own investigations into costs and benefits.[20]

This paper seems to justify several specific suggestions for the (approximate) taxes and subsidies on some pollutants toward which our political process is moving. First, as stated in Theorem 3, when many are affected by the same pollutant, the tax share going to each injured party (generally different for each) may be paid to the government and not redistributed. This convenience in a world of positive administrative costs makes particular sense when the parties ultimately responsible for the pollution (e.g., consumers of electricity) form the majority of those injured by it. Second, the optimal tax will typically be less for one polluter farther from pollution centers than another producer of identical pollutants. Finally, this work shows the importance of devising a complete set of taxes and subsidies on interconnected externalities. Taxes on one or a few pollutants will often cause manufacturers to switch from one pollutant to another. For example, public pressure against the use of phosphates in laundry

[19] As Mishan [13] shows, externality levels that are Pareto optimal under one state of law (such as a law banning the externality) are not Pareto optimal under another state of law (a law permitting externalities).

[20] The most notable example of an informationally decentralized shadow pricing scheme applied to externalities is that of Davis and Whinston [9].

detergents has already caused some manufacturers to substitute carbon compounds which apparently result in the same eutrophication of bodies of water charged against phosphates. If the government enacts a reasonably comprehensive set of taxes and show its determination to react quickly to newly discovered pollutants, it will be in the self-interest of firms to investigate carefully the results of any substitution of inputs before engaging in capital expenditures and promotional campaigns.

REFERENCES

1. Apostol, T., *Mathematical Analysis*, Reading, Massachusetts: Addison-Wesley, 1957.
2. Bator, M., "The Anatomy of Market Failure," *The Quarterly Journal of Economics*, August 1958, **72**, 351–379.
3. Baumol, J., "External Economies and Second-Order Optimality Conditions," *American Economic Review*, June 1964, **54**, 358–372.
4. Baumol, J., and D. F. Bradford, "Detrimental Externalities and Non-Convexity of the Production Set," *Economica N.S.*, May 1972, **39**, 160–176.
5. Buchanan, J. M., "External Diseconomies, Corrective Taxes, and Market Structure," *American Economic Review*, March 1969, **59**, 174–177.
6. Buchanan, J. M., and W. C. Stubblebine, "Externality," *Economica*, November 1962, **29**, 371–384.
7. Coase, R. H., "The Problem of Social Cost," *Journal of Law and Economics*, October 1960, **3**, 1–44.
8. Davis, O. A., and A. B. Whinston, "Externalities, Welfare, and the Theory of Games," *Journal of Political Economy*, June 1962, **70**, 241–262.
9. Davis, O. A., and A. B. Whinston, "On Externalities, Information and the Government-Assisted Invisible Hand," *Economica*, August 1966, **33**, 303–318.
10. Henderson, J. M., and R. E. Quandt, *Microeconomic Theory – A Mathematical Approach*, New York: McGraw-Hill, 1958; 2nd ed., 1971.
11. Meade, J. E., "External Economies and Diseconomies in a Competitive Situation," *Economic Journal*, March 1952, **62**, 54–67.
12. Mishan, E. J., "The Relationship Between Joint Products, Collective Goods and External Effects," *Journal of Political Economy*, May–June 1969, **72**, 329–348.
13. Mishan, E. J., "The Postwar Literature on Externalities: An Interpretive Essay," *Journal of Economic Literature*, March 1971, **9**, 1–28.
14. Pigou, A. C., *The Economics of Welfare*, New York: Macmillan, 4th ed., 1932, reprinted, 1952.
15. Ridker, G., *Economic Costs of Air Pollution: Studies in Measurement*, New York: Praeger, 1967.
16. Samuelson, P. A., "The Pure Theory of Public Expenditure," *Review of Economics and Statistics*, November 1954, **36**, 387–389.
17. Shapley, L. S., and M. Shubik, "On the Core of and Economic System with Externalities," *American Economic Review*, September 1969, **59**, 678–684.
18. Starrett, D. A., "Fundamental Nonconvexities in the Theory of Externalities," *Journal of Economic Theory*, April 1972, **4**, 180–199.
19. Turvey, R., "On Divergencies Between Social Cost and Private Cost," *Economica*, August 1963, **30**, 309–313.

20. Wellisz, S., "On External Diseconomies and the Government-Assisted Invisible Hand," *Economica*, November 1964, **31**, 345–362.
21. Whitcomb, D. K., *Externalities and Welfare*, New York: Columbia Univ. Press, 1972.

Discussion

JAMES T. LITTLE

Washington University

Of the many unsolved problems related to externalities, perhaps none is so important as the problem of design of institutions and institutionally imposed constraints that might contribute to higher levels of economic welfare. Thus, the Lin–Whitcomb paper falls in a highly significant area of research.

Briefly, their suggested procedure is to modify the reported profit functions by a system of tax–subsidy functions that represent "prices" for interfirm effects, solve for the conditions for maximization of the modified profit functions, and solve for the optimal externality "prices" by substituting the optimal levels of the inputs in these first order conditions. In conception, this approach is close to Arrow's formation of auxiliary markets through the definition of property rights on externalities [1]. In the Lin–Whitcomb procedure, however, "prices" are determined by the central authority under the implicit assumption that property rights exist.

Clearly, the central problem with this procedure is one of information. The central authority requires the correct profit functions of the firms both to set the optimal input levels and to establish the optimal tax–subsidy scheme. However, quite aside from the informational requirements, the procedure depends critically on the assumption of convexity of the cost functions. Theorem 1 demonstrates that the tax–subsidy scheme defined by the algorithm will enforce optimal output decisions on the part of all firms. Actually, the result proved is somewhat stronger: firms will *uniquely* prefer the efficient input levels. The key step in the proof of this theorem, however, uses the fact that the first partial derivatives of differentiable, *strictly* convex functions are one-to-one. In economic terms, the assumption implies that all firms have a unique maximum of their modified profit functions at the Pareto efficient input levels.

The assumption of convex cost functions, as with most assumptions of great power, is somewhat suspect, and it is difficult to justify the assumption particularly when externalities are present. Taking into account both the informational requirements and the severity of the assumptions as to the technological relationships, it must be concluded that the specific approach developed here is somewhat limited in its applicability.

The second of Lin and Whitcomb's main results is that when the number of firms receiving an externality is "large" and the effect of the externality on the profits of recipient firms is "small," then the tax or subsidy need not be paid in order for the stable optimum to be enforced.

While their argument is intuitively plausible, it is difficult to know just how "large" the number of firms must be and how "small" must be the effect on recipient firms' profits resulting from a change.

Consider the following example: suppose there is a single externality X_J produced by firm J and received by n other firms. Profit functions of all firms are functions of X_J alone. The control authority sets the tax or subsidy at a level such that the functions

$$E_J = \Pi_J(X_J) + \sum_i S^*_{Ji} X_J \qquad \text{and} \qquad E_i = \Pi_i(X_J) + S^*_{Ji} X_J \qquad (i = 1, \ldots, n)$$

are maximized at X_J^* where X_J^* is the point of maximized joint profits.

Now suppose firm J is taxed (or subsidized) while the n recipient firms do not receive a subsidy (or pay a tax). For any level X_J of the externality other than X_J^*, they are willing to pay J the difference between their profits at X_J and X_J^* Taking these bribes into account, firm J attempts to maximize

$$B_J = \Pi_J(X_J) + \sum S^*_{Ji} X_J + \sum_i (\Pi_i(X_J) - \Pi_i(X_J^*)) - (\Pi_J^*) + \sum S^*_{Ji} X_J^*).$$

Hence

$$B_J = P(X_J) - P(X_J^*) + \sum S^*_{Ji}(X_J - X_J^*),$$

where $P(X_J)$ is joint profits at externality level X_J. Since joint profits are maximized at X_J^*, for any $X_J \neq X_J^*, P(X_J) - P(X_J^*)$ is negative, and therefore the potential for bargaining depends on $\sum S^*_{Ji}$. The external economy case is illustrated in Figure 1.

At any level of X_J in the interval $(X_J^*, \hat{X}_J)$ both firm J's profits and total industry profits are higher than at X_J^*. Profits are maximized at $\tilde{X}_J$ where

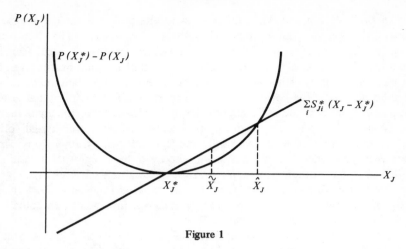

Figure 1

$dP(X_J)/dX_J = -\Sigma S^*_{ji}$. Because firm J receives a per unit subsidy without an offsetting tax on the n recipient firms, there is a net subsidy to the group of firms. It is for this reason that the potential for bargaining away from X_J^* exists.

The crux of the Lin—Whitcomb argument is that firm J will continue to produce at X_J^* rather than some other level such as $\tilde{X}_J$ because the benefit each firm receives from the change is small, and therefore it is in its self-interest not to contribute but to encourage other firms to do so. However, the incentive to contribute also depends on the total gains that might result from moving to another level of X_J. Not all firms need contribute in order that firm J have sufficient incentive to move to another level of production such as $\hat{X}_J$. In fact, through the per unit subsidy, the central authority is a major contributor. The higher the marginal effect on profits of J of a change in X_J (at X_J^*), the larger is the contribution of the central authority at levels of production above X_J^*. Thus, the contributions of a relatively small number of firms, together with the implicit contribution of the central authority, may provide sufficient incentive to firm J. While firms may recognize the "publicness" of contribution, they will also take self-interest into account. The larger the potential gains, the greater is the incentive for the necessary coalition of recipient firms to form.

It is worth noting that without the subsidy, "efficient" bargaining by the firms would imply production at X_J^* (i.e. $S^*_{ji} = 0$ for all i). It is the existence of the per unit subsidy or tax that effectively creates the incentive to produce at levels other than the Pareto efficient level. This still does not answer the question of how "large" the number of recipient firms must be nor how "small" must be the marginal effect on this profits. However, it does suggest that in the presence of a nonbalanced tax—subsidy system, the possibility of effective interfirm bargaining is higher than in a situation without the subsidy and the effective bargaining will lead to inefficient allocations.

The third of Lin and Whitcomb's main results is that even in the case of nonseparable externalities, optimal tax–subsidy schemes exist. The basis of this claim in Theorem 1 which shows that modified profits of each firm are maximized by choosing those levels of inputs maximizing joint profits given the optimal tax–subsidy scheme. There is, however, an important proviso: the variables not under the control of the firm must be set at their optimal level if the firm is to choose the optimal input levels. Davis and Whinston argue that in the nonseparable case, no single strategy exists which dominates all other strategies but rather is dependent on the strategy followed by other firms. Thus, there is no assurance that the firms will choose optimal input levels. Lin and Whitcomb, on the other hand, argue that the optimal tax subsidy scheme gives firms perfect predictors of other firms' strategies. That is, given the externality price, the optimal level of the externality for each firm will be the predicted level of the externality.

What really is at issue is the question of whether optimal decisions will be made in the absence of direct coordination but through decentralized decision making given the optimal tax–subsidy system. Clearly, it is to the advantage of all firms to inform other firms as to their intentions; and should all firms behave this way, modified profits of each firm will be higher at optimal input levels. However, the existence of the tax–subsidy system does not assure that all firms will behave in this way. Furthermore, a few firms' decisions to set inputs at nonoptimal levels is likely to signal other firms that the levels of inputs not subject to their control are uncertain. This suggests that the system is unstable and that there is no reason that the group of firms should move toward the optimal allocation should they begin at any nonoptimal allocation. Thus, at least intuitively, the Lin–Whitcomb argument appears to be incorrect. However, a definitive answer requires a more rigorous proof of the assertion within the context of noncooperative games.

In summary, the Lin–Whitcomb paper represents a promising beginning to solutions of a difficult and important set of problems. Just how far the approach can be carried is uncertain, but if useful techniques for the internalization of externalities are to be developed, the Lin and Whitcomb approach merits substantially more research.

REFERENCES

1. Arrow, K. J., "The Organization of Economic Activity: Issues Pertinent to the Choice of Market versus Nonmarket Allocation," in R. Haveman and J. Margolis, eds., *Public Expenditure and Policy Analysis*, Chicago, Illinois: Markham Publ., 1970.
2. Davis, O. A., and A. B. Whinston, "Externalities, Welfare and the Theory of Games," *Journal of Political Economy*, June 1962, **70**, 241–262.
3. Lin, S. A. Y., and Whitcomb, D. K., "Externality Taxes and Subsidies," this volume.

Information, Incentives, and the Internalization of Production Externalities

THEODORE GROVES

Northwestern University

I. INTRODUCTION

The coordination of economic agents' decisions having external effects (hereafter referred to as *external decisions*) has been a central issue of the theory of externalities. Two distinct approaches to this problem have been followed by most of the literature: one emphasizing the incentives agents have to coordinate or internalize their external decisions on their own and the other proposing different explicit mechanisms for achieving the coordination. In both approaches the problems of what information agents must have to achieve the coordination and how this information is to be acquired often have been ignored, assumed away, or treated in an informal manner making it difficult or impossible to verify the claims made.

The first approach emanated from the seminal paper of Coase [6]. The Coasian tradition has emphasized that, in the absence of transaction costs, since a lack of coordination of external decisions is inefficient in the Pareto sense, rational agents will, *on their own*, seek out each other in ways not offered by traditional markets and conclude such agreements that lead to efficiency. Thus if one agent is damaged by a decision of another agent, the damaged party would be expected to offer the damaging agent a deal, commonly called a "bribe," to reduce the level of the damages. If the agents are sufficiently skilled in their negotiations to leave no opportunity for mutual improvement unexplored, efficiency will result. A change in legal liability requiring damaging agents to compensate the damaged parties would, income effects aside, not affect the resulting coordinated decisions if the compensation rules are efficient. Thus, if income effects are negligible, bribes and damage compensation are symmetric; both lead to the same coordinated efficient decisions; only the distribution of benefits is affected.[1]

However, even though economic agents might have an incentive to negotiate efficient agreements, precisely how the negotiation process occurs and what information is required are questions that remain, especially when there are many agents and many external decisions to coordinate. Also, once transaction costs are allowed, the particular mechanism is of crucial importance in order to compare the benefits of coordination with the cost of achieving it. There is no reason to believe that a lack of coordination and a reliance on traditional market incentives to motivate decisions including those with external effects imply that the transaction costs associated with any mechanism capable of achieving efficiency are greater than the benefits to be realized. It may be that an appropriate mechanism for coordination has not yet been considered.

The second approach to the coordination of external decisions has focused on various explicit mechanisms for achieving coordination. Although much of the discussion has been cast in the context of government rules such as tax and subsidy formulas,[2] direct regulation, and the creation of additional markets for, say, pollution rights,[3] the particular coercive authority of government has not been the central issue. The focus of this Pigouvian tradition has been to devise explicit behavioral rules for the economic agents, including an additional agent (e.g. "government" or "central planning board"), such that if all agents follow the prescribed rules, efficient decisions will result.

Two important questions that invariably arise with such formulations and that are often not fully explicated or explored are the informational requirements of the decision rules and the incentives the economic agents have to follow the prescribed decision rules. For example, in a typical two firm model where one firm's output adversely affects the other firm's cost (e.g., a negative externality

[1] The symmetry property of the Coase theorem has been a subject of much controversy in the literature. See Buchanan and Stubblebine [4], Wellisz [21], Calabresi [5], Demsetz [8], Gifford and Stone [9], Kamien, Schwartz and Dolbear [14], Bramhall and Mills [3], Tybout [20], and Marchand and Russell [15].

[2] The literature on the classical remedy of corrective taxes and/or subsidies is voluminous. The classic work is by Pigou [17]; a later classic paper is by Meade [16].

[3] See Dales [7]. More generally the possibility of augmenting the economy with auxiliary markets was proposed by Arrow [1]; see however Starrett [19] for a discussion of the difficulties.

such as pollution produced in fixed proportions with output), an appropriate tax may be levied on the output of the externality producing firm so that individual firm profit maximization will lead to optimal (joint-profit maximizing) decisions. However, since the appropriate tax depends on substantial information regarding the technological, cost, and demand conditions facing the two firms, the authority responsible for setting the tax rate must acquire this information in some manner If, as seems most reasonable, the tax authority must depend at least in part on information supplied by the firms, they typically would have considerable incentives to distort or communicate false information to the taxing authority The damaged firm would typically have an incentive to overstate the damages inflicted on it, and the damaging firm would typically have an incentive to overstate the benefits of its activity that damages the other firm.

This paper follows the spirit of the Pigouvian tradition in formulating explicit mechanisms to coordinate external decisions. Considered is an n-firm production model in which some decisions of the firms have external effects on other firms. In Section II, a general scheme for coordinating the external decisions is formulated and the twin problems of the informational requirements of any mechanism and the incentives the agents have to communicate the correct information are posed. In Section III a specific mechanism is proposed to coordinate the external decisions that takes into account both the informational limitations and the agents' incentives to communicate correct information. Additionally, the mechanism is interpreted as a scheme both for the voluntary coordination or internalization of external decisions and for imposed coordination by a government relying on governmental coercive authority. As a voluntary scheme the mechanism may be viewed in the Coasian tradition of emphasizing the mutual self-interest of the agents to coordinate their external decisions.

II. THE COORDINATION OF EXTERNAL DECISIONS OF MANY FIRMS

Consider a collection of n firms that are interdependent in some aspects of their operations. In order to isolate for attention the interdependencies, we distinguish among three types of decisions each firm may take. First, denote by x_i a vector of firm i's "local" input and/or technique decisons; that is, each element of x_i is the quantity of some input or the level of some variable specifying a choice of technique for firm i and is such that the decision has no direct effect on any of the other firms. Second, denote by y_i a vector of firm i's "local" output decisions; each element of y_i is the quantity of some output of firm i and is also such that it has no direct effect on any of the other firms. Third, denote by z_i a vector of all those decisions of firm i that do have a direct effect on at least one other firm. Letting $z = (z_1, \ldots, z_n)$ denote the n-tuple of all firms' external decisions, the external effects of these decisions is represented by including the entire n-tuple z in every firm's production relation and revenue and cost functions.

Each firm i has a production relation $f_i(x_i, y_i; z) \leqslant 0$ that defines the feasible decision choices (x_i, y_i, z_i) of the firm given the external decisions z_j of each of the other firms. Examples of external decisions affecting the production relation of firm i might be the level of pollution discharged by firm j into a river whose water is used as an input by firm i, or the quantity of some input that is public in the sense that firm j cannot exclude firm i from also consuming the input.

In addition to the production relation, associated with each firm i is a revenue function $P_i(y_i, z)$ and a cost function $C_i(x_i, z)$. The external decisions z are included as arguments of these functions to capture various types of possible pecuniary externalities.[4] For example, if the output of firm j affects the price received by firm i, then z_j would include that output variable. Also, if firm j imposes external costs on firm i and is legally liable to firm i for these costs, then the cost and revenue functions of firms i and j would include the legally required compensation from j to i.

Assuming the firms are profit maximizing and choose their local decisions (x_i, y_i) after the level of all external decisions z are known, we may confine our attention to each firm's profit function, as a function of the external decisions z_j, that is, to the functions $\pi_i(z)$ defined by

$$\pi_i(z) = \max_{(x_i, y_i)} [P_i(y_i, z) - C_i(x_i, z)] \quad \text{subject to} \quad f_i(x_i, y_i; z) \leqslant 0. \quad (2.1)$$

We assume henceforth that the functions $\pi_i(\cdot)$ exist.

In the absence of any coordination of the n firms' choices of their external decisions z, the n profit functions $\pi_i(\cdot)$ define the payoff functions of an n-person noncooperative game. A natural though not unique solution concept for this game is the Nash equilibrium, namely, $\bar{z} = (\bar{z}_1, \ldots, \bar{z}_n)$ is a Nash equilibrium if, for every i, z_i maximizes $\pi_i(\bar{z}/z_i)$ over all possible z_i, where $\bar{z}/z_i \equiv (\bar{z}_1, \ldots, \bar{z}_{i-1}, \bar{z}_{i+1}, \ldots, \bar{z}_n)$.

In general, a Nash equilibrium, even if one exists, will not maximize the joint profits of the n firms, $\Sigma_i \pi_i(z)$, and thus there are potential benefits to the firms individually and collectively from voluntarily coordinating their choices of the external decision. Additionally, if the n firms are perfectly competitive and the external effects of the decisions z do not extend beyond the group of n firms then external decisions that maximize joint profits are efficient from a social welfare point of view; and hence there are social benefits to be gained by

---

[4] See Scitovsky [18] for the distinction between "technological" and "pecuniary" externalities.

coordinating the choices of the external decisions through, perhaps, governmental intervention.[5] In either case, the goal of coordination adopted here is to choose external decisions that maximize the n firms' joint profits. Henceforth, it is assumed that there exists an n-tuple of external decisions, denoted by z^*, that maximizes joint profits:

$$\text{There exists a } z^* \text{ that maximizes } \sum_i \pi_i(z) \text{ over all possible } z. \qquad (2.2)$$

To accomplish the task of coordinating the external decisions, an additional agent, hereafter called the center, is introduced into the model. The center may be thought of as an agent hired by the n-firms to help coordinate the choices of external decisions in the case of voluntary coordination or as a government agency in the case of imposed coordination.

Since the center is assumed to be dependent on information acquired from the n firms, an elementary process of communication between the firms and the center is specified. Each firm i is required to send the center a message, denoted m_i, that is chosen from a "language" set, denoted M, of all possible messages.[6] Upon receipt of the n-tuple of messages $m = (m_1, \ldots, m_n)$, the center selects an n-tuple of external decisions in accordance with a rule denoted $z(\cdot)$; that is $z = z(m)$ are the external decisions selected by the center if it receives the message m.

Although there are many ways to coordinate the external decisions, the process envisioned here requires that the actual external decisons z taken by the firms are sufficiently visible or capable of being monitored at negligible cost to permit the center to announce the external decisions chosen $z(m)$ to the firms and verify subsequently whether or not they have taken these decisions. Sufficiently high penalties are assumed to be assessed against a firm that takes a decision z_i different from the one $z_i(m)$ selected and announced by the center. Thus any self-interested firm may be assumed to take the selected decisions. This assumption is analogous to the assumption that no firm will release more pollution than a system of standards permits or than it has purchased rights for in a system of auxiliary markets for purchase and sale of pollution rights. It is also similar to the implicit assumption of models with taxation schemes that the required tax will in fact be paid. Obviously the costs of enforcing compliance with such types of rules may not be negligible. However, consideration of enforcement costs are ignored in this paper in order to focus on the prior issue of the selection of the optimal external decisions. This is the analogous problem

---

[5] Governmental coordination, of course, would not be socially desirable in cases of pecuniary externalities. In fact, governmental coordination of the external decisions in cases of pecuniary externalities should be prohibited from a social welfare point of view.

[6] The formalization of a "language" and the communication process is based on Hurwicz [13].

to the selection of an optimal pollution standard an optimal quantity of pollution rights to create, or an optimal tax.

Now, in order for the center's coordination to be successful, the language set M and the center's rule $z(\cdot)$ must be selected with reference to the objective of choosing the joint-profit maximizing or optimal external decisions z^*. Since the optimal decisons z^* depend on the firms' profit $\pi_i(\cdot)$, the language set M must be sufficiently large so that for every allowable[7] collection of profit functions $\pi_i(\cdot)$, $i = 1, \ldots, n$, there are messages m_i^* in M such that if sent the center's rule $\hat{z}(\cdot)$ will select the optimal decisions z^* for the particular collection of profit functions; that is,

$$\text{given } (\pi_1, \ldots, \pi_n), \text{ there exists for every } i, m_i^* \in M$$
$$\text{such that } z^* = \hat{z}(m^*) \text{ maximizes } \sum_i \pi_i(z). \tag{2.3}$$

It should be noted that the relation between the allowable profit functions $\pi_i(\cdot)$ and the messages m_i^* defines the concept of "truth" with reference to the decision rule $\hat{z}(\cdot)$. Truthful reporting or sending true messages consists of sending messages that yield optimal decisions.

A simple example may help clarify these concepts. Suppose the language set M is a set of all allowable profit functions $\pi_i(\cdot)$; that is every message m_i in M is an allowable (profit) *function* of the decisions z. Further, suppose that the center's rule $\hat{z}(\cdot)$ for selecting the external decisions is defined by

$$\hat{z}(m) = \text{the } z \text{ that maximizes } \sum_i m_i(z). \tag{2.4}$$

Such a rule is optimal if the actual profit functions $\pi_i(\cdot)$ are identical with the messages m_i. Thus "truth" in this case consists of sending the center the firm's actual profit function $\pi_i(\cdot)$, i.e. $m_i^* = \pi_i$, since $\hat{z}(m^*)$ maximizes $\sum_i m_i^*(z) = \sum_i \pi_i(z)$.

Now given a general language set M and the center's rule $\hat{z}(\cdot)$, a firm may or may not have any reason to send the correct or truthful message m_i^* corresponding to its profit function π_i. Furthermore since the center does not know the firm's actual profit function, it is unable to ascertain whether or not the message it receives is the truthful message. The essence of the incentive problem is to provide the firms with some reason to choose truthful messages over all other messages, even when the center is unable to verify subsequently whether or not it was sent these messages.

From the point of view of any firm, its interest in communicating its truthful message depends on the consequences to it of not sending this message. In order to provide an incentive to the firms, the center is assumed to have the authority

---

[7] The allowable collection of profit functions are those admitting a solution to the joint-profit maximization.

to levy charges or make payments to the firms in addition to its role in choosing the external decisions $\hat{z}(m)$. However, since the center's only information consists of the messages m received from the firms, the charges or payments selected by the center can depend, at most, on this information. Thus the center selects charges or payments, hereafter called *transfers*, in accordance with n rules $T_i(\cdot)$, $i = 1, \ldots, n$, each of which is a real-valued function of the n-tuple of messages m. Given the message m the transfer $T_i(m)$ is a charge levied against the ith firm if it is negative and a payment to the ith firm if it is positive.

Given the center's decision rule $\hat{z}(\cdot)$ and transfer rules $T_i(\cdot)$, the outcome or payoff to each firm is the firm's after-transfer profits realized when the message m is sent:

$$\omega_i(m; T_i) \equiv \pi_i[\hat{z}(m)] + T_i(m), \qquad i = 1, \ldots, n. \qquad (2.5)$$

Since both the decisions $\hat{z}(m)$ and the transfers $T_i(m)$ depend on the messages sent by all the firms, the consequence to firm i of sending a message m_i other than its truthful message m_i^* depends on the messages of the other firms and is given by

$$\omega_i(m; T_i) - \omega_i(m/m_i^*; T_i) \qquad \text{where} \qquad m/m_i^* \equiv (m_1, \ldots, m_i^*, \ldots, m_n). \qquad (2.6)$$

The incentive problem in this framework is then to find transfer rules $T_i(\cdot)$ such that each firm maximizes its own after-transfer profit (payoff) by sending its truthful message m_i^*, *regardless of the messages sent by the other firms.*[8] Formally, we call a collection of n transfer functions $\hat{T} = \{\hat{T}_i, i = 1, \ldots, n\}$ an *optimal incentive structure* relative to the decision rule $\hat{z}(\cdot)$ and language set M if

$$m_i^* \text{ maximizes } \omega_i(m/m_i; \hat{T}_i) \text{ over } M \text{ for any}$$
$$\qquad\qquad (2.7)$$
$$m\backslash m \equiv (m_1, \ldots, m_{i-1}, m_{i+1}, \ldots, m_n) \qquad \text{where} \qquad m_j \in M, \quad j \neq i.$$

Summarizing, the problem of coordinating the external decision choices subject to the informational limitations of the center and the incentives of the n firms is to choose (1) a language set M and a decision rule $\hat{z}(\cdot)$ such that (2.3) holds and (2) an optimal incentive structure $\hat{T}$ relative to the decision rule $\hat{z}(\cdot)$ and language set M.[9]

Several properties of an optimal incentive structure deserve emphasis. First, the only information required by the center to make the transfers (and choose

---

[8] Thus, the incentive problem requires that a truthful message from a firm be defined independently of the messages of the other firms. Furthermore, the n-tuple of truthful messages m^* must be a stronger equilibrium than a Nash equilibrium of the game defined by the n payoff functions $\omega_i(m; T_i)$, $i = 1, \ldots, n$.

[9] Implicitly assumed in this model is that the center automatically follows the rules selected; in other words, there is no consideration given to the center's incentives to follow the rules. See Alchian and Demsetz [2] for a discussion of this issue.

the decisions as well) is the messages received from the firms, and furthermore the center does not have to know whether or not it was sent the correct messages. An optimal incentive structure provides a rationale for it to assume the messages are the correct ones. Second, the transfers made according to an optimal incentive structure do not depend on the external decisions that the firms actually make. As noted above, it is assumed that the center can monitor the firms' external decisions at negligible cost and severely penalize any firm that does not take the decisions selected by the center. Nevertheless, no firm need worry that its transfer given by an optimal incentive structure will be affected by another firm's failure to implement the selected decision. Third, under an optimal incentive structure, the best message for any firm is completely independent of the messages the other firms are sending to the center. Thus a firm needs to know only what its own truthful message is and that its transfer will be computed according to an optimal incentive structure.[10]

For an optimal incentive structure, a fourth property that is less desirable is that there is no guarantee that the center's budget exactly balances; that is, that the sum of all the transfers will be identically zero, even when all firms respond to the incentives and send their truthful messages. This issue is discussed at length in the next section. As shown there, however, the center's net balance (the sum of all charges less the sum of all payments) can be guaranteed to always be nonnegative so that the financial feasibility of the center can be assured. Also, it can be shown that in special cases,[11] if the profit functions $\pi_i(\cdot)$ are known to have a special structure, it is possible to ensure a zero net balance for the center. For example, for some special cases, the language set M may be taken to be a Euclidean space and an optimal incentive structure $\hat{T}$ can be exhibited with the property that the sum of all transfers $\Sigma \hat{T}_i(m)$ is a polynomial function of the vectors m_i of finite degree K less than the number of firms n. Also, any optimal incentive structure $\hat{T}$ may be modified without altering its incentive properties by adding to each transfer rule $\hat{T}_i(\cdot)$ a function of the messages, say $R_i(\cdot)$, that is constant in the ith firm's message m_i, i.e.,

$$R_i(m/m_i) = R_i(m/m_i') \quad \text{for all} \quad m_i, m_i' \in M. \tag{2.8}$$

Thus, since $\Sigma \hat{T}_i(m)$ is a polynomial function of degree K less than n, it is easy to find polynomial functions $R_i(\cdot)$ constant in m_i such that

$$\sum_i [\hat{T}_i(m) + R_i(m)] = 0 \quad \text{for every} \quad m \in M^{(n)}. \tag{2.9}$$

---

[10] The firms, therefore, do not even have to know what the center's rules are.
[11] See Groves and Loeb [12] for a detailed example

III. A GENERAL SOLUTION OF THE COORDINATION
PROBLEM

Given the model of Section II it is not difficult to solve the coordination problem posed subject to the informational limitations of the center and the incentives of the firms.[12] For a very general solution, the set Z of external decisions z is assumed to be a compact space and the language set M the collection of all upper semicontinuous real-valued functions $m_i(\cdot)$ of z. The firms' actual profit functions π_i are assumed to be members of the set M also. Given M, the center's rule $\hat{z}(\cdot)$ for choosing the external decisons z is defined by:

$$\text{for every} \quad m \in M^{(n)}, \quad \hat{z}(m) \quad \text{maximizes} \quad \sum_i m_i(z) \qquad (3.1)$$

Note that although each message m_i is a function of z, $\hat{z}(m)$ is an n-tuple of external decisions.

Given the language set M and the rule $\hat{z}(\cdot)$, the firms' actual profit functions $\pi_i(\cdot)$ are truthful messages, that is, $m_i^* = \pi_i$. These are, of course, not the only "truthful" messages since, for example, the addition of a constant to $m_i(\cdot)$ will not change the value $\hat{z}(m)$. Truthful messages, it will be recalled, are defined as any messages m_i^* such that

$$\hat{z}(m^*) \quad \text{maximizes} \quad \sum_i \pi_i(z), \qquad (3.2)$$

where $\pi_i(\cdot)$ is the ith firm's actual profit function.

The rule $\hat{z}(\cdot)$ is easily interpreted as a rule that selects external decisions that maximize the joint reported profits of the n firms. If each firm reports its profit function, the rule will select the optimal external decisions. It is the purpose of an optimal incentive structure to provide the firms with a reason to tell the truth or report their actual profit functions.

Consider an incentive structure $\hat{T} = \{\hat{T}_i, i = 1, \ldots, n\}$ defined by

$$\hat{T}_i(m) \equiv \sum_{j \neq i} m_j[\hat{z}(m)] - R_i(m), \qquad i = 1, \ldots, n, \qquad (3.3)$$

where $R_i(\cdot)$ is any real-valued function of the message m that is constant in its ith component m_i. Note that although m_j is a function of z, $R_i(m)$ is a real number that depends only on the functions m_j and not on the values of these functions at $\hat{z}(m)$. For example, $R_i(m)$ might be defined by

$$R_i(m) = \sum_{j \neq i} m_j(\bar{z}) \quad \text{where } \bar{z} \text{ is some fixed value of } z. \qquad (3.4)$$

---

[12] The general incentive problem in this form was posed and solved by Groves [10] In Groves and Loeb [12] the solution was applied to the case of a public input. Ledyard has extended these results to a general equilibrium model with public (consumption) goods; see Groves and Ledyard [11].

To show $\hat{T}$ is an optimal incentive structure, it is only necessary to recall that $\hat{z}(m/m_i^*)$ maximizes the joint profits $\pi_i(z) + \Sigma_{j \neq i} m_j(z)$. Thus, from the definition of $\omega_i(\cdot, \hat{T}_i)$ (see (2.5)),

$$\omega_i(m/m_i^*; \hat{T}_i) + R_i(m/m_i^*) = m_i^*[\hat{z}(m/m_i^*)] + \sum_{j \neq i} m_j[\hat{z}(m/m_i^*)]$$

$$\geq m_i^*(z) + \sum_{j \neq i} m_j(z)$$

for all z. In particular, the inequality holds for $\hat{z}(m/m_i)$ for all m_i. Thus

$$\omega_i(m/m_i^*; \hat{T}_i) + R_i(m/m_i^*) \geq \omega_i(m/m_i; \hat{T}_i) + R_i(m/m_i)$$

or, since $R_i(m/m_i)$ is constant in m_i,

$$\omega_i(m/m_i^*; \hat{T}_i) \geq \omega_i(m/m_i; \hat{T}_i) \qquad \text{for all} \quad m_i \text{ in } M,$$

which is the requirement for an optimal incentive structure.

The optimal incentive structure $\hat{T}$ is interpreted most easily by defining the transfers independently of the particular rule used to determine the level of the external decisions z. Specifically, for every level z, define transfer rules T_i' of z and the messages m by

$$T_i'(z, m) \equiv \sum_{j \neq i} m_j(z) - R_i(m), \qquad i = 1, \ldots, n, \qquad (3.5)$$

where R_i is, as above, constant in m_i. Note that $T_i'(z, m)$ is also constant in m_i. That is, the message m_i affects firm i's transfer only through the selection of z.

When the center uses the rule $\hat{z}(\cdot)$ to select the level of z, the transfers defined by T_i' are the same as those given by the optimal incentive structure $\hat{T}$:

$$T_i'[\hat{z}(m), m] = \hat{T}_i(m) \qquad \text{for all } m \in M^{(n)}, \qquad i = 1, \ldots, n. \qquad (3.6)$$

To interpret the transfer rules T_i', recall that the center interprets each firm's message m_i as the firm's profit function. Thus, T_i' transfers to firm i the full amount of "reported" profits of the other firms less an amount $R_i(m)$ that is independent of firm i's message. The role of the function $R_i(\cdot)$ is examined below in connection with the budget balance question.

Now, each firm's after-transfer profits in terms of the transfer rules T_i' are given by a function $\omega_i'(\cdot)$ of the decisions z, the message m, and the rule T_i':

$$\omega_i'(z, m; T_i') = \pi_i(z) + T_i'(z, m). \qquad (3.7)$$

Assuming the external decisions are real variables and all profit functions (the actual π_i and reported m_j) are differentiable, the marginal profitability of any external decisions z_{jk} (the kth external decision of the jth firm) and hence the value to the ith firm of the marginal unit of z_{jk} is

$$\frac{\partial \omega_i'}{\partial z_{jk}} = \frac{\partial \pi_i}{\partial z_{jk}} + \sum_{l \neq i} \frac{\partial m_l}{\partial z_{jk}}. \qquad (3.8)$$

However, when the center receives the messages m_j from the firms and endeavors to maximize joint (reported) profits, the marginal joint profitability of the external decision z_{jk} as perceived by the center is $\Sigma_{l=1}^n \, \partial m_l(z)/\partial z_{jk}$. Thus if firm i reports truthfully, i.e. sends $m_i^* = \pi_i$, the center will value the marginal unit of z_{jk} at every level of z the same as firm i. Also, when all firms communicate truthfully, each firm's after-transfer profit $\omega_i'(z, m^*; T_i')$ is maximized at the same quantity $\hat{z}(m^*) = z^*$ — the true joint-profit maximizing quantity — although there is no reason for the firms' profits to be all equal at this quantity since the amounts $R_i(m^*)$ need not be identical for all i.

Summarizing this interpretation, the optimal incentive structure may be viewed as a scheme to induce each firm to evaluate each external decision in terms of its true marginal joint profitability $\Sigma_l \partial \pi_l(z)/\partial z_{jk}$.

As noted in Section II, the center's choice of transfer rules T_i is not forced to satisfy a budget constraint

$$\sum_i T_i(m) = 0. \tag{3.9}$$

Thus, under any particular optimal incentive structure $\hat{T}$, the center may run a surplus or a deficit. The magnitude of the surplus or deficit, for an optimal incentive structure of the form $\hat{T}$ given by (3.3), depends on the functions $R_i(\cdot)$ chosen, since the *net surplus* for any such $\hat{T}$ may be defined as

$$\text{net surplus} \equiv -\sum_i \hat{T}_i(m) = \sum_i R_i(m) - (n-1)\sum_i m_i[\hat{z}(m)]. \tag{3.10}$$

Although in special cases, as noted in Section II, it is possible to find functions $R_i(\cdot)$ that will ensure a zero net surplus, in general such functions do not exist. However, the importance of this difficulty depends on the interpretation of the model.

If the center is viewed as a government agency imposing the coordination on the n firms with the authority to levy taxes, the budget balancing property is not of crucial significance, expecially since the center can at least guarantee that its surplus is nonnegative. For example, consider the functions $R_i^0(\cdot)$ defined by

$$R_i^0(m) \equiv \max_z \sum_{j \neq i} m_j(z), \qquad i = 1, \ldots, n. \tag{3.11}$$

The transfer functions $\hat{T}_i^0(\cdot)$ with this specification of $R_i(\cdot)$ are then defined by

$$\hat{T}_i^0(m) = \sum_{j \neq i} m_j[\hat{z}(m)] - \max_z \sum_{j \neq i} m_j(z), \qquad i = 1, \ldots, n, \tag{3.12}$$

and it is obvious by inspection that the transfer of each firm is nonpositive, i.e. each firm is charged or taxed. Thus, the center's net surplus is always nonnegative. This specific optimal incentive structure may be interpreted as assessing each firm for the full impact that its existence has on the optimal joint profits of all the other firms.

If the center is interpreted as an agent hired by the n firms in an attempt to coordinate voluntarily the choice of the external decisions, the budget balance issue is more important. Even though the center can be guaranteed a nonnegative net surplus and the external decisions that maximize the joint *before-transfer* profits will be selected by the center, the firms' *after-transfer* profits *may* be lower than what they would have been in the absence of the coordination of the external decisions. In assuring the center a nonnegative surplus in some cases it could accumulate a positive surplus larger than the total joint profits foregone by uncoordinated decision making by the n firms. Although the surplus could always be redistributed back to the firms in such a way that they would all be better off than with no coordination, the optimal incentive property of the scheme would be destroyed since any firm would then take into account the effect of its message on its share of the center's surplus.

One method for avoiding this problem in cases of repeated decision periods is to require only that the center balance its budget in the long run, permitting it to run surplusses or deficits in any one period. If this could be accomplished, then total joint profits over many periods will be received as total after-transfer profits by the n firms. It might be additionally hoped that each firm in the long run would receive greater aggregate profits than it would have in the absence of the coordination. If this could be assured, it would not be unreasonable to expect that all the firms could agree to participate in such a voluntary coordination arrangement.

A way to formalize a long-run budget balance requirement for the center is to require that the center's budget be balanced in *expectation*. To be specific, suppose in each period the n firms' true profit functions $\pi_i(\cdot)$, $i = 1, \ldots, n$, are given as the realization of some fixed probability law. Further, relaxing the assumption of the center's total ignorance, assume that the center knows the probability distribution of the n profit functions, here a distribution over $M^{(n)}$, the n-fold product of the language set M. Given this distribution, the center can select the functions $R_i(\cdot)$ in such a way that its expected net surplus is zero; i.e. such that

$$\sum_i E[\hat{T}_i(\pi)] = 0 \qquad (3.13)$$

where E is the expected value operator with respect to the probability distribution over $M^{(n)}$.

An interesting example of such functions $R_i(\cdot)$ is

$$R_i^1(m) = \sum_{j \neq i} E[m_j(\hat{z}(m)) \mid m \backslash m_i], \qquad i = 1, \ldots, n, \qquad (3.14)$$

or the sum of the *conditional* expected reported profits of all the firms excepting firm i, conditioned on the reported messages of these firms. The transfer functions $\hat{T}_i^1$ for this specification of $R_i(\cdot)$ are then

$$\hat{T}_i^1(m) = \sum_{j \neq i} \{ m_j[\hat{z}(m)] - E[m_j(\hat{z}(m)) \mid m \backslash m_i] \}, \qquad i = 1, \ldots, n,$$

(3.15)

and may be interpreted as transferring to firm i the full amount by which its message m_i changes the center's expectation of all the other firms', $j \neq i$, reported profits.

It is easy to verify that these transfer rules provide the center with a zero expected net surplus. However, in any one period, the net surplus is likely to be different from zero. An initial reserve could be provided the center to cover deficits uncovered by previous surplusses. If either consistent deficits or surplusses are realized over time, the center could reasonably infer that its probability distribution was biased and that some adjustment would be necessary. The optimality of the transfer rules $\hat{T}_i^1(\cdot)$ would not be destroyed as long as such revisions occurred sufficiently infrequently so that no firm would be likely to consider the effect of its current message on its future transfers as affected by any revisions of the probability distribution.

Since the transfer rules $\hat{T}_i^1(\cdot)$ defined in (3.15) balance the center's budget in expectation, the expected total of all firms' after-transfer profits is greater than their expected profits if their decisions were uncoordinated. However, any one firm might expect to do worse under these rules than with no coordination at all.

For example, suppose the conditional distribution of m_i given all the other m_j is concentrated in a small subset of M; i.e., knowing all the other firms' profit functions gives the center a very close, but not exact, idea of what firm i's profit function must be. In this case, the transfer rule $\hat{T}_i^1(\cdot)$ defined by (3.15) will define a transfer to (from) firm i that is very close to zero. Thus the *after*-transfer profit of firm i will be very similar to its *before*-transfer profit $\pi_i(\hat{z}(m))$ where $\hat{z}(m)$ is the optimal external decisions selected by the center.

In addition, suppose that firm i's own external decision z_i (the ith component of the n-tuple z) has a large negative impact on the other firms' joint profits. A major effect of the coordination might well be to choose a level of $z_i = \hat{z}_i(m)$ that significantly reduces firm i's (before-transfer) profits $\pi_i(z)$ from what firm i could achieve if it were not a party to the coordination effort. Since firm i, under the transfer rule $\hat{T}_i^1(\cdot)$ would not share in the increases in joint profits realized through the coordination, it would likely not agree to participate in a voluntary coordination effort with rules such as these.

Thus, an optimal incentive structure, in addition to the zero expected net surplus property, should have the property that each firm can at least *expect* to benefit from the coordination. It would be unlikely that a voluntary coordination effort could otherwise be acceptable to all the firms. However, it is possible to find such an optimal incentive structure under the same assumptions as made for $\hat{T}^1$ above.

Suppose that, in the absence of any coordination, the external decisions chosen by the n firms would be $\bar{z}(m)$ if m is the n-tuple of the firm's profit functions. For example $\bar{z}(m)$ might be the Nash equilibrium of the n-person noncooperative game defined by the n payoff functions $m_i(\cdot)$, $i = 1, \ldots, n$ of $z = (z_1, \ldots, z_n)$ if one exists. Next consider the transfer functions $\hat{T}_i^2(\cdot)$ defined by

$$\hat{T}_i^2(m) \equiv \sum_{j \neq i} \{ m_j[\hat{z}(m)] - E[m_j(\hat{z}(m)) \mid m \backslash m_i] \}$$

$$+ E \{ m_i[\bar{z}(m)] - m_i[\hat{z}(m)] + w_i \sum_j [m_j(\hat{z}(m)) - m_j(\bar{z}(m))] \mid m \backslash m_i \},$$

$$\tag{3.16}$$

$i = 1, \ldots, n$, where the w_i are fixed positive weights summing to unity. The first term is, of course, identical to the transfer specified above by $\hat{T}_i^1$ (see (3.15)). Since $\hat{T}_i^1$ is an optimal incentive structure and the second term does not depend on m_i (having been "expected out"), the incentive structure $\hat{T}^2$ is also optimal. Further, taking the expected value of the entire expression and summing over all i demonstrates that under $\hat{T}^2$ the center's expected net surplus is also zero.

These transfer functions may be interpreted as follows: the first term transfers to (from) firm i the full amount by which its message m_i changes the center's expectations of all the other firms', $j \neq i$, reported profits. The last term consists of two parts; the first part transfers to (from) firm i any loss (gain) the center *expects* the firm to suffer (receive) as a result of the coordination. The second part transfers to firm i a fixed share of the total expected gain in joint profits resulting from the center's coordination. It should be noted that the expectations defining the transfer $\hat{T}_i^2(m)$ are taken only with respect to the message m_i and are conditioned on the actual messages received from the other firms m_j, $j \neq i$. Since the fixed weights w_i, $i = 1, \ldots, n$, are arbitrary in part, they could be selected through some type of initial bargaining process among the n firms.

With the transfer rules $\hat{T}_i^2$, every firm can expect over the long run to receive greater (after-transfer) profits than it would in the absence of any coordination. The expected after-transfer profits of firm i are

$$E[\omega_i(m; \hat{T}_i^2)] = E[\pi_i[\bar{z}(m)] + w_i \sum_j [m_j(\hat{z}(m)) - m_j(\bar{z}(m))]] \tag{3.17}$$

or are equal to the expected noncooperative profits of the firm plus a share of the expected total gain in joint profits realized from the coordination. Thus, a voluntary coordination effort among the n firms to hire an agent (the center) that would use these transfer rules might be expected to be agreed to by every firm.

As a postscript, it should be emphasized that the assumption of knowledge by the center of the probability distribution of the firms' profit functions is a very strong assumption and is somewhat contrary to the spirit of the prior discussion in this paper where the only information the firms had was their own profit function and the center was entirely dependent on the firms for its information. For this reason, the results for the interpretation of the center as an agent hired in a voluntary effort of the firms to coordinate their decisions must be, perhaps, viewed cautiously.

More generally, finding incentive compatible rules for voluntary coordination of external decisions seems much more difficult than finding them for imposed coordination. The key source of the difficulty is that an optimal incentive structure for voluntary coordination must compensate firms whose before-transfer profits are decreased from what they would be under no coordination if they are expected to agree to participate in the coordination effort. No compensation is necessary for the other firms since their before-transfer profits are increased by the coordination. In fact, to maintain the budgetary viability of the center, the gainers from the coordination must provide the compensation paid to the losers. This means that optimal incentive rules for voluntary coordination cannot treat all firms symmetrically. Yet the center, unless it has independent information regarding which firms will gain and which will lose such as the independent knowledge of the probability distribution of the firms profit functions, must rely exclusively on information provided it by the firms themselves.

An imposed coordination scheme can avoid this problem and treat all firms symmetrically since losers are not provided the option of not participating in the scheme. Furthermore, if the government is the center agent imposing the coordination, the budgetary feasibility problem is not essential, especially since it can assure a nonnegative net surplus with an optimal incentive structure such as $\hat{T}^0$ defined by (3.12).

APPENDIX   ON THE UNIQUENESS OF THE TRUTHFUL MESSAGE EQUILIBRIUM

In some comments on the previous sections of this paper, Professor Trout Rader raised an interesting question regarding the uniqueness of the equilibrium consisting of the truthful messages $m_i{}^* \equiv \pi_i$ (see (2.7)). In particular, considering the n-person game defined by the payoff functions $\omega_i(m; \hat{T}_i)$ (see (2.6) and (3.3)) where the language set M is a set of real-valued functions $m_i(\cdot)$ of the external decisions z, Rader pointed out that there are in general many noncooperative equilibria and that there is no assurance any particular noncooperative equilibrium $\bar{m} = (\bar{m}_1, \ldots, \bar{m}_n) \in M^{(n)}$ will yield external decisions $\bar{z} = \hat{z}(\bar{m})$ that maximize true joint profits $\sum_i \pi_i(z)$. Furthermore, Rader suggested that under stronger conditions on the functions m_i and the message space M a uniqueness theorem could be proved.

Under the restrictions assumed in Section III that the set of decisions Z is compact, that every element $m_i(\cdot)$ of the language set is an upper semi-continuous function of z and that the true profit functions $\pi_i(\cdot)$ belong to this set, two results can be proved. First, as pointed out by Rader, a noncooperative equilibrium $\bar{m}$ may exist that does not maximize true joint profits. Second, however, the n-tuple of truthful messages $m^* = (m_1^*, \ldots, m_n^*)$ is the unique (up to the addition of arbitrary constants to the functions $m_i^* \equiv \pi_i$) noncooperative equilibrium with the additional property that each firm's truthful message m_i^* maximizes its after-transfer profits $\omega_i(m/m_i; \hat{T}_i)$ *for every* $(n-1)$-*tuple of the other firms' messages* $m \setminus m_i \equiv (m_1, \ldots, m_{i-1}, m_{i+1}, \ldots, m_n)$. Thus, since the addition of a constant to the truthful message $m_i^* \equiv \pi_i$ does not change the values of the external decisions $\hat{z}(m^*)$ maximizing reported joint profits, any noncooperative equilibrium with this additional property yields external decisions $\hat{z}(m^*)$ maximizing true joint profits.

Concerning the first result an intuitive counterexample will be given. Suppose the external decision z to be coordinated is the level of some real variable that cannot assume negative values. Under the further restriction that each firm's true profit function π_i and message m_i are strictly concave and differentiable functions of z, a zero level of the decision z will maximize *reported* joint profits if the sum of the *reported* marginal profitabilities evaluated at zero is nonpositive; i.e.,

$$z = \hat{z}(m) = 0 \text{ maximizes } \sum_i m_i(z) \qquad \text{if} \quad \sum_i \partial m_i(z)/\partial z \Big|_{z=0} \leqslant 0. \quad \text{(A.1)}$$

Now suppose that the sum of the *true* marginal profitabilities is strictly greater than zero; i.e.,

$$\sum_i \partial \pi_i(z)/\partial z \Big|_{z=0} > 0 \qquad\qquad \text{(A.2)}$$

so that the *true* joint profit maximizing level of z is strictly positive. Now consider any n-tuple of messages $\bar{m} = (\bar{m}_1, \ldots, \bar{m}_n)$ such that, for every i,

$$\frac{\partial \pi_i(z)}{\partial z}\Big|_{z=0} + \sum_{j \neq i} \frac{\partial \bar{m}_j(z)}{\partial z}\Big|_{z=0} < 0. \qquad\qquad \text{(A.3)}$$

That is, each message $\bar{m}_j$ sufficiently understates the marginal profitability of the decision z such that, even if a firm i reports the truth (sends $m_i^* \equiv \pi_i$ instead of $\bar{m}_i$), the level maximizing the reported joint profits (here, $\pi_i(z) + \sum_{j \neq i} \bar{m}_j(z)$) is zero. It follows that $\bar{m}$ is a noncooperative equilibrium that yields the zero decision, $\hat{z}(\bar{m}) = 0$, which is not *true* joint profit maximizing. However it should be noted that since the true messages $m_i^* \equiv \pi_i$ maximize after-transfer profits $\omega_i(m/m_i, \hat{T}_i)$ for every $m \backslash m_i$ (as proved in Section III), *including* $\bar{m} \backslash \bar{m}_i$, the message m_i^* would be no worse for the firm to send than the message $\bar{m}_i$. Furthermore, in the event that the other firms are, in fact, reporting truthfully, the truthful message $m_i^* \equiv \pi_i$ is better, in general, than $\bar{m}_i$. Thus, the true message m_i^* dominates any other message, even though some other message m_i may be no worse given some *particular* messages of the other firms.

To prove the second result, suppose $m^0 = (m_1{}^0, \ldots, m_n{}^0)$ is any non-cooperative equilibrium with the additional property that $m_i{}^0$ is best for any $m \backslash m_i$

$$m_i{}^0 \text{ maximizes } \omega_i(m/m_i; \hat{T}_i) \qquad \text{for every} \quad m \backslash m_i \in M^{(n-1)}. \quad \text{(A.4)}$$

To be shown is that $m_i{}^0(z) = \pi_i(z) + \text{constant}$, or, equivalently, that

$$m_i{}^0(z^1) - m_i{}^0(z^2) = \pi_i(z^1) - \pi_i(z^2) \qquad \text{for every} \quad z^1 \text{ and } z^2. \quad \text{(A.5)}$$

Suppose the contrary and without loss in generality that

$$\text{for some } z^1 \text{ and } z^2, m_i{}^0(z^1) - m_i{}^0(z^2) > \pi_i(z^1) - \pi_i(z^2). \quad \text{(A.6)}$$

It can be shown that there exist messages from the other firms $j \neq i$ such that, if firm i's message is $m_i^* \equiv \pi_i$, the decision z^2 will maximize reported joint profits, whereas if the firm's message is $m_i{}^0$, the decision z^1 will maximize reported joint profits. Furthermore, after-transfer profits of firm i when m_i^* is sent are greater than when $m_i{}^0$ is sent, thus contradicting (A.4). A brief sketch of the proof follows.

Let P be any number satisfying

$$m_i{}^0(z^1) - m_i{}^0(z^2) > P > \pi_i(z^1) - \pi_i(z^2). \quad \text{(A.7)}$$

Define the quantities C and D by

$$C \equiv \min \{m_i(z^1), \pi_i(z^1), m_i(z^2) + P, \pi_i(z^2) + P\}$$

$$D \equiv \max\{\max_z \pi_i(z), \max_z m_i(z)\} + \epsilon, \text{ for some small } \epsilon > 0. \quad \text{(A.8)}$$

The quantity D is well defined since π_i and $m_i{}^0$ are upper semicontinuous functions. Now let $\hat{m} \backslash \hat{m}_i$ be any $(n-1) - \text{tuple}$ in $M^{(n-1)}$ such that

$$\sum_{j \neq i} \hat{m}_i(z) = \begin{cases} -C & \text{if} \quad z = z_1 \\ P - C & \text{if} \quad z = z_2 \\ -D & \text{otherwise.} \end{cases} \quad \text{(A.9)}$$

The existence of such an $\hat{m} \backslash \hat{m}_i$ is clear. It is straightforward to verify that when firms $j \neq i$ send the messages $\hat{m}_j$, if firm i sends $m_i^* \equiv \pi_i$, z^2 is chosen and, if $m_i{}^0$

is sent, z^1 is chosen; i.e.,

$$z(\hat{m}/\pi_i) = z_2 \qquad \text{and} \qquad \hat{z}(\hat{m}/m_i^0) = z_1. \tag{A.10}$$

Then using the definition of $\omega_i(m; \hat{T}_i)$ and P it follows that

$$\omega_i(\hat{m}/\pi_i; \hat{T}_i) - \omega_i(\hat{m}/m_i^0; \hat{T}_i) = \pi_i(z^2) + P - \pi_i(z^1) > 0. \tag{A.11}$$

Thus, m_i^0 does not maximize $\omega_i(\hat{m}/m_i; \hat{T}_i)$ contradicting (A.4).

REFERENCES

1. Arrow, K., "The Organization of Economic Activity: Issues Pertinent to the Choice of Market versus Non-Market Allocation," in Joint Economic Committee, *The Analysis and Evaluation of Public Expenditures: The PPB System*, Washington, D.C.: Gov. Printing Office, 1969, 47–64.
2. Alchian, A., and H. Demsetz, "Production, Information Costs, and Economic Organization," *American Economic Review*, December 1972, **62**, 777–795.
3. Bramhall, D., and E. Mills, "A Note on the Asymmetry Between Fees and Payments," *Water Resources Research*, 1966, **2**, 615–616.
4. Buchanan, J., and W. Stubblebine, "Externality," *Economics N.S.*, November 1962, **29**, 371–384.
5. Calabresi, G., "Transaction Costs, Resource Allocation and Liability Rules – A Comment," *Journal of Law and Economics*, April 1968, **11**, 67–73.
6. Coase, R., "The Problem of Social Cost," *Journal of Law and Economics*, October 1960, **3**, 1–44.
7. Dales, J., *Pollution, Property, and Prices*, Toronto: Univ. of Toronto Press, 1968.
8. Demsetz, H., "When Does the Rule of Liability Matter?" *Journal of Legal Studies*, 1972, **1**, 13–28.
9. Gifford, A., and C. Stone, "Externalities, Liability and the Coase Theorem: A Mathematical Analysis," *Western Economic Journal*, September 1973, **11**, 260–269.
10. Groves, T., "Incentives in Teams," *Econometrica*, July 1973, **41**, 617–631.
11. Groves, T., and J. Ledyard, "Optimal Allocation of Public Goods: A Solution to the 'Free Rider Problem'," *Econometrica* (forthcoming).
12. Groves, T., and M. Loeb, "Incentives and Public Inputs," *Journal of Public Economics*, July 1975, **4**, 211–226.
13. Hurwicz, L., "Optimality and Information Efficiency in Resource Allocation Processes," in K. Arrow, S. Karlin, and P. Suppes, eds., *Mathematical Methods in the Social Sciences*, Stanford, California: Stanford Univ. Press, 1960, 27–46.
14. Kamien, M., N. Schwartz, and F. Dolbear, "Symmetry Between Bribes and Charges," *Water Resources Research*, 1966, **2**, 147–157.
15. Marchand, J., and K. Russell, "Externalities, Liability, Separability, and Resource Allocation," *American Economic Review*, September 1973, **63**, 611–620.
16. Meade, J., "External Economies and Diseconomies in a Competitive Situation," *Economic Journal*, March 1952, **62**, 54–67.
17. Pigou, A. C., *The Economics of Welfare*, New York: Macmillan, 4th ed., 1932, reprinted 1952.
18. Scitovsky, T., "Two Concepts of External Economies," *Journal of Political Economy*, April 1954, **17**, 143–151.

19. Starrett, D., "Fundamental Nonconvexities in the Theory of Externalities," *Journal of Economic Theory*, April 1972, 4, 180–199.
20. Tybout, R., "Pricing Pollution and Other Negative Externalities," *Bell Journal of Economics and Management Science*, Spring 1972, 3, 252–266.
21. Wellisz, S., "On External Diseconomies and the Government Assisted Invisible Hand," *Economica N.S.*, November 1964, 31, 345–362.

Discussion

JAMES T. LITTLE

Washington University

Perhaps the most difficult problem in the coordination of decisions when externalities or public goods are present is the design of a system that produces valid information as to firms' production and cost functions and individuals' preferences. An important property of the competitive system is that in the absence of externalities or public goods, agents have an incentive to reveal the true conditions for private optimization. The reason for this is quite obviously not public spiritedness on the part of the agents, but rather that only through revealing this information can private optimization be achieved. Since all commodities and decisions are subject to the "discipline" of the market, cost and production functions and preference orderings generating the decisions can, in principle, be inferred from the observed behavior.

In the externalities/public goods case, on the other hand, there is no incentive for agents to reveal their true decision parameters. In fact, if such information were to be employed in the enforcement of efficient resource allocation, there is an incentive for agents to deliberately misinform. Nor can this information be inferred from decisions as in the competitive case. Since externalities are by their very nature not subject to the market, there are not sufficient data from which valid information can be derived.

Given the importance of the information problem, the Groves paper represents a highly significant contribution to the externalities literature. Groves has succeeded in designing a method for coordinating decisions that not only achieves efficient allocation on the basis of reported cost and production functions, but also, through the accompanying incentive system, assures that profit maximizing agents will provide valid information concerning their profit functions.

Clearly, some problems remain in the application of the technique to actual externality situations; for example, firms themselves may have difficulty in estimating their profit functions in the presence of many externalities and, as a result of problems in balancing the center's budget, control may necessarily be externally imposed. Nonetheless, Groves' incentive structure goes a considerable distance in solving the informational problems in externality control and should the forthcoming application to the public goods case prove as powerful (Groves and Ledyard [1]), the most difficult of the problems of externalities and public goods has been solved.

REFERENCE

1. Groves, T., and J. Ledyard, "Optimal Allocation of Public Goods: A Solution to the Free Rider Problem'," *Econometrica* (forthcoming).

A Generalized Cost Allocation Scheme

EDNA T. LOEHMAN

University of Florida

ANDREW B. WHINSTON

Purdue University

The proper definition of charges for use of a common facility is an important problem in achieving efficiency in the production of services characterized by economies of scale. The importance of this issue lies in the fact that charges that are too high will give disincentives for use of such facilities, while if charges are too low, costs of use will not be covered. Charges must also be in some sense "fair" in order that there be agreement among users of a common facility. The problem of defining a cost allocation scheme satisfying these properties has been previously discussed by Loehman and Whinston [2, 3].

The cost allocation scheme given in [2] was derived under the assumption that it is possible for all subgroups of a group of users of a common facility to occur and that each ordering of arrival of members within a subgroup is equally likely. Under these assumptions, the calculation of the cost allocation for a given user was obtained by weighting each possible definition of incremental cost by the probability of that order occurring. The charge formula is then the expected incremental cost due to a user when all orders of arrival are equally likely, and it is identical to the Shapley value of a cooperative game (Shapley [5]) where savings to a group of users is the characteristic value function for the game. The subsequent use of this formula in determing the size and charges for a common facility as a Lindahl-type equilibrium was also discussed in [2].

In [3], the same charge formula was derived axiomatically using the axiom that users causing the same incremental costs should be charged the same amount; that is, only the demands and not the ordering of users is important in computing the charge. The axiom system serves as a constitution to which users of a common facility must agree before deciding to cooperate in building a common facility. Obviously, if a user would receive a loss by being in this game, he would not join the coalition to build the common facility. Therefore, [3] also discussed how the optimal number of members in such a coalition might be determined.

Thus, there are three related questions to be settled before agreement to build a common facility can occur: what will be the charge scheme for covering costs, how many users of the facility will there be, and what will be the size of the facility based on users' demands? This paper will take the same approach as our previous studies (Loehman and Whinston [2, 3]) and discuss the formulation of the charge scheme independently of questions of size and number of users; this in effect separates equity from efficiency issues. Though the discussion will be in terms of fixed demands and numbers of users, it is not meant to imply that such a charge scheme could only be used under fixed conditions. Rather, the size and number of users are determined, as illustrated in [2] and [3], once the charge scheme is determined.

Unlike the earlier papers we will not make the assumption here that all orders of arrival in a coalition are equally likely (or use the equivalent axiom that users with the same demands are to be charged equally). In reality, given a group of potential users of a common facility, it can be supposed that some subcoalitions are not possible and hence the ordering of users is important. In such a case, not all orders of users within the group will be equally likely. The use of the charge formula derived in [2] and [3] may then not be appropriate.

The following example of this sort of situation will be analyzed in this paper. Given a group of three potential users of a water treatment plant as indicated in Figure 1, suppose that users 1 and 3 are located so far apart that the cost of one user piping wastes to a treatment plant at the site of the other user would exceed his savings due to the economies of scale of a joint treatment plant. Thus, a subcoalition of users 1 and 3 would not occur. However, suppose the presence of user 2 allows the location of a treatment plant there with a lower piping cost for wastes so that the three users would agree to use a joint treatment plant and economies of scale can be captured. In this situation, it seems that a charge

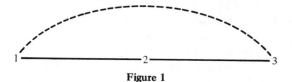

Figure 1

scheme should be defined so as to give user 2 some extra incentives to join the coalition beyond his savings due to economies of scale because users 1 and 3 realize savings from economies of scale only when he is present. That is, the presence of user 2 provides an external economy to users 1 and 3, and so his use should be subsidized to some extent according to the theory of externalities.

A cost allocation scheme for this situation will be developed by generalizing some game theory concepts used in deriving the Shapley value (Shapley [5]) and extending the probability notions used in Loehman and Whinston [2]. The form of the Shapley value was derived in [5] by first decomposing a game into subgames and then using some axioms to develop a value for a player in the game from this decomposition. This paper will follow the same outline, considering both decomposition of a game and the role of axioms, but at each point will generalize the Shapley results by applying some concepts of linear algebra. In this presentation a game will be viewed as an element of a vector space and an imputation as a linear transformation.

I. DECOMPOSITION OF A GAME

A game in characteristic function form is defined by a set function v from subsets S of the set of players N into the positive real numbers R:

$$v: S \to R, \qquad S \subseteq N. \tag{1}$$

The set function is usually also required to satisfy the property

$$v(A \cup B) \geqslant v(A) + v(B) \qquad \text{for} \quad A \cap B = \phi; \qquad A, B \subseteq N \tag{2}$$

in order to define a superadditive game.

To decompose such a game, Shapley [5] defined some subgames $v_R(S)$ such that

$$v_R(S) = \begin{cases} 1 & \text{if} \quad R \subseteq S \\ 0 & \text{otherwise,} \end{cases} \tag{3}$$

and showed that a game v may then be written as a linear combination of the v_R:

$$v_R = \sum_{R \subseteq N} c_R(v) v_R, \tag{4}$$

where

$$c_R(v) = \sum_{T \subseteq R} (-1)^{r-t} v(T). \tag{5}$$

This result was proved by means of an identity and was independent of any axioms. As we will show here, the form (4) can be generalized by using definitions other than Shapley's for $c_R(v)$ and $v_R(S)$.

With addition and multiplication by positive scalars defined for games, the set of all games on N is a subset of a vector space V of all mappings from subsets of N to the real numbers. (The set of all games on N is not a subspace of V since only multiplication by positive scalars is allowed.) Since V is a vector space, it has a basis $\{v_R\}$ such than any element v of V (in particular a game) can be represented by

$$v = \sum_{R \subseteq N} \tilde{c}_R(v)v_R. \tag{6}$$

The set $\{v_R\}$ used by Shapley [5] is one choice of basis for V. It is proved to be a basis since any v can be written as a linear combination of the v_R and the v_R are linearly independent. Each $\{v_R\}$ itself satisfies the definition of a superadditive game given by (1) and (2). Other choices of bases for V are possible. In general, since $\{v_R\}$ in (3) is a basis, an element of any other basis $\{\nu_R\}$ can be expressed as

$$\nu_R = \sum_{X \subseteq N} p_{RX}v_X \qquad \text{or} \qquad [\nu_R] = P[v_X], \tag{7}$$

where the p_{RX} are elements of an invertible matrix of P of rank $2^n - 1$. For example, we may have a basis $\{\nu_R\}$ such that

$$\nu_R(S) = \begin{cases} k & \text{if} \quad R \subseteq S \\ 0 & \text{otherwise,} \end{cases} \tag{8}$$

where k is some constant greater than 0. Alternatively, we may have a basis defined such that $\nu_R(S) > 0$ when $R \nsubseteq S$. If the p_{RX} in (7) are ≥ 0 for all x, $R \subseteq N$, then the basis elements of $\{\nu_R\}$ will be superadditive games. Otherwise, the basis elements may not be games.

The coordinates $\tilde{c}_R(v)$ in (6) depend on the choice of basis $\{v_R\}$. For a given v and basis $\{v_R\}$, the coordinates may be obtained by solving a set of linear equations; this is illustrated below in (9) using the basis $\{v_R\}$ given in (3). For $N = \{1, 2, 3\}$, evaluating (6) for each subgroup in N gives the systems of equations

$$\begin{bmatrix} v(1) \\ v(2) \\ v(3) \\ v(12) \\ v(13) \\ v(23) \\ v(123) \end{bmatrix} = \begin{bmatrix} 1 & 0 & 0 & 0 & 0 & 0 & 0 \\ 0 & 1 & 0 & 0 & 0 & 0 & 0 \\ 0 & 0 & 1 & 0 & 0 & 0 & 0 \\ 1 & 1 & 0 & 1 & 0 & 0 & 0 \\ 1 & 0 & 1 & 0 & 1 & 0 & 0 \\ 0 & 1 & 1 & 0 & 0 & 1 & 0 \\ 1 & 1 & 1 & 1 & 1 & 1 & 1 \end{bmatrix} \begin{bmatrix} c_1 \\ c_2 \\ c_3 \\ c_{12} \\ c_{13} \\ c_{23} \\ c_{123} \end{bmatrix}; \tag{9}$$

(9) may be written in matrix notation as

$$[v(S)] = [v_R(S)] [c_R]$$

or

$$[c_R] = [v_R(S)]^{-1}[v(S)].$$ (10)

The matrix $[v_R(S)]$ is invertible because the $\{v_R\}$ are independent. The solution for c_R in (10) gives the same result as (5) but is obtained by linear algebra instead of by identities. Using a different choice of basis $\{\nu_R\}$, instead of (9) we have

$$[\tilde{c}_R] = [\nu_R(S)]^{-1}[v(S)] = [P']^{-1}[v_R(S)]^{-1}[v(S)] = [P']^{-1}[c_R].$$ (11)

Thus, a choice of basis different from (3) results in different coordinates $\tilde{c}_R(v)$.

A priori, there is no reason to choose one basis over another. However, the results for a value of a game may be interpretable and reasonable for some choices and not interpretable for others. In the Shapley case all subgroups $R \subseteq N$ are assumed to be possible and R can form within any subgroup containing it, so that $v_R(S)$ serves as an indicator of probability of subgroup formation. $c_R(v)$ in the Shapley case can be interpreted as the excess value that would be available to distribute to the members of R after paying off each subgroup of R that could form. An obvious extension would be the situation where some subgroups R would never occur, as in the treatment plant example above; in such a case $v_R(\cdot)$ would be identically zero and $c_R(v)$ would be zero since there would be no members of R to pay. A further generalization would be to take $\nu_R(R)$ to be the probability that subgroup R would form independently of $N - R$ and $\nu_R(S)$ to be the probability of formation of R as a subgroup of S where these probabilities could be less than one, i.e., $0 \leqslant \nu_R(S) \leqslant 1$. The probabilities would have to be determined by observations about the environment of the game. If R will form within some subgroups S and not in others, then this definition may lead to a nonsuperadditive situation.

II. GENERALIZED VALUE OF A GAME

By a *generalized value* for a game we will mean a vector $(Q_1, \ldots, Q_n)$, where each component Q_i is a mapping from the subset of games in V to the positive real numbers R

$$Q_i : V \to R$$ (12)

that satisfies[1]

$$\sum_{i \in N} Q_i(v) = v(N)$$ (13)

---

[1] A cost allocation problem can be viewed as a constrained game. Equation (13) corresponds to the constraint that total charges equal total costs of the facility.

for a game v with carrier N. (The "carrier" for v is the minimum set of members for which the value of a game is achieved.) In addition, we shall restrict our attention to those values for which the components Q_i satisfy[2]

$$Q_i(cv + w) = cQ_i(v) + Q_i(w) \tag{14}$$

for a scalar c and games $v, w, cv + w$. Since (13) and (14) are respectively Shapley's axioms 2 and 3 (Shapley [5]), the generalized value to be derived here will satisfy these two axioms but is not required to satisfy Shapley's axiom 1.

The set V^* of all linear transformations from V into the field of real numbers with addition and scalar multiplication defined by

$$
\begin{aligned}
(Q^1 + Q^2)(v) &= Q^1(v) + Q^2(v) \qquad \text{for} \quad v \in V; \qquad Q^1, Q^2 \in V^* \\
(cQ)(v) &= cQ(v) \qquad \text{for } c \text{ a scalar,} \qquad Q \in V^*
\end{aligned}
\tag{15}
$$

is a vector space called the dual space of V. Since V^* is a vector space, there exist bases for V^*. By a theorem in linear algebra (see Hoffman and Kunz [1]) there is a unique basis for V^*, called the dual basis, corresponding to a choice of basis for V. The properties of this dual basis, denoted by $\{\tilde{c}_R\}$, are that for a given basis $\{\nu_R\}$ of V,

$$
\tilde{c}_R(\nu_S) = \begin{cases} 1 & \text{if} \quad R = S \\ 0 & \text{otherwise.} \end{cases}
\tag{16}
$$

and

$$v = \sum_{R \subseteq N} \tilde{c}_R(v)\nu_R \tag{17}$$

$$Q(v) = \sum_{R \subseteq N} Q(\nu_R)\tilde{c}_R(v) \tag{18}$$

for any v in V and Q in V^*. That is, $\tilde{c}_R(v)$ are the coordinates of v in the basis $\{\nu_R\}$ of V and also $\{\tilde{c}_R\}$ is the dual basis for V^*; $Q(\nu_R)$ are the coordinates of Q in the basis $\{\tilde{c}_R\}$. By (17), the dual basis $\{\tilde{c}_R\}$ can be found as described in the preceding discussion by solving a set of linear equations.

In particular, the representations (17) and (18) hold for a game v and component $Q_i(v)$ of a value. A generalized representation of a component of a value for a game is thus

$$Q_i(v) = \sum_{R \subseteq N} Q_i(\nu_R)\tilde{c}_R(v) \tag{19}$$

where $\{\nu_R\}$ is a basis for V such that ν_R are games and $\{\tilde{c}_R\}$ is the corresponding

---

[2] As indicated in Loehman and Whinston [3], it should be possible to weaken requirement (14) to only require linear homogeneity of Q_i and obtain the same results for the form of Q_i using calculus instead of linear algebra.

dual basis. Only (14), Shapley's axiom 3, has been required to obtain this form for the generalized value.

It can easily be seen that the values of $\{c_R\}$ in (5) satisfy the properties of the dual basis corresponding to the Shapley basis $\{v_R\}$ for V. For other choices of basic subgames $\{v_R\}$, other dual bases $\{\tilde{c}_R\}$ are obtained. Hence (19) provides a generalization of the form of the Shapley value.

From (19), the dependence of the form of the generalized value on the choice of basic subgames is now obvious. A value is completely specified by defining[3]

(1) a basis $\{v_R\}$ which then determines the dual basis $\{\tilde{c}_R\}$, and
(2) the coordinates $Q_i(v_R)$.

The sole purpose of Shapley's axioms 1 and 2 is to define the values $Q_i(v_R)$.

III. DEFINITION OF WEIGHTS

From the property[4]

$$\sum_{i \in N} Q_i(v_R) = v_R(N), \tag{20}$$

(13) holds automatically since

$$\sum_{i \in N} Q_i(v) = \sum_{i \in N} \sum_{R \subseteq N} Q_i(v_R)\tilde{c}_R(v) = \sum_{R \subseteq N} \tilde{c}_R(v) \sum_{i \in N} Q_i(v_R)$$

$$= \sum_{R \subseteq N} \tilde{c}_R(v) v_R(N) = v(N). \tag{21}$$

If in addition R is a carrier for v_R with $v_R(R) = 1$, then by (13)

$$\sum_{i \in R} Q_i(v_R) = 1.$$

The $Q_i(v_R)$ may then be interpreted as relative weights on members of subgroup R.[5]

---

[3] Since Q_i is a linear functional, $\{v_R\}$ is a linear transformation of $\{v_R\}$, and $\{\tilde{c}_R\}$ is linearly related to $\{c_R\}$, then any specification of $Q_i(v)$ in terms of $\{v_R\}$ different from $\{v_R\}$ will result in an equivalent formulation, i.e.,

$$Q_i(v) = \sum_{R \subseteq N} Q_i(v_R)\, \tilde{c}_R(v) = \sum_{R \subseteq N} Q_i(v_R) c_R(v).$$

This suggests that the basis $\{v_R\}$ and dual $\{c_R\}$ are completely adequate to specify $Q_i(v)$ for all purposes. However, for some games it may be more rational to use some basis other than $\{v_R\}$.

[4] If some $v_R(\cdot)$ equals zero, then (12) and (13) imply that $Q_i(v_R) = 0$.

[5] If $v_R(R) \neq 1$ but is not zero then a transformation $v_R'(S) = v_R(S)/v_R(R)$ can be made to define a basis with $v_R(R) = 1$.

Shapley's axiom 1 serves to define the values of the weights $Q_i(v_R)$ since

$$Q_i(v_R) = Q_j(v_R), \quad i, j \in R; \qquad Q_i(v_R) = 0, \quad i \notin R \qquad (22)$$

derived from his axiom 1 combined with (20) yield that

$$Q_i(v_R) = 1/ |R| \qquad \text{for} \quad i \in R. \qquad (23)$$

For any basis $\{v_R\}$, if the rules

$$Q_i(v_R) = Q_j(v_R), \quad i, j \in R; \qquad Q_i(v_R) = 0, \quad i \notin R \qquad (24)$$

are taken as an axiom, then (20) implies that

$$Q_i(v_R) = 1/ |R| \qquad \text{for} \quad i \in R \qquad (25)$$

will also hold for a general basis $\{v_R\}$. Note that if the weights specified by (25) are used with a general basis $\{v_R\}$, the generalized value $Q_i(v)$ will differ from the Shapley value since the $\bar{c}_R(v)$ differ.

As a generalization, it is plausible to have weights $Q_i(v_R)$ that are not equal for members of a subgroup R. Unequal weights would correspond to an axiom different from (24). For example, another rule that satisfies (20) is

$$Q_i(v_R) = \text{probability } (i \text{ follows } R - i \text{ in } N). \qquad (26)$$

This is a generalization of (25) for the case that all orders of arrival are not equally likely.

An alternative way to define weights $Q_i(v_R)$ could be based on observations of prior gaming situations. If the same group N of n users has been previously involved in $2^n - 1$ games $v^1, v^2, \ldots, v^{2n-1}$ with values $Q_i(v^1), Q_i(v^2), \ldots, Q_i(v^{2n-1})$, $i = 1, \ldots, n$, then given a basis $\{v_R\}$, and corresponding dual $\{\bar{c}_R\}$, the linear equations

$$Q_i(v^1) \quad = \sum_{R \subseteq N} Q_i(v_R)\bar{c}_R(v^1)$$

$$Q_i(v^2) \quad = \sum_{R \subseteq N} Q_i(v_R)\bar{c}_R(v^2)$$

$$\vdots \qquad\qquad\qquad\qquad\qquad (27)$$

$$Q_i(v^{2n-1}) = \sum_{R \subseteq N} Q_i(v_R)\bar{c}_R(v^{2n-1})$$

could be solved for $Q_i(v_R)$, $i = 1, \ldots, n$. Assuming the weights do not change from game to game, the representation (19) thus gives a way of calculating bargaining power for groups. In the case of $n = 3$, observations of seven games would be necessary. Clearly, this process could get quite cumbersome for a large group, and there may not be enough observations of previous games, especially if members of N had not previously been in a game situation together. This way of determining weights does not seem very practical in general.

Thus, the weights $Q_i(v_R)$ required to define a value may be derived in a variety of ways, either axiomatically or based on observations of bargaining power. It seems the choice of method to define weights depends on the game situation as to what seems most reasonable and how much prior information is available.

IV. INCREMENTAL VALUES

As done in the Shapley paper [5], once weights $Q_i(v_R)$ are defined, it is possible to manipulate the formulation (19) so that it is in terms of incremental values $(v(T) - v(T - i))$ instead of $\bar{c}_R(v)$.[6] This may provide a more readily interpretable value for a game. For example, when the Shapley basis (3) is being used, (5) holds to define $c_R(v)$ and (19) may then be written as

$$Q_i(v) = \sum_{i \in R} Q_i(v_R) \sum_{T \subseteq R} (-1)^{r-t} v(T) = \sum_{T \subseteq N} v(T) \sum_{i \cup T \subseteq R} (-1)^{r-t} Q_i(v_R).$$
(28)

Defining

$$\gamma_i(T) = \sum_{i \cup T \subseteq R} (-1)^{r-t} Q_i(v_R),$$
(29)

it can be shown for $T' = T \cup \{i\}$, $i \notin T$, that

$$\gamma_i(T') = -\gamma_i(T),$$
(30)

so that

$$Q_i(v) = \sum_{T \subseteq N, i \in T} \gamma_i(T) [v(T) - v(T - i)].$$
(31)

Thus (31) provides a generalization of the Shapley value when axiom 1 is not required. In the Shapley case, $\gamma_i(T)$ is the probability of i joining $T - i$ in N assuming all orders of arrival are equally likely; in this case $\gamma_i(T)$ depends on the definition of $Q_i(v_R)$.

For a given i, $\gamma_i(T)$ in (29) has the property that

$$\sum_{T \subseteq N} \gamma_i(T) = \sum_{T \subseteq N} \sum_{T \subseteq R \subseteq N} (-1)^{r-t} Q_i(v_R)$$

$$= \sum_{R \subseteq N, i \in R} Q_i(v_R) \sum_{s=0}^{r-1} (-1)^s \binom{r-1}{s} = Q_i(v_{\{i\}}) = 1.$$
(32)

If $\gamma_i(T) \geqslant 0$ for all i and $T \subseteq N$, then by (32), the $\gamma_i(T)$ may be interpreted to be probabilities.

---

[6] This is not a change of basis for V^* since the set $\{v(T) - v(T - i)\}$ is not independent.

V. VALUE, IMPUTATIONS, AND THE CORE

Just because we may define a generalized value for a game as in (19) or (31), it does not mean such a value would necessarily be a solution of a game, i.e., an equilibrium outcome. Certain additional requirements must be added to (12) and (13) in order to obtain a value that qualifies as a solution.

One requirement is individual rationality, or $Q_i(v) \geqslant v(\{i\})$ for all $i \in N$. (This condition plus (12) and (13) mean that $Q_i(v)$ is called an imputation.) From (19), if $\bar{c}_R(v) \geqslant 0$ for all $R \subseteq N$, then

$$Q_i(v) \geqslant Q_i(v_{\{i\}})\bar{c}_{\{i\}}(v) = \bar{c}_{\{i\}}(v) \tag{33}$$

Also, if $v_R(S) = 0$ for $R \not\subseteq S$, then by (17), $v(\{i\}) = \bar{c}_{\{i\}}(v)$ and individual rationality holds. Thus the conditions on v_R and v, that $v_R(S) = 0$ for $R \not\subseteq S$ and $\bar{c}_R(v) \geqslant 0$, are sufficient but not necessary conditions for $Q_i(v)$ to be an imputation. Using the definition of $c_R(v)$ in (5) as an example, it can be seen that superadditivity of v is not sufficient to assure nonnegativity of $c_R(v)$. Note also that there is no requirement on $Q_i(v_R)$ except nonnegativity and $Q_i(v_{\{i\}}) = 1$. A different sufficient condition, in the case that the Shapley basis is being used, is obtained from (31). If $\gamma_i(T) \geqslant 0$ for all i and T and if v is superadditive so that $v(T) - v(T - i) \geqslant v(i)$, then by (31) and (32)

$$Q_i(v) \geqslant \sum_{T \subseteq N, i \in T} \gamma_i(T)v(i) = v(i) \sum_{T \subseteq N, i \in T} \gamma_i(T) = v(i), \tag{34}$$

so that $Q_i(v)$ is then an imputation. The nonnegativity of $\gamma_i(T)$ depends on the definition of $Q_i(v_R)$ by (29). Other sufficient conditions could be derived similarly depending on the definition of v_R and $c_R(v)$.

The condition that $Q_i(v)$ be in the core is a still more restrictive solution concept. In addition to (12) and (13), a collective rationality property is required:

$$\sum_{i \in S} Q_i(v) \geqslant v(S), \qquad S \subset N. \tag{35}$$

(This requirement implies that $Q_i(v)$ is also an imputation.) By (19),

$$\sum_{i \in S} Q_i(v) = \sum_{i \in S} \sum_{R \subseteq N} Q_i(v_R)\bar{c}_R(v) = \sum_{R \subseteq N} \bar{c}_R(v) \sum_{i \in S} Q_i(v_R), \tag{36}$$

and by (17)

$$v(S) = \sum_{R \subseteq N} \bar{c}_R(v)v_R(S). \tag{37}$$

Clearly, one sufficient condition for $Q_i(v)$ to be in the core is that $\bar{c}_R(v) \geqslant 0$ and

$$\sum_{i \in S} Q_i(v_R) \geqslant v_R(S) \qquad \text{for all} \quad R, S. \tag{38}$$

There are four cases to consider for (38): $R \subset S, S \subset R, R \cap S = \phi, R \cap S \neq \phi$. If $v_R(S) = 0$ for $R \nsubseteq S$, R is a carrier for v_R, and $Q_i(v_R) = 0$ for $i \notin R$, then (38) holds in all cases since then

$$\sum_{i \in S} Q_i(v_R) = \sum_{i \in R} Q_i(v_R) = v_R(R) = v_R(S) \qquad \text{for all} \quad R \subseteq S \qquad (39)$$

$$\sum_{i \in S} Q_i(v_R) \geqslant 0 = v_R(S) \qquad \text{in all other cases.}$$

Thus, $\tilde{c}_R(v) \geqslant 0$, R a carrier for v_R, $v_R(S) = 0$ for $R \nsubseteq S$, and $Q_i(v_R) = 0$ for $i \notin R$ are sufficient conditions for $Q_i(v)$ to be in the core. Again, these conditions are not necessary and there are other sufficient conditions.

Clearly, more work is needed to determine necessary and sufficient conditions for when a generalized value for a game is or is not an imputation and is or is not in the core.

VI. A COST ALLOCATION EXAMPLE

Using the concepts about the generalized value of a game presented in the previous two sections, we may now develop an allocation of costs for the treatment plant example. The agreement to build a common facility and the allocation of costs of this facility can be viewed as a cooperative game among users of the common facility. The characteristic function for this game is the savings to group G

$$v(G) = \sum_{i \in G} C(i) - C(G) \qquad (40)$$

where $C(i)$ is the minimum cost to user i if he has to build his own facility and $C(G)$ is the minimum cost to supply the demand of subgroup G. (The minimum cost could correspond to noncooperation for some subgroups.) This definition satisfies the properties of a superadditive game. The value $Q_i(v)$ for this game is the allocation of total savings $v(N)$ among users. Since savings for a user are his cost $C(i)$ of building his own facility minus his charge for use of the common facility $\mathscr{C}(i)$

$$Q_i(v) = C(i) - \mathscr{C}(i), \qquad (41)$$

the allocations of costs to a user is found from

$$\mathscr{C}(i) = C(i) - Q_i(v). \qquad (42)$$

The sum of cost shares defined in this way equals total costs.

$$\sum_{i \in N} \mathscr{C}(i) = \sum_{i \in N} C(i) - \sum_{i \in N} Q_i(v) = \sum_{i \in N} C(i) - v(N)$$

$$= \sum_{i \in N} C(i) - \left[\sum_{i \in N} C(i) - C(N) \right] = C(N). \qquad (43)$$

The charge scheme is then specified once $Q_i(v)$ is determined. As discussed in the previous section, to define the allocation of savings we need only define a set of basic subgames $\{v_R\}$ and a set of weights $\{Q_i(v_R)\}$.

To illustrate this process, we consider the allocation of costs for the treatment plant example presented initially in this paper. The case that users 1 and 3 would never cooperate can be indicated by defining the characteristic function for the basic subgame $v_{13}(\cdot) \equiv 0$. In the dual space, the corresponding dual basis element $c_{13}(\cdot)$ is defined to be identically zero. The other basis elements are defined by (3) since all other subsets are assumed to form. The rest of the dual basis elements are then obtained from evaluating (6) to obtain the equations

$$\begin{bmatrix} 1 & 0 & 0 & 0 & 0 & 0 \\ 0 & 1 & 0 & 0 & 0 & 0 \\ 0 & 0 & 1 & 0 & 0 & 0 \\ 1 & 1 & 0 & 1 & 0 & 0 \\ 0 & 1 & 1 & 0 & 1 & 0 \\ 1 & 1 & 1 & 1 & 1 & 1 \end{bmatrix} \begin{bmatrix} c_1 \\ c_2 \\ c_3 \\ c_{12} \\ c_{23} \\ c_{123} \end{bmatrix} = \begin{bmatrix} v(1) \\ v(2) \\ v(3) \\ v(12) \\ v(23) \\ v(123) \end{bmatrix}, \qquad (44)$$

which have the solution

$$
\begin{array}{ll}
c_1(v) = v(1) & c_{12}(v) = v(12) - v(1) - v(2) \\
c_2(v) = v(2) & c_{23}(v) = v(23) - v(2) - v(3) \qquad (45) \\
c_3(v) = v(3) & c_{123}(v) = v(123) - v(12) - v(23) + v(2)
\end{array}
$$

(Since $v(13) - v(1) - v(3) = 0$ due to the fact that there are no gains from cooperation of users one and three, we may also define $c_{13}(v) = v(13) - v(1) - v(3)$.) The formula to allocate savings for user i will then be specified by (19) once we define the weights $Q_i(v_R)$, $i = 1, 2, 3$.

Instead of defining equal weights, the probabilistic definition (26) will be used. Using this definition

$$Q_1(v_1) = 1, \qquad Q_2(v_2) = 1, \qquad Q_3(v_3) = 1.$$

Since the subgroup $\{13\}$ does not form,

$$Q_1(v_{13}) = Q_3(v_{13}) = 0.$$

In the subgroups $\{12\}$ and $\{23\}$ any order is equally likely, therefore

$$Q_1(v_{12}) = Q_2(v_{12}) = \tfrac{1}{2}, \qquad Q_2(v_{23}) = Q_3(v_{23}) = \tfrac{1}{2}.$$

However, in the formation of the grand coalition $N = \{123\}$, any order of arrival is not equally likely; the possible orders of arrival are limited to only eight cases if subgroups formations are considered:

$$1\overline{23}, \quad 1\overline{32}, \quad \overline{123}$$
$$\overline{213}, \quad \overline{231}$$
$$3\overline{12}, \quad 3\overline{21}, \quad \overline{321}$$

(The notation $1\overline{23}$ indicates that coalition $\{123\}$ was formed by user 1 joining first, followed by the subcoalition of users 2 and 3; in the subcoalition $\overline{23}$ user 2 is the first member.) From these eight orders, the probabilities of arrivals are

$$Q_1(v_{123}) = \tfrac{3}{8}, \qquad Q_2(v_{123}) = \tfrac{2}{8}, \qquad Q_3(v_{123}) = \tfrac{3}{8}.$$

Now, using these values of $Q_i(v_R)$ and $c_R(v)$ from (45), we obtain the savings allocation formulas by substituting in (19):

$$Q_1(v) = 1\,[v(1)] + \tfrac{1}{2}\,[v(12) - v(1) - v(2)] + \tfrac{3}{8}\,[v(123) - v(23) - v(12) + v(2)]$$

$$Q_2(v) = 1\,[v(2)] + \tfrac{1}{2}\,[v(12) - v(1) - v(2)] + \tfrac{1}{2}\,[v(23) - v(2) - v(3)]$$
$$+ \tfrac{2}{8}\,[v(123) - v(12) - v(23) + v(2)]$$

$$Q_3(v) = 1\,[v(3)] + \tfrac{1}{2}\,[v(23) - v(2) - v(3)] + \tfrac{3}{8}\,[v(123) - v(12) - v(23) + v(2)].$$

$$(46)$$

Substituting (40) and (42), the charge allocation formulas are then

$$\mathscr{C}(1) = C(1) + \tfrac{1}{2}\,[C(12) - C(1) - C(2)] + \tfrac{3}{8}\,[C(123) - C(23) - C(12) + C(2)]$$

$$\mathscr{C}(2) = C(2) + \tfrac{1}{2}\,[C(12) - C(1) - C(2)] + \tfrac{1}{2}\,[C(23) - C(2) - C(3)]$$
$$+ \tfrac{2}{8}\,[C(123) - C(12) - C(23) + C(2)]$$

$$\mathscr{C}(3) = C(3) + \tfrac{1}{2}\,[C(23) - C(2) - C(3)] + \tfrac{3}{8}\,[C(123) - C(12) - C(23) + C(2)].$$

$$(47)$$

These cost allocation formulas may also be manipulated to be in terms of incremental costs $C(G) - C(G - i)$. The above formulas for $\mathscr{C}(i)$ can be transformed[7] (for $C(13) = C(1) + C(3)$) to

$$\mathscr{C}(1) = \tfrac{3}{8}\,C(1) + \tfrac{1}{8}\,[C(12) - C(2)] + \tfrac{1}{8}\,[C(13) - C(3)] + \tfrac{3}{8}\,[C(123) - C(23)]$$

$$\mathscr{C}(2) = \tfrac{2}{8}\,C(2) + \tfrac{2}{8}\,[C(12) - C(1)] + \tfrac{2}{8}\,[C(23) - C(3)]$$
$$+ \tfrac{2}{8}\,[C(123) - C(1) - C(3)]$$

$$\mathscr{C}(3) = \tfrac{3}{8}\,C(3) + \tfrac{1}{8}\,[C(13) - C(1)] + \tfrac{1}{8}\,[C(23) - C(2)] + \tfrac{3}{8}\,[C(123) - C(12)].$$

$$(48)$$

---

[7] Actually, this transformation is not unique since $C(13) - C(3) - C(1) = 0$. In $\mathscr{C}(1)$, any coefficients may be chosen for $C(1)$ and $C(13) - C(3)$ as long as their sum is ½; likewise for $C(3)$ and $C(13) - C(1)$ in $\mathscr{C}(3)$.

Note that in (48) each possible definition of the incremental cost $C(G) - C(G - i)$ is weighted by the probability of user i joining the coalition immediately after $G - i$. Thus the cost allocation formula corresponds to the expected value of the incremental cost due to a user. Comparing this example to the cost allocation scheme for the equally likely case in [2], a higher proportion of the cost allocation for users 1 and 3 is based on their cost outside the coalition (e.g., $\frac{3}{8}C(1)$ compared to $\frac{1}{3}C(1)$); this is because there is a greater likelihood that users 1 and 3 would not be in the coalition; likewise, a lower portion of the cost allocation for user 2 is based on what his cost would be outside the coalition ($\frac{1}{4}C(2)$ as opposed to $\frac{1}{3}C(2)$). This corresponds to the notion that user 2 is given extra incentives to join the coalition because his presence allows savings to occur to other users.

When there are economies of scale ($C(G) - C(G - i) \leqslant C(i)$ for each G), it can be shown that using the expected incremental cost formula, each user will pay less than his costs would be outside the coalition; for example,

$$\mathscr{C}(1) \leqslant \tfrac{3}{8}C(1) + \tfrac{1}{8}C(1) + \tfrac{1}{8}C(1) + \tfrac{3}{8}C(1) = C(1). \tag{49}$$

(This is because in the expected incremental cost formula, the probabilities of user i joining after $G - i$ for each $G \subseteq N$ must sum to 1.) Thus, each user would have incentives to join the coalition using this cost allocation formula. As was already discussed, total costs will be covered using this scheme. "Fairness" was another property of cost allocation schemes considered in [2] and [3]. However, in this scheme, as opposed to the equally likely case, users with the same demands are not necessarily charged the same. Here, two users will be charged the same amount only if they have the same demands for service and carry the same weight in the coalition. Though this system may not be "fair," it corresponds more closely to what would happen in a bargaining situation since it takes into account the bargaining power of coalition members.

It still needs to be determined in general what requirements on weights and basic subgames are needed in order that the charge allocation formula results in the expected incremental cost. Other properties of using the expected incremental cost also need to be considered. These topics should provide material for other papers.

VII. CONCLUSIONS

This paper has demonstrated the form of the most general cost allocation formula based on game theoretic and linear algebra concepts. The form of the cost allocation was shown to depend on both the choice of basic subgames and the choice of weights on users in these subgames. Using this general formulation, cost allocation schemes different from that given in Loehman and Whinston [2,

3] could be obtained by: (1) using a definition of basic subgames different from Shapley's while using the Shapley axioms that define equal weights; (2) changing the axioms that define weights, while using the Shapley basis; or (3) changing both weights and basic subgames. By allowing these changes in the basic subgames and weights, it is possible to develop cost allocation schemes for nonsuperadditive game situations and situations where not all combinations of users are possible. By making these alternations, although it is possible theoretically to obtain many different cost allocations schemes that would cover costs in a given situation, only some schemes will be "acceptable." *Acceptable* means that the charge scheme gives the proper incentives for coalition formulation to build a common facility when there are economies of scale and the scheme is compatible both with costs of meeting demands and with bargaining power of members of a coalition.

Some alternative definitions of basic subgames and weights were considered in this paper. It was shown by means of an example that probabilistic definitions result in a charge scheme based on expected incremental cost. This expected incremental cost scheme is acceptable in the above sense since it covers costs and takes into account both the incremental cost and relative bargaining power of potential users of a common facility. These probabilistic definitions are generalizations of methods used in [2] to derive a cost allocation formula.

REFERENCES

1. Hoffman, K., and R. Kunze, *Linear Algebra*, Englewood Cliffs, New Jersey: Prentice-Hall, 1965.
2. Loehman, E. T., and A. B. Whinston, "A New Theory of Pricing and Decision Making for Public Investment," *Bell Journal of Economics and Management Science*, Autumn 1971, 2, 606–625.
3. Loehman, E. T., and A. B. Whinston, "An Axiomatic Approach to Cost Allocations for Public Investment," *Public Finance Quarterly*, April 1974, 2.
4. Owen, G., *Game Theory*, Philadelphia, Pennsylvania: Saunders, 1968.
5. Shapley, L. S., "A Value for *n*-person Games", in H. W. Kuhn and A. W. Tucker, eds., *Contributions to the Theory of Games Vol. 2, Annals of Mathematical Studies No. 28*, Princeton, New Jersey: Princeton Univ. Press, 1953.

Discussion

ARYE LEO HILLMAN

Tel-Aviv University

Since Loehman and Whinston (henceforth L & W) have not placed their paper within the context of the existing literature, I have decided that it would be useful, before going on to consider the substance of their paper, to develop briefly the relationship between their work and the results that we currently have.

L & W's cost allocation scheme is directed toward a solution to an externalities problem that arises when there are decreasing costs. The question they are concerned with is, if because of decreasing costs there are gains from cooperating to secure output collectively, how are such gains to be distributed among consumers? So the problem is one of the production externalities variety. There appears to be no restriction on the characteristic of the goods consumed, which may be private, intermediately rivalrous, or pure public goods.

L & W's decreasing cost problem is distinct from the general equilibrium decreasing cost market failure, where the concern is with establishing an optimal vector of market prices when sufficient subsidies are not forthcoming to facilitate pricing of output at marginal cost. In the context of this general equilibrium problem, once the price vector that minimizes the aggregate dead-weight-loss of departing from marginal cost pricing is secured, all consumers are charged the same price. L & W's decreasing cost problem is specifically a partial equilibrium one, and they set out to establish a pricing scheme that discriminates across consumers by disparities in their demands and allows for any monopolistic power individual consumers or subcoalitions may have in coalition formation.

By its nature, the L & W cost allocation problem has much in common with the peak-load pricing problem, where the objective is also to secure some discriminatory pricing scheme for output. The authors would have much better motivated their paper had they expounded on the connection between their formulation and the peak-load pricing problem, on which a considerable literature exists. The fundamental characteristic of the L & W problem is the existence of potential gains from cooperative action in securing output. Such gains also exist in the peak-load pricing problem which is motivated by the desire to establish a cost allocation scheme when some subcoalitions of users, indexed with respect to the point of time of use, require more fixed capacity than do other subcoalitions. L & W's motivating question can be phrased as: if total cost is necessarily to be covered, what price should a large user of a facility pay relative to a smaller user, when the magnitude of the large user's demand facilities low per unit costs? Their objective may be viewed as that of seeking a cost allocation scheme that gives the large user an incentive to participate in a production coalition rather than have him set up his own independent facility. Note that by contrast, in the peak-load pricing problem, it is generally the large user coalition that gains by the presence of the smaller user (off-peak) coalition since the latter defray part of the cost of a facility capacity which without off-peak demand would have been idle waiting for the peak-load time period to occur.

The L & W paper is an interesting exercise. The authors transform the derivation of the Shapley value to a linear algebraic formulation, note that the Shapley value is based on but one of an infinite number of ways of decomposing a game, and then use this generalization of decomposition to allow for monopolistic power in coalition formation. However, there would appear to be at least two sets of problems with the L & W cost allocation scheme, the first interpretative and the second quite fundamental to the nature of the problem they are considering.

The interpretative problems arise once one departs from the Shapley basis. The Shapley value has the intuitively appealing property of assigning to each individual in a cooperative game the expected net benefit from his participation in the coalition. However, once monopolistic power in coalition formation is introduced, difficulties would appear to arise in the a priori interpretation of the basic subgames v_R and weights $Q_i(v_R)$ employed in a cost allocation solution. Since only some special choices of v_R and $Q_i(v_R)$ yield incremental cost as a solution, it is of interest to establish what the general requirements on v_R and $Q_i(v_R)$ are for a generalized Shapley value to be capable of the same interpretation as the specific Shapley value for a particular game. Yet as L & W acknowledge, at this point they have not established what these general requirements are. But without such knowledge, we cannot identify a priori the subset of generalized Shapley values that are of interest.

We are also confronted with the interpretive problem of establishing the conditions under which L & W's proposed generalized Shapley value yields solutions that are imputations – or for subgroups, solutions that are in the core. Although L & W present us with some sufficient conditions for solutions being imputations and in the core, it would be revealing to establish the common characteristics of these diverse sufficient conditions.

A quite basic question is, even if a choice of v_R and $Q_i(v_R)$ *does* yield expected incremental cost – with (a) $Q_i(v) \geqslant v\{i\}$ and (b) $\Sigma_i Q_i(v) = v(N)$ satisfied – what are the desirable characteristics of the L & W generalized Shapley value, as compared to the outcome of any criterion that proceeds to allocate the gains from cooperative action such that (a) and (b) hold? The condition $Q_i(v) \geqslant v\{i\}$ ensures Pareto optimality. Once the additional exhaustion condition $\Sigma_i Q_i(v) = v(N)$ is satisfied, the traditional way of looking at outcomes is in terms of equity: via cooperation in coalition formation, we can establish a set of states Pareto superior to the outcomes obtained when individuals act alone, and we are then confronted with the traditional problem of choosing an equitable distribution of the gains from coaltion formation. As a prerequisite to obtaining a solution via their generalized cost allocation scheme, L & W require us to choose v_R and $Q_i(v)$ so as to reflect both volume of demand by users and individuals' monopolistic power in coalition formation. Certainly, we would expect to be able to obtain determinate outcomes every time if we had unequivocal measures of bargaining power which we could parametrically impose upon our solutions. The difficulty, of course, is in knowing which v_R and $Q_i(v_R)$ to use; i.e., in obtaining the a priori measures of bargaining power necessary in order to be able to apply the L & W generalized cost allocation formula.

Finally, and most fundamentally, there is an apparent problem with the way in which demand enters L & W's cost allocation scheme. Demand is predetermined for each user *before* the cost allocation scheme determines the prices to be assigned to users. As a *general* cost allocation scheme, L & W's procedure is therefore unsatisfactory, in that it requires consumers' demands to be known before consumers are aware of prices, which themselves are not known until the outcome of the application of the scheme is determined. Accordingly, the cost allocation scheme as developed by L & W in their paper is appropriate only when demand is infinitely inelastic with respect to price.

This is not to say that an equilibrium might not exist where the prices assigned as the consequence of the application of the cost allocation scheme were indeed compatible with demands presupposed as data for the problem's solution. However, an investigation of the existence and general properties of such an equilibrium is a much more complicated task than the inelastic demand formulation of the L & W paper. The truly general problem would appear to be of the following form. Let q_i denote the dimension of the facility desired (or the flow of output demanded) by the ith consumer, and following L & W, let e_i denote the price assigned to the ith consumer. Then a solution not confined to completely inelastic demand is in principle obtainable from the following system of equations — if a solution exists:

$$q_i = f_i(e_i), \qquad i = 1, \ldots, N \tag{1}$$

$$\bar{q} = \sum_i q_i \tag{2}$$

$$e_i = g[v_R, Q_i(v_R), \bar{q}], \qquad i = 1, \ldots, N. \tag{3}$$

(1) is the set of demand functions of all potential users, specified to depend only upon the price charged to the individual. (3) is the set of price determination equations which are established as L & W's generalized Shapley values by the choice of basic subgames v_R and the individual's coalition weight for coordinates v_R, $Q_i(v_R)$; but in addition the vector of cost allocations depends upon total demand $\bar{q}$ as given by the identity (2). For $\bar{q}$ indicates the equilibrium scale of output, and with decreasing costs, this clearly affects prices charged to consumers.

In (1)–(3), v_R and $Q_i(v_R)$ have been left, as proposed by L & W, to be exogenous. However, we can suppose that at different prices assigned to consumers and with then different demands, monopoly power in coalition formation will vary. Consequently, both v_R and $Q_i(v_R)$ would then themselves be endogenously determined by the equilibrium values of the q_i and e_i.

These extensions would appear to complicate substantially L & W's cost allocation scheme, causing much of the neatness and simplicity of their formulation to disappear. However, a much more appealing frame of reference does result if the amount demanded by each consumer is specified to depend upon the price assigned to him via the cost allocation scheme.

IV

Externalities in
General Equilibrium

The analysis of externality including the private bargain approach has always been carried out within a partial equilibrium framework. Mishan in his recent paper [7] touches upon an analytic difficulty of the partial analysis. In addition, he argues that the conclusion reached after mutual agreement between producers and spillover victims produces an optimal output that commonly ignores the consumer interest.

As it is observed in the "General Theory of Second Best" (Lipsey and Lancaster [5]), there is no certainty that the output satisfying optimal conditions with the application of the social marginal cost pricing rule in the sector(s) under consideration will move the entire economy closer to the Pareto optimum, unless all the optimum conditions are already met in the rest of the economy. The price—marginal cost ratio, nevertheless, can be invoked to justify this partial procedure (Farrell [3], Green [4], Mishan [6], Davis and Whinston [2]). Ayres and Kneese's study [1] is one exception to the prevailing partial equilibrium analysis of externalities.

Solutions are considered by Bergstrom for the allocation of resources in an economy with public goods and interdependent preferences. These solutions are similar to the "Lindahl solution" suggested by Wicksell and developed by Lindahl. It is shown that a "generalized Lindahl equilibrium" exists under very general circumstances and that there is a correspondence between the set of such equilibria and the set of Pareto optimal allocations.

The model is somewhat more general in its assumptions about tastes and technology than Arrow and Foley's, and applies to a broader class of institutional arrangements. There is a discussion of the specification and measurement of commodities and of the circumstances under which aggregation can be legitimately performed. An effort also is made to illuminate the special difficulties for the existence problem appearing in a nonindividualistic economy.

Rader analyzes efficiency from a decentralized viewpoint in social systems with externalities. The necessary and sufficient conditions for Pareto optimality are analyzed in detail.

Pairwise optimality refers to the situation where each pair of traders exploits all mutual gains given their position with respect to others. This approach to efficiency is claimed to have considerable computational advantage over the usual competitive equilibrium approach. Of course pairwise optimality does not have the nice properties shown by Debreu and Scarf for competitive equilibrium. A pairwise optimal choice need not be equitable nor in the core.

In his paper, Rader derives a general theorem for exchange economies that contains both his previous study in this subject and Feldman equivalence theorems as special cases. He also applies the concept of pairwise optimality to economic systems related to, but different from, trade in pure exchange economies. In analyzing efficiency from a decentralized viewpoint in social systems with externalities, it is shown that pairwise optimality has to be replaced with more general decision systems. For bilateral externalities only, efficient exchange between every triple of agents will suffice. For multilateral externalities, one will also need to have an efficient operation of the so-called public externalities, namely those affecting two or more individuals.

Shapley presents a model of trade with a "money" as a noncooperative game of a variety related to the Cournot type of economic model. The effect on feasibility and optimality caused by trading with "money" in markets with a price system is examined in detail. The markets and the price system form of trading is viewed as constituting an economic *externality* to all traders in the sense that the prices paid by any trader are always dependent on the actions of all others.

The restrictions imposed upon individual economic behavior by being required to trade in "money," how they influence the strategies of individuals, and the feasible outcomes from economic activity are the central focuses of discussion.

Shapley's conclusions can be summarized as follows. A noncooperative equilibrium point is shown to exist. There is less volume of trade at a noncooperative equilibrium than at the corresponding competitive equilibrium. The noncooperative equilibrium is not only not Pareto optimal, but it is quite possible that the competitive equilibrium is not even attainable if no "credit" is granted. "Credit" refers to the fact that an individual, say, the first trader, is permitted to bid more of the means of payment commodity than he has.

REFERENCES

1. Ayres, R. V., and A. V. Kneese, "Production, Consumption, and Externalities," *American Economic Review*, June 1969, 59, 282–297.
2. Davis, O. A., and A. B. Whinston, "Piecemeal Policy in the Theory of Second Best," *Review of Economic Studies*, July 1967, 34, 323–331.
3. Farrell, M. J., "In Defence of Public Utility Pricing," *Oxford Economic Papers*, Feb. 1958, 10, 109–123.
4. Green, H. A. J., "The Social Optimum in the Presence of Monopoly and Taxation," *Review of Economic Studies*, 1961, 29, 66–78.
5. Lipsey, R. G., and K. Lancaster, "The General Theory of Second Best," *Review of Economic Studies*, 1956–1957, 24, 11–32.
6. Mishan, E. J., "Second Thoughts on Second Best," *Oxford Economic Papers*, October 1962, 14, 205–217.
7. Mishan, E. J., "The Post War Literature on Externalities: An Interpretive Essay," *Journal of Economic Literature,* March 1971, 9, 1–28.

Collective Choice
and the Lindahl
Allocation Method

THEODORE C. BERGSTROM†

Washington University
St. Louis

INTRODUCTION

The cornerstone of traditional economic theory is the elegant and paradoxical result that in an economy of selfish men, resources can be allocated efficiently if consumers are allowed to pursue their own interests in competitive trading. This result is purchased at the cost of strong assumptions about the extent to which technology and preferences are compatible with individualism. It is assumed that commodities can be allocated among consumers in such a way that preferences of each consumer are concerned only with the quantity of commodities allocated to him. The individualistic consumer is not interested in the total supply of any commodity or in the quantities allocated to others.

It has been recognized, largely in the literature on "public goods," that there are commodities that do not lend themselves well to the individualistic

This is a revised version of a paper of the same title, which was written in 1970. I am grateful for useful suggestions and encouragement from Professors Trout Rader of Washington University, James Barr of University of Pennsylvania, David Bradford of Princeton, and David Starrett of Stanford.

†Present address: Department of Economics, University of Michigan, Ann Arbor, Michigan,

formulation. This may be true because of the physical nature of commodities such as fireworks or impurities in the air, or it may be because of such psychological interactions as sympathy, envy, or emulation. In such cases it may be impossible to partition private rights or consumption in such a way that consumers are interested only in the commodities allocated to them. When commodities and preferences do not conform to the individualistic model, efficiency considerations may suggest the usefulness of collective action.

This paper suggests a formulation of the choice space that seems appropriate to a wide range of problems of joint consumption and interdependence of preference. There is a discussion of the specification and measurement of commodities and of the circumstances under which aggregation can be legitimately performed. Solutions are considered for the allocation of resources in any economy with public goods and interdependent preferences. These solutions are similar to the "Lindahl solution" suggested by Wicksell [25] and developed by Lindahl [16]. It it shown that what we call a "generalized Lindahl equilibrium" exists under very general circumstances and that there is a correspondence between the set of such equilibria and the set of Pareto optimal allocations. Some special assumptions on the nature of preferences are shown to lead to interesting simplifications of the structure of Lindahl equilibria.

Arrow [1] and Foley [14] have shown that the Arrow—Debreu proof of the existence of competitive equilibrium can be adapted to show the existence of a Lindahl equilibrium. The model presented here is somewhat more general in its assumptions about tastes and technology, and applies to a broader class of institutional arrangements. An effort is made to illuminate the special difficulties for the existence problem appearing in a nonindividualistic economy. Other discussions of Lindahl equilibrium appear in Milleron [19], Dreze and Poussin [13], Malinvaud [17], Starrett [24], Rader [22], and Bergstrom [4–6].

I.

Samuelson [23] suggests an interesting view of the public goods problem in which "public" and "private" commodities are treated as polar extremes. The analysis of efficient resource allocation then permits an elegant formal duality. Some question remains as to whether the "public goods" with which actual governments must be concerned fall neatly into the Samuelson polar case or whether such commodities are typically "mixed cases" which are neither purely private nor purely public.

The formulation that is chosen in this paper is one in which all commodities can be formally treated as purely public.[1] To avoid confusing connotations of

[1] This formulation is similar to that of Arrow [1].

the term "public goods," the basic commodities shall here be called communal commodities. Pure private commodities will appear as special cases of communal commodities. The so-called mixed cases turn out to be rather awkwardly specified aggregates of communal commodities. In order to subject the mixed cases to analysis it is necessary to disaggregate them into the communal commodities of which they are composed.

An attempt is made in the discussion to separate the formal theory from its economic interpretation. The discussion of the latter, which proceeds on an informal level is intended to illustrate that the theory when carefully applied has a reasonably "realistic" economic interpretation. The confusion that exists in the terminology of theoretical and applied public finance perhaps justifies this somewhat laborious examination.

A. Communal Commodities and Consumer Preference

There are *n consumers* (where *n* is a positive integer) indexed by the set $I = \{1, \ldots, n\}$. There are *m communal commodities* (where *m* is a positive integer) indexed by the set $J = \{1, \ldots, m\}$. An *allocation* is a point in nonnegative orthant Ω^m of the *m*-dimensional vector space, E^m. If $x = (x_1, \ldots, x_m)$ is an allocation, then where $j \in J$, x_j is said to be the *quantity of communal commodity j in allocation x*. For each consumer $i \in I$, there is a *preference relation* R_i defined on Ω^m that is complete, transitive, and reflexive. The corresponding *strict preference* and *indifference relations* P_i and I_i are defined in the usual way.

An economic interpretation of these terms is as follows. A consumer is a decision making unit, usually thought of as an individual or a family. There is a set A of conceivable states of the world. For any state of the world $\alpha \in A$, a vector $x \in \Omega^m$ can be found that lists the quantities of each of *m* distinct goods and services which appear in state of the world α. These vectors are called allocations. Each of the distinct goods and services is called a communal commodity. Communal commodities may be distinguished by time and location of availability as well as by to whom they are made available. The set A can be partitioned into subsets, each of which is characterized by a different vector in Ω^m. The statement "$x \, R_i \, y$" is interpreted to mean that if α and β are states of the world characterized by the vectors x and y respectively, then consumer i finds state of the world α at least as satisfactory as state β.

B. Aggregation and the Choice of Communal Commodities

When this interpretation is placed on the above definitions, the seemingly innocuous assumption "R_i is reflexive" requires that the set J of communal commodities be very carefully chosen if the economic interpretation of the theory is to be plausible. In particular, the equivalence classes that are generated by the set Ω^m of allocations must be sufficiently fine so that if any two states of the world are characterized by the same allocation, *everyone* finds them equally satisfactory.[2] For example, in the traditional theory where all consumers are "selfish," each consumer cares not how much bread is present in total but only how much bread is made available to him. Clearly, if there are k "private commodities" of the traditional sort, these must be represented in our model by nk communal commodities, a typical one of which is a particular private commodity available to a specified consumer.

In the aggregation of public goods, considerable care must be taken. It would not be reasonable to treat national defense as a communal commodity. Almost certainly, different consumers will place different relative importance on various aspects of defense expenditure. It is, therefore, most unlikely that any aggregation of armament efforts into a single scalar index would have the characteristic that for any two states of the world differing only in the aspect of armaments and for which the national defense index is identical, *all* consumers agree that the two states are equally satisfactory. Yet this is precisely what is required if R_i is to be reflexive for all $i \in I$.

These observations can be summarized in more formal terms. Consider a partition $\{A, B\}$ of the set J such that A consists of a commodities where $1 \leqslant a \leqslant m$. Allocations may be represented (x_A, x_B) where x_A and x_B are vectors of commodities in A and B respectively. Preferences of consumer i are said to be separable on A if whenever $(x_A, x_B') R_i (x_A', x_B')$ for some $x_B' \in \Omega^{m-a}$, it must be that $(x_A, x_B) R_i (x_A', x_B)$ for all $x_B \in \Omega^{m-a}$. If preferences are separable on A, one can unambiguously define the *projection* $\gtrsim_i^A$ of R_i on E^a so that $x_A \gtrsim_i^A x_A'$ if and only if $(x_A, x_B) R_i (x_A', x_B)$ for some $x_B \in \Omega^{m-a}$. One can also define the corresponding strict preference and indifference relations $>_i^A$ and $\sim_i^A$ in the natural way.

Preferences of consumers i and j are said to be *similar on A* if preferences of both consumers are separable on A and if for all x_A and x_A', $x_A \sim_i^A x_A'$ if and only if $x_A \sim_j^A x_A$. If preferences of i and j are separable on A and if $x_A \gtrsim_i^A x_A'$ if and only if $x_A \gtrsim_j^A x_A'$ then preferences of i and j are said to be *identical on A*.

Theorem 1 *If preferences of all consumers are representable by a continuous utility function U defined on Ω^m, then there exists a continuous real-valued aggregator function v defined on Ω^a such that preferences can be represented by a function U_i^* defined on Ω^{m-a+1} where $U_i(x) = U_i^*(v(x_A), x_B)$ for all $x \in \Omega^m$ if and only if preferences of all consumers are similar on A.*

Proof It is a well-known result that preferences of consumer i can be represented in the form of $U_i^*(v_i(x_A), x_B)$ if and only if preferences of i are

---

[2] It is here assumed that it is possible to generate a sufficiently fine partition of states of the world from a finite-dimensional commodity space. This might not be the case if one wishes, for example, to treat time as a continuum.

separable on A (see Gorman [15]). It is easily verified that one can choose identical v_i functions for each i if and only if preferences of all consumers are similar on A. q.e.d.

If preferences of all consumers are identical on A, then U_i^* will be monotonic in the same direction with respect to v for all $i \in I$. If preferences are similar but not identical, this is not true since some consumers may like and some may dislike increases in v.

C. Survival Sets and Feasible Allocations

For each consumer $i \in I$, there is a set $C_i \subset \Omega^m$ called the *survival set of i.* There is also a set $Z \subset \Omega^m$ called the *set of feasible allocations.*

The set C_i may be interpreted as the set of all allocations that enable consumer i to survive physically for at least some short period of time. Although it is convenient to assume that consumer preference is defined on all allocations in Ω^m, it will be useful to assume stronger properties for preferences on C_i than could reasonably be assumed for preferences over the entire nonnegative orthant. For example, the economic interpretations of the assumptions of local nonsatiation and continuity of preferences at all points in Ω^m is quite implausible (see Bergstrom [4]). If these properties are assumed only at points in C_i, the economic interpretation is more reasonable. Of course, in the formal theory, C_i is simply a set that has the properties attributed to it by the axioms in which it is mentioned. The theorems in this paper do not necessarily require that C_i be coextensive with the set of allocations that enable i to survive physically although this interpretation may be useful.

The set Z can be interpreted as the set of all allocations that can be attained given the resources and technological capabilities of the economy. The institutional framework of production is deliberately left unspecified. This enables us to develop a general theorem on the existence of equilibrium that will apply under many forms of industrial organization. There may, for example, be several firms operating with or without externalities as well as several governmental activities.

D. Prices, Wealth Distribution, and Lindahl Equilibrium

In "voluntaristic" collective decision models of the Wicksell–Lindahl type, unanimous agreement is gained for a single allocation by the device of confronting different consumers with (in general) different price vectors. An equilibrium allocation maximizes the preferences of *each* consumer subject to his budget constraint at equilibrium prices.[3] Furthermore, the value of the

---

[3] This method presents an interesting formal contrast to the competitive pricing of "private goods" where all consumers face the same prices but may choose different quantities.

equilibrium allocation when valued at the sum of the individual prices must be at least as high as that of any other feasible allocation.

A *Lindahl price vector* is a point $p = (p^1, \ldots, p^n) \in E^{mn}$ where for all $i \in I$, $p^i = (p_1{}^i, \ldots, p_m{}^i) \in E^m$. A wealth distribution function is a function W from E^{mn} to E^n such that for $p \in E^{mn}$,

$$W(p) = (W_1(p), \ldots, W_n(p)) \qquad \text{and} \qquad \sum_{i \in I} W_i(p) = \max_{z \in Z} \sum_{i \in I} p^i z.$$

The *budget correspondence* B_i of consumer i is a mapping from E^{mn} to the set of subsets of Ω^m such that $B_i(p) = \Omega^m \cap \{x \mid p^i x \leqslant W_i(p)\}$.

An example of a wealth distribution function is that of a "private ownership economy" (e.g., Debreu [12] in which all commodities are private and in which a consumer's wealth is the value of a vector of commodities that he owns before trade occurs plus some historically predetermined fraction of the (maximized) profits of each firm). Where there are communal commodities that are not private commodities, there is a great variety of conceivable arrangements of claims to commonly enjoyed commodities. For this reason it is useful to consider a very general wealth distribution function.

A *generalized Lindahl equilibrium* under the wealth distribution function W is a point $(\bar{p}, \bar{z}) \in E^{mn} \times Z$ such that:

(i) For all $i \in I$, $\bar{z}$ maximizes R_i on $\Omega^m \cap B_i(\bar{p})$.
(ii) $\sum_{i \in I} \bar{p}^i \bar{z} \geqslant \sum_{i \in I} \bar{p}^i z$ for all $z \in Z$.

Notice that if an individual regards a communal commodity as unpleasant, we would expect his equilibrium Lindahl price for that commodity to be negative.

II. THE EXISTENCE OF LINDAHL EQUILIBRIUM

Since the requirements for an allocation to be in equilibrium are rather intricate, it is not at all obvious that they can be simultaneously met for reasonable economies. It is shown here that generalized Lindahl equilibrium does exist for a large class of economies. The assumptions employed to prove existence are similar to those used in traditional proofs of the existence of competitive equilibrium. There are, however, some interesting novelties of interpretation which are due to the nonindividualistic nature of the economy. After the statement of our existence theorem, these interpretations will be discussed.

Theorem 2   *In an economy with a set I of n consumers and a set J of m communal commodities, there exists a generalized Lindahl equilibrium if the following assumptions are satisfied:*

(A)   (Individual preferences) *For each $i \in I$, there is a preference ordering R_i and a survival set $C_i \subset \Omega^m$ such that:*

A–I R_i *is a complete quasi-ordering defined on Ω^m.*

A–II   (Weak convexity and regularity)   *For all $x \in \Omega^m$, the set $R_i(x) = \{x' \mid x'R_i x\}$ is closed and convex.*

A–III   (Continuity along straight lines in C_i)   *If $x, x' \in C_i$ and $xP_i x'$, then for some λ such that $0 < \lambda < 1$, $(\lambda x + (1 - \lambda)x') P_i x'$.*[4]

A–IV   *The set C_i is closed and convex.*

A–V   (Local nonsatiation on C_i)   *If $x \in C_i$, then in every open neighborhood of x there is an allocation x' such that $x' P_i x$.*

A–VI   *There is a nonzero vector, $\hat{v}^i \in \Omega^m$ such that for $x \in C_i$, and all real valued $\lambda \geq 0$, $x + \lambda \cdot \hat{v}^i \in C_i \cap R_i(x)$.*[5]

(B)   (Technology)   *There is a closed, bounded, convex set $Z \subset \Omega^m$ of feasible allocations.*

(C)   (Wealth distribution)   *There is a wealth distribution function W such that $W(p) = (W_1(p), \ldots, W_n(p))$ is continuous and homogeneous of degree one, and $\Sigma_{i \in I} W_i(p) = \max_{z \in Z} \Sigma_{i \in I} p^i z$.*

(D)   (Social compatibility)   *The set $\cap_{i \in I} C_i \cap Z$ has a nonempty interior.*

(E)   (Preference minimal allocation)   *There exists an allocation $w \in \cap_{i \in I} C_i \cap Z$ called a "preference minimal allocation" such that for all $i \in I$, $R_i(w) \subset C_i$ and for all $p \in E^{mn}$, $B_i(p) \cap R_i(w) \neq \phi$.*

(F)   (Social conflict)   *For all $h \in I$, if $x R_h w$ and $x \in Z$, then there exists $\hat{x} \in \cap_{i \in I} C_i \cap Z$ such that $\hat{x} P_i x$ for all $i \neq h$, $i \in I$.*

The interpretations of assumptions A–I – A–VI are familiar from the literature on competitive equilibrium (Debreu [12]). The only novelty is the interpretation of the set C_i discussed in Section I.C. Assumption B requires that the aggregate set of technically possible transformations be convex. As mentioned above, this formulation of the technology could apply to a variety of institutional arrangements. It might be observed that assumption B does allow any commodity whether private or not to be used in the production of other commodities.

Assumption C specifies the class of wealth distribution functions for which the theorem applies. As the discussion of Section I.D suggests, it is useful to consider a broader class of wealth distribution functions than simply those appropriate for a private ownership economy.

Assumption D demands a minimal amount of social compatibility in the sense that there must be some feasible allocation such that every individual can survive

---

[4] This assumption is slightly weaker than the familiar assumption that lower contour sets are closed. See Rader [21].

[5] Assumption A–VI involves no substantial loss of generality since an artificial commodity could be introduced which is both harmless and useless.

at that allocation or any allocation sufficiently close to it. A similar assumption is contained in the traditional models of private competitive equilibrium (see e.g. McKenzie [18, Assumption 5]). Where there are nonprivate commodities, assumption D requires also that there be no "public good" that is one man's necessity and another man's poison.

Assumption E places an additional restriction on the wealth distribution function. It is assumed that at any price vector, each individual's budget constraint allows him the choice of some allocation that he likes at least as well as the preference minimal allocation. The preference minimal allocation in the private ownership economy of the traditional models is the "initial" allocation. There the equivalent of assumption E is obtained by assuming that each consumer could survive with his initial holdings. Here the term *preference minimal* rather than *initial* is used because there is nothing in the formal structure requiring that the allocation w would persist in the absence of social intercourse. In fact it may be useful to interpret w as an allocation in which some communal commodities that provide at least a minimal social infra-structure are present by mutual agreement.

Assumption F requires conflict of interest in the economy in the following sense. If any consumer likes a feasible allocation x as well as the preference minimal allocation, then there exists another feasible allocation that is preferred by all other consumers to x. Thus it would be in the interest of all other consumers to "enslave" him if they could. In the individualistic private ownership economy, assumption F would follow either from the assumption that all consumers have initial holdings interior to their consumption sets and have locally nonsatiated preferences (Arrow and Debreu [2]) or the assumption that everyone can surrender some commodity vector which can be transformed into something desirable for each other consumer (McKenzie [18] or Bergstrom [13]). Since our model allows the possibility of benevolence or more complicated interactions between consumers, it might be that even if a consumer could surrender a quantity of a good desirable to all others, the others would not wish him to do so because of benevolent feelings for him. An example that illustrates this difficulty is presented in Bergstrom [4, p. 394].

The proof of Theorem 2 will be aided by the following lemmas. Lemma 1 is proved by Debreu [10].

Lemma 1 *Let P be the intersection of the unit sphere $\{p \mid p \in E^{mn}$ and $\Sigma_{i=1}^{mn} p_i^2 = 1\}$ with a convex cone in E^{mn} that is not a linear manifold. Let E be an upper semicontinuous mapping from P to the set of subsets of E^{mn} such that $E(p) = E(\lambda p)$ for all $\lambda > 0$ and all $p \in P$ and such that $px \leqslant 0$ whenever $x \in E(p)$. Then there exists a $\bar{p} \in P$ such that $E(\bar{p}) \cap -P^* \neq \phi$, where $P^* = \{x \mid px \geqslant 0$ for all $p \in P\}$.*

Lemma 2 *The assumptions of Theorem 2 excluding A–III, D, and F imply* *that there exists a feasible allocation* $\bar{z} \in Z$ *and a nonzero Lindahl price vector* $\bar{p} \in E^{mn}$ *such that:*

(i) *For all* $i \in I$, $\bar{z} \in C_i \cap \{x \mid \bar{p}^i x \leqslant W_i(\bar{p})\}$ *and if* $x \in \Omega^m \cap \{x \mid \bar{p}^i x < W_i(\bar{p})\}$, *then* $\bar{z} \, R_i \, x$.

(ii) $\sum_{i \in I} \bar{p}^i \bar{z} \geqslant \sum_{i \in I} \bar{p}^i z$ *for all* $z \in Z$.

If in part (i) of the conclusion $\leqslant$ were substituted for $<$, then the conclusion would state that $(\bar{p}, \bar{z})$ is a generalized Lindahl equilibrium. An allocation and a Lindahl price vector satisfying Lemma 2 is exactly analogous to what Debreu calls a "quasi-equilibrium" for a private economy (Debreu [11]).

Following the procedure of Debreu [11], we first restrict attention to choice on a bounded subset of Ω^m. Assumption B allows one to choose a closed bounded cube $\tilde{Z}$ in Ω^m that contains $Z \cap \Omega^m$ in its interior. Assumption A–VI allows us to restrict attention to a set of price vectors of the kind required for Debreu's lemma. For each $i \in I$, let $\hat{v}^i$ be the vector mentioned in A–VI. Define the set $V \equiv \{v \mid v = (\lambda_1 \hat{v}^1, \ldots, \lambda_n \hat{v}^n)$ and $\lambda_i \geqslant 0$ for all $i \in I\}$. Clearly V is a closed convex cone in Ω^{mn} that contains points other than the origin. Define the set $V^* \equiv \{p \mid p \in E^{mn}$ and $pv \geqslant 0$ for all $v \in V\}$. Then V^* is a closed convex cone that is not a linear manifold and if $p = (p^1, \ldots, p^n) \in V^*$, then $p^i v^i \geqslant 0$ for all $i \in I$. Define the set $P \equiv V^* \cap \{p \mid |p| = 1\}$.

Define the mappings, M, F_i, and E with domain P so that:

$$M(p) \equiv Z \cap \{z \mid \sum_{i \in I} p^i z \geqslant \sum_{i \in I} p^i z' \text{ if } z' \in Z\}.$$

$$F_i(p) \equiv \tilde{Z} \cap R_i(w) \cap B_i(p) \cap \{x \mid x \, R_i \, x' \text{ if } p^i x' < W_i(p) \text{ and } x' \in \tilde{Z}\}.$$

$$E(p) \equiv \{(z^1 - z, \ldots, z^n - z) \mid z^i \in F_i(p) \text{ for all } i \in I \text{ and } z \in M(p)\}.$$

It is not difficult to show that the assumptions of Lemma 2 imply that each mapping is upper semicontinuous and has nonempty convex image sets.

For all $i \in I$, if $z^i \in F_i(p)$, then $p^i z^i \leqslant W_i(p)$. Hence

$$\sum_{i \in I} p^i z^i \leqslant \sum_{i \in I} W_i(p) = \max_{\hat{z} \in Z} \sum_{i \in I} p^i \hat{z}.$$

Therefore, if $z \in M(p)$ and $x = (z^1 - z, \ldots, z^n - z) \in E(p)$, it must be that

$$px = \sum_{i \in I} p^i z^i - \max_{\hat{z} \in Z} \sum_{i \in I} p^i \hat{z} \leqslant 0.$$

Since W is homogeneous of degree 1, $E(\lambda p) = E(p)$ for all $\lambda > 0$.

The set P and the correspondence E thus satisfy the hypothesis of Lemma 1. Therefore for some $\bar{p} \in P$, $E(\bar{p}) \cap -P^* \neq \phi$. Since V is a closed convex cone, it follows from the duality theorem for closed convex cones that $-P^* = -V$. Therefore there exist $\bar{p} \in P$, $\bar{z} \in M(\bar{p})$, $(\bar{z}^1, \ldots, \bar{z}^n) \in \Pi_{i \in I} F_i(\bar{p})$, and $(\bar{v}_1, \ldots, \bar{v}_n) \in V$ such that for all $i \in I$, $\bar{z}^i + \bar{v}^i = \bar{z}$.

Since $\bar{z}^i \in F_i(\bar{p})$ and $\bar{z} = \bar{z}^i + \bar{v}^i \, R_i \, \bar{z}^i$, we can be assured for all $i \in I$, that

$\bar{z} \in F_i(\bar{p})$ if $\bar{p}^i \bar{z} \leqslant W_i(\bar{p})$. This is demonstrated as follows. Since $\bar{z} \in Z \subset$ int $\tilde{Z}$ and since $\bar{z}^i \in F_i(\bar{p})$, and $\bar{z}\ R_i\ \bar{z}^i$, it follows from the assumption of local nonsatiation that $\bar{p}^i \bar{z} \geqslant W_i(\bar{p})$ for all $i \in I$. But

$$\sum_{i \in I} \bar{p}^i \bar{z} = \max_{z \in Z} \sum_{i \in I} \bar{p}^i \bar{z} = \sum_{i \in I} W_i(\bar{p}).$$

Therefore $\bar{p}^i \bar{z} = W_i(\bar{p})$ for all $i \in I$. Hence $\bar{z} \in F_i(\bar{p})$ for all $i \in I$. Since, also $\bar{z} \in M(\bar{p})$, conditions (i) and (ii) of the lemma are satisfied except for the restriction of choice to $\tilde{Z}$. To remove the artificial bounding cube $\tilde{Z}$, simply follow the procedure of Debreu [11].   q.e.d.

We can now complete the proof of Theorem 2. It remains to show that an allocation z that satisfies Lemma 2 actually maximizes preferences on $B_i(\bar{p})$ for all $i \in I$. If for any consumer $i \in I, \bar{z}$ does not maximize R_i on $B_i(\bar{p})$, then it follows by a well-known argument of Debreu [12] that $\min_{x \in C_i} \bar{p}^i x = W_i(\bar{p})$. Suppose that for some $h \in I, \min_{x \in C_h} \bar{p}^h x = W_h(\bar{p})$.

Since $z\ R_h\ w$, there is an allocation $\hat{z} \in \cap_{i \in I} C_i \cap Z$ such that $\hat{z}\ P_i\ \bar{z}$ for all $i \in I, i \neq h$. Since $\hat{z} \in C_h$, $\bar{p}^h \hat{z} \geqslant W_h(\bar{p})$. Since $\hat{z}\ P_i\ \bar{z}$ for all $i \in I, i \neq h$, it must be that $\bar{p}^i \hat{z} \geqslant W_i(\bar{p})$ for all $i \in I$ and that strict inequality obtains for every $i \in I$, such that $\min_{x \in C_i} \bar{p}^i x < W_i(\bar{p})$. Assumption D implies that for some $i \in I$, $\min_{x \in C_i} \bar{p}^i x < W_i(\bar{p})$. [6] Therefore

$$\sum_{i \in I} \bar{p}^i z > \sum_{i \in I} W_i(\bar{p}) = \max_{z \in Z} \sum_{i \in I} \bar{p}^i z.$$

But since $\hat{z} \in Z$, this is a contradiction. Therefore we must conclude that for all $i \in I, \min_{x \in C_i} \bar{p}^i x < W_i(\bar{p})$. It then follows that for all $i \in I, \bar{z}$ maximizes R_i on $B_i(\bar{p})$.   q.e.d.

The next result is a stronger version of Theorem 2, which will be useful for showing that when preferences and/or production possibility sets have special structure, there can be found Lindahl equilibrium prices that have special form. For example, we shall wish to show that where there are classical private goods, these will have "private" prices and where there is crowding of an impersonal sort, the corresponding Lindahl prices can take the form of uniform "tolls" for users.

Theorem 3   *For each $i \in I$, let S_i be a linear subspace of E^m such that for all $z^i \in C_i$, $(z^i + S_i) \cap C_i \subset R_i(z_i)$. Let Y be a linear subspace in E^m such that $(Z + Y) \cap C_I \subset Z$ (where $C_I = \cap_{i \in I} C_i$). If $\cap_{i \in I} (C_i + S_i) \subset C_I$, and if the assumptions of Theorem 2 hold, then there exists a Lindahl equilibrium $(\bar{p}, \bar{z})$*

---

[6] Suppose that for all $i \in I$, $\bar{p}^i x \geqslant W_i(\bar{p})$ for all $x \in C_i$. Then if $x \in \cap_{i \in I} C_i$, $\sum_{i \in I} \bar{p}^i x \geqslant \sum_{i \in I} W_i(\bar{p}) = \max_{z \in Z} \sum_{i \in I} \bar{p}^i z$. But this means that $\cap_{i \in I} C_i$ and Z are separated by $\sum_{i \in I} \bar{p}^i$ which is impossible if $\cap_{i \in I} C_i \cap Z$ has a nonempty interior.

such that for all $i \in I$, $\vec{p}^i x = 0$ *for all* $x \in S_i$ *and such that* $\Sigma_{i \in I} \vec{p}^i y = 0$ *for all* $y \in Y$.

Proof   Let $S = \Pi_{i \in I} S_i$ and   let $T = \{(y, \ldots, y) \mid y \in Y\}$.   Let $Q = \{p \in E^{mn} \mid |p| = 1\} \cap V^* \cap S^* \cap T^*$.[7] Since S and T are linear subspaces, if $p \in Q$, then $p^i x^i = 0$ for all $x^i \in S_i$, and $\Sigma_{i \in I} p^i y = 0$ for all $y \in Y$. Thus Theorem 3 will be established if we demonstrate the existence of Lindahl equilibrium $(\bar{p}, \bar{z})$ where $\bar{p} \in Q$. To do this we need only to show that there exists $(\bar{p}, \bar{z})$ where $\bar{p} \in Q$ which satisfies conditions (i) and (ii) of Lemma 2. The same argument used to prove Theorem 2 from Lemma 2 can then be applied to show that $(\bar{p}, \bar{z})$ is a Lindahl equilibrium.

Replacing the set P by the set Q in the arguments of the first part of the proof of Lemma 2 leads us to conclude that there exists $\bar{p} \in Q$ such that $E(\bar{p}) \cap -Q^* \neq \phi$. From the theory of convex cones, it is known that

$$Q^* = (V^* \cap S^* \cap T^*)^* = V^{**} + S^{**} + T^{**} = V + S + T.$$

Thus for some $\bar{p} \in Q$, $E(\bar{p}) \cap - V - S - T \neq \phi$.

Therefore   there   exists $(\bar{z}^1, \ldots, \bar{z}^n) \in \Pi_{i \in I} F_i(\bar{p})$, $(\bar{x}^1, \ldots, \bar{x}^n) \in S$, $(\bar{v}^1, \ldots, \bar{v}^n) \in V$, $\bar{z} \in M(\bar{p})$, and $\bar{y} \in Y$ such that for all $i \in I$, $\bar{z}^i - \bar{z} = -\bar{v}^i - \bar{x}^i - \bar{y}$, or equivalently $\bar{z} - \bar{y} = \bar{z}^i + \bar{v}^i + \bar{x}^i$. Since $\bar{z}^i + \bar{v}^i \in C_i$ for all $i \in I$, $\bar{z} - \bar{y} \in \cap_I (C_i + S_i) \subset C_i$.   Therefore $\bar{z} - \bar{y} \in (Z + Y) \cap C_I \subset Z \cap C_I$.   Let $\bar{\bar{z}} = \bar{z} - \bar{y}$. Since $\Sigma_{i \in I} \bar{p}^i \bar{y} = 0$, $\bar{\bar{z}} \in M(\bar{p})$. For all $i \in I$, $\bar{\bar{z}} R_i \bar{z}^i$ since $\bar{\bar{z}} \in C_i \cap \bar{z}^i + V_i + S_i$. Also $\bar{z}^i \in F_i(\bar{p})$ and $\bar{\bar{z}} \in Z \subset -\mathrm{Int}\, \bar{Z}$. From the assumption of local nonsatiation it follows that $\bar{p}^i \bar{\bar{z}} \geqslant W_i(\bar{p})$ for all $i \in I$. But since $\bar{\bar{z}} \in M(\bar{p})$, it must be that $\Sigma_{i \in I} \bar{p}^i \bar{\bar{z}} = \Sigma_{i \in I} W_i(\bar{p})$. Therefore for all $i \in I$, $\bar{p}^i \bar{\bar{z}} = W_i(\bar{p})$ and hence $\bar{\bar{z}} \in \cap_{i \in I} F_i(\bar{p}) \cap M(\bar{p})$. Thus $(\bar{p}, \bar{\bar{z}})$ satisfies the conditions of Lemma 2.   q.e.d.

III. SPECIAL LINDAHL EQUILIBRIA

A. Private Commodities

Private commodities will be treated as special cases of communal commodities, and it will be shown that there exist Lindahl equilibria with a corresponding special structure.

In the classical model of a private goods economy, one man's bread can be costlessly transformed into another man's bread. Furthermore each individual is interested in his own bread consumption but not in the bread consumption of others. These notions motivate the following definitions.

Consumer i is said to be *not concerned with commodity j* if whenever $x \in C_i$, and $x' \in O^m$ such that $x_k{}' = x_k$ for all $k \neq j$, it follows that $x' \in C_j$ and $x' I_i x$.

---

[7] For any set X, X^* denotes the polar cone of X.

Otherwise consumer j is said to be *concerned with commodity j*. A *private commodity specific to consumer i* is a communal commodity j such that i is concerned with commodity j but no consumer other than i is concerned with j.

A set $k = \{k_1, \ldots, k_s\}$ of communal commodities is said to be *freely exchangeable* if $(Z + T_k) \cap \Omega^m \subseteq Z$ where $T_k = \{x \in E^m \mid x_j = 0$ for $j \notin k$ and $\Sigma_{k_i \in k} x_{k_i} = 0\}$. A *nonspecific exchangeable private commodity* is a freely exchangeable set $k = \{k_1, \ldots, k_n\}$ of communal commodities such that for each $i \in I$, k_i is a private commodity specific to consumer i. Let K be the set of all nonspecific exchangeable private commodities. Then where $k \in K$ and $i \in I$, the communal commodity k_i is an *exchangeable private commodity specific to consumer i*.

These definitions simply define in formal language the properties of private commodities that are implicitly assumed in the classical theory. Thus if k is the nonspecific, exchangeable private commodity "bread," then k_i is the specific exchangeable private commodity "bread for consumer i."

It will be seen that the pricing of specific exchangeable private commodities in Lindahl equilibrium is similar to that of private commodities in a competitive economy. A *Lindahl–Samuelson* equilibrium is a generalized Lindahl equilibrium $(\bar{p}, \bar{z})$ such that for every nonspecific exchangeable commodity $k \in K$ and for all $i, j \in I$, $\bar{p}^i_{k_i} = \bar{p}^j_{k_j} \equiv \bar{p}_k$ and if $i \neq j$, $p^i_{k_j} = 0$. In a Lindahl–Samuelson equilibrium, then Mr. i pays the same price for the commodity, "bread for i," as Mr. j pays for the commodity "bread for j." Also Mr. i pays nothing for the commodity "bread for j." In the special case where all communal commodities are specific exchangeable private commodities, a Lindahl–Samuelson equilibrium is a competitive equilibrium.

Theorem 4 *If the assumptions of Theorem 2 hold, there exists a Lindahl–Samuelson equilibrium.*

Proof   We apply Theorem 3. For each $i \in I$, let $S_i = \{x^i \in E^m \mid x^i_j = 0$ if $j \neq k_h$ for some $k \in K$ and some $h \neq i\}$. Let $Y = \Sigma_{k \in K} T_k$. Clearly the sets S_i and Y are linear subspaces in E^m. Since for all $i \in I$, $C_i \subset \Omega^m$, the definition of exchangeable private commodities implies that for all $z^i \in C_i$, $(z^i + S_i) \cap C_i \subset R_i(z^i)$ and that $(Z + Y) \cap C_I \subset Z$. If $z \in \cap_{i \in I}(C_i + S_i)$, then $z \in \Omega^m$. Therefore

$$\underset{i \in I}{\cap} (C_i + S_i) = \underset{i \in I}{\cap} ((C_i + S_i) \cap \Omega^m) = \underset{i \in I}{\cap} C_i.$$

Thus the hypothesis of Theorem 3 is true. It follows that there exists a generalized Lindahl equilibrium $(\bar{p}, \bar{z})$ such that for all $i \in I$, $\bar{p}^i x = 0$ for all $x \in S_i$ and such that $\Sigma_{i \in I} \bar{p}^i y = 0$ for all $y \in Y$. If $\bar{p}^i x = 0$ for all $x \in S_i$, then evidently $\bar{p}^i_{k_h} = 0$ for all $k \in K$ and all $h \neq i$. If $\Sigma_{i \in I} \bar{p}^i y = 0$ for all $y \in Y$, then for all $k \in K$ and all $h, h' \in I$, $\Sigma_{i \in I} \bar{p}^i_{k_h} = \Sigma_{i \in I} \bar{p}^i_{k_{h'}}$. But since $\bar{p}^i_{k_h} = 0$ if $i \neq h$, it must be that for all $k \in K$ and all h, $i \in I$, $\bar{p}_{k_h}^h = \bar{p}_{k_i}^i \equiv \bar{p}_k$. Thus $(\bar{p}, \bar{z})$ is a Lindahl–Samuelson equilibrium.   q.e.d.

B. Congestion and Impersonal Externalities

It is of some interest to examine the way in which congested public facilities can be treated within our model. Where a public facility such as a highway or park is subject to crowding, the commodity space must be sufficiently disaggregated so that allocations describe not only the size of the facility but also the amount of crowding. If, for example, each consumer's enjoyment of a park depends on the size of the park, the extent to which he uses it, and the extent to which each other consumer uses it, we would wish to include as distinct communal commodities the utilization of the park by each consumer (possibly treating use at different times as different commodities) as well as the size of the park.

Often it would seem reasonable to suppose that individuals do not care *who* is crowding them but are interested only in the size of the facility, the *total* use of the facility by others, and in the extent to which they themselves use it. If this is the case, the system of Lindahl prices can be somewhat simplified.

An *impersonal externality* is a set $m = \{m_1, \ldots, m_n\} \subset J$ such that for all $i \in I$, if z, $z' \in C_i$ and if $z_j = z_j'$ for all $j \notin m$, $z_{m_j} = z'_{m_j}$, and $\Sigma_{h \in I} z'_{m_h} = \Sigma_{h \in I} z'_{m_h}$, then $z \, I_i \, z'$. Thus the impersonal externality m might be use of a park. The communal commodity m_i is use of the park by consumer i. Consumer i is indifferent between any two allocations that differ in the distribution of park use among others, but which have the same use by himself, the same *total* use by others, and the same quantities of all other communal commodities.

A further simplification of the system of Lindahl prices can be made if we are willing to assume that use of a particular public facility by any individual does not directly affect aggregate production possibilities for other commodities. This assumption is made explicit as follows. A communal commodity j is *independently produced* if $Z + Y_j \cap C_I \subset Z$ where Y_j is the linear subspace $\{y \in E^m \mid y_k = 0 \text{ if } k \neq j\}$. In effect, all restrictions on the feasible quantities of commodity j are expressed as restrictions on the sets C_i. As an example, suppose that commodity j is use of a specified park by a certain individual. Of course this individual cannot possibly spend more than 24 hours a day in the park. Furthermore, time he spends in the park cannot be spent using other public facilities, nor can this time be spent working. These constraints can be incorporated in the model by obvious restrictions on the sets C_i. Once this is done, there is no reason to suppose that use of the park, as such, has any direct effect on production possibilities for other commodities. Thus we may reasonably assume that $Z + Y_j \cap C_I \subset Z$.

It turns out that if m is an impersonal externality such that m_i is independently produced for each $i \in I$, then there exists a Lindahl equilibrium $(\bar{p}, \bar{z})$ such that for each $i \in I$, there is some scalar $\bar{p}_m{}^i$ such that $\bar{p}_{m_k}^i = \bar{p}_m{}^i$ for all $k \neq i$, and such that for all $i \in I$, $\Sigma_{j \in I} \, \bar{p}_{m_j}^i = 0$. When this is the case, the portion of consumer i's budget constraint that relates to the impersonal externality is

$$\bar{p}_{m_i}^i x_{m_i} + \sum_{j \neq i} \bar{p}_j^i x_{m_j} = \bar{p}_{m_i}^i x_{m_i} + \bar{p}_{\overline{m}}^i \sum_{j \neq i} x_{m_j}$$

$$= - \sum_{j \in I} \bar{p}_{\overline{m}}^j x_{m_i} + \bar{p}_m^i \sum_{j \in I} x_{m_j}$$

$$= \bar{q}_m x_{m_i} - t_m{}^i \bar{q}_m \sum_{j \in I} x_{m_j}$$

where $\bar{q}_m = -\Sigma_{j \in I} \, \bar{p}_{\overline{m}}^j$ and $t_m{}^i = \bar{p}_{\overline{m}}^i / \Sigma_{j \in I} \, \bar{p}_{\overline{m}}^j$. Suppose, for example, the impersonal externality m is use of a public facility and that each individual dislikes being crowded by others. Then the $\bar{p}_{\overline{m}}^i$ will all be negative. The Lindahl prices reduce to a system of uniform tolls for use of the facility where each consumer pays at the rate $\bar{q}_m = -\Sigma_{j \in I} \, \bar{p}_{\overline{m}}^j$ for the use of the facility. Revenue from the toll is disbursed in such a way that consumer i receives the fraction $t_m{}^i$ of the total revenue from tolls for each i.

It is of some interest to look at the very special case where preferences are identical so that there is a Lindahl equilibrium in which for some $\bar{p}_m, p_{\overline{m}}^i = \bar{p}_m$ for all $i \in I$. Where there are n consumers, $\bar{q} = n\bar{p}_m$ and $t_m{}^i = 1/n$. Each consumer i in equilibrium chooses the same value $x_{m_j}^i = x_m$ for all $j \in I$. Thus he pays tolls amounting to $\bar{q} x_m = n\bar{p}_m x_m$. He receives $n^{-1} \bar{q} n x_m = n\bar{p}_m x_m$ from the total toll revenue.

Thus his receipts from tolls precisely equal his payments. Of course his behavior is by no means the same as in a system without tolls. The cost to him of using the road by an extra amount Δ is

$$\bar{q}\Delta - t_m{}^i \bar{q}\Delta = \bar{p}_m n \left(1 - \frac{1}{n}\right)\Delta = \bar{p}_m(n-1)\Delta.$$

Thus the marginal private cost is $\bar{p}_m(n-1)$, which is in turn equal to marginal social cost.

Theorem 5 proves the assertions we have made about the special structure of Lindahl prices for impersonal externalities and independently produced commodities.

Theorem 5 *If the assumptions of Theorem 2 are true and if m is an impersonal externality, then there exists a generalized Lindahl equilibrium $(\bar{p}, \bar{z})$ in which for all $i \in I$ there is some $\bar{p}_{\overline{m}}^i$ such that $\bar{p}_{m_j}^i = \bar{p}_{\overline{m}}^i$ for all $j \neq i$. Furthermore if the communal commodity m_i is independently produced, then $\Sigma_{j \in I} \, \bar{p}_{m_j}^i = 0$.*

Proof Let $\quad S_i = \{x^i \in E^m \mid x_i^i = 0 \quad$ if $\quad j \neq m_k \quad$ for $\quad$ some $\quad k \neq i\} \cap$

$\{x_i \in E^m \mid \Sigma_{h \in I} x^i_{m_h} = 0\}$. Let N be the set $\{m_j \in m \mid m_j$ is independently produced$\}$ and let $Y = \Sigma_{m_j \in N} Y_{m_j}$. The sets S_i and Y are linear subspaces. Also $Z + Y \cap C_I \subset Z$ and $\cap_{i \in I} (C_i + S_i) \subset C_I$. We can therefore apply Theorem 3. There exists a generalized Lindahl equilibrium $(\bar{p}, \bar{z})$ such that for all $i \in I$ and all $x \in S_i$, $\bar{p}^i x = 0$ and such that for all $y \in Y$, $\Sigma_{i \in I} \bar{p}^i y = 0$. But this implies that for all $i \in I$ and for all $h, k \in I$ such that $h \neq i$, $k \neq i$, $\bar{p}^i_{m_k} = \bar{p}^i_{m_h} \equiv \bar{p}_{\bar{m}}{}^i$ and that for all $m_j \in N$, $\Sigma_{i \in I} \bar{p}^i = 0$.   q.e.d.

C. Aggregation and Decentralized Lindahl Equilibrium

In Section I, conditions were stated under which it is possible to aggregate commodities in some subset A of the commodity space. It seems reasonable that one might be able to find a simplified structure for the Lindahl equilibrium price vectors allowing some decentralization of decision making on subsets of the commodity space that admit aggregation. Theorem 6 below states a result of this kind.

A *decentralized Lindahl equilibrium* for the partition $\{A_1, \ldots, A_r, B\}$ of J is a generalized Lindahl equilibrium $(\bar{p}, \bar{x})$ such that for each A_k, $k = 1, \ldots, r$, there exists a nonnegative vector $(\bar{\lambda}_k{}^1, \ldots, \bar{\lambda}_k{}^n)$ where $\Sigma_{i \in I} \bar{\lambda}_k{}^i = 1$ and such that for all $i \in I$ and all $j \in A_k$, $\bar{p}_j{}^i = \bar{\lambda}_k{}^i \bar{p}_j$ where $\bar{p}_j \equiv \Sigma_{i \in I} \bar{p}_j{}^i$.

Theorem 6   *If the assumptions of Theorem 2 are true, if $W(p) = W(\hat{p})$ whenever $\Sigma_{i \in I} p^i = \Sigma_{i \in I} \hat{p}^i$, and if for the partition $\{A_1, \ldots, A_r, B\}$ of J, preferences of all consumers are identical on A_k for each $k = 1, \ldots, r$, then there exists a decentralized Lindahl equilibrium for the partition $\{A_1, \ldots, A_r, B\}$.*

Proof   It will be shown that Theorem 3 holds in the case where $r = 1$. A simple induction argument extends the result to $r \geqslant 1$. Suppose that J is partitioned into sets A and B such that preferences of all consumers are identical on A. Let $(\bar{p}, \bar{x})$ be a generalized Lindahl equilibrium. Define $\bar{p}_A \equiv \Sigma_{i \in I} \bar{p}_A{}^i$. Let

$$V \equiv \{(z_1, \ldots, z_n, y_1, \ldots, y_n) \mid \text{for all } i \in I, z_i = \bar{p}_A(x_A{}^i - \bar{x}_A)$$
$$\text{and } y_i = \bar{p}_B{}^i(x_B{}^i - \bar{x}_B) \text{ where } (x_A{}^i, x_B{}^i) R_i \bar{x}\}.$$

Let

$$H = \{(\underbrace{z, \ldots, z}_{n \text{ times}}, y_1, \ldots, y_n) \mid z + \sum_{i \in I} y_i \leqslant 0\}.$$

It is easily verified that H and V are convex sets in E^{2n} containing the origin. We now show that V does not intersect the interior of H. Suppose $(z, \ldots, z, y_1, \ldots, y_n) \in V$. Then for each $i \in I$, there exists an $(\hat{x}_A{}^i, \hat{x}_B{}^i)$ such that $(\hat{x}_A{}^i, \hat{x}_B{}^i) R_i \bar{x}$ and such that $\bar{p}_A(\hat{x}_A{}^i - \bar{x}_A) = z$ and $p_B{}^i(\hat{x}_B{}^i - \bar{x}_B) = y_i$. Since preferences of all consumers are identical on A, the projection of each preference ordering R_i on A gives the same ordering $\gtrsim_A$, on A for each $i \in I$. Choose a bundle $\hat{x}_A$ that maximizes $\gtrsim_A$ subject to $\bar{p}_A(x_A - \bar{x}_A) < z$. Clearly

$(\hat{x}_A, \hat{x}_B) R_i \bar{x}$ for all $i \in I$. But this implies that for all $i \in I$,

$$\bar{p}_A{}^i(\hat{x}_A - \bar{x}_A) + \bar{p}_B{}^i(\hat{x}_B - \bar{x}_B) \geqslant 0.$$

Hence

$$\left(\underset{i \in I}{\Sigma} \bar{p}_A{}^i \right) (\hat{x}_A - \bar{x}_A) + \underset{i \in I}{\Sigma} \bar{p}_B{}^i(\hat{x}_B{}^i - \bar{x}_B) \geqslant 0.$$

But

$$z = \left(\underset{i \in I}{\Sigma} \bar{p}_A{}^i \right) (\hat{x}_A - \bar{x}_A).$$

Therefore $z + \Sigma_{i \in I} y_i \geqslant 0$. It follows that $(z, \ldots, z, y_1, \ldots, y_n)$ cannot be in the interior of H. By the separation theorem for convex sets, there is a vector $(\bar{\lambda}^1, \ldots, \bar{\lambda}^n, \bar{\mu}^1, \ldots, \bar{\mu}^n)$ such that:

   (i) $(\Sigma_{i \in I} \bar{\lambda}^i) z + \Sigma_{i \in I} \bar{\mu}^i y_i \leqslant 0$ if $(z, \ldots, z, y_1, \ldots, y_n) \in H$; and

   (ii) $\Sigma_{i \in I} \bar{\lambda}^i z_i + \Sigma_{i \in I} \bar{\mu}^i y_i \geqslant 0$ if $(z_1, \ldots, z_n, y_1, \ldots, y_n) \in V$.

But (i) implies that for some such vector, $\Sigma_{i \in I} \bar{\lambda}^i = 1$ and $\bar{\mu}^i = 1$ for all $i \in I$. It is easily shown that (ii) implies that for all $i \in I$, $\bar{\lambda}^i \geqslant 0$ and that if $(x_A, x_B) R_i \bar{x}$ then $\bar{\lambda}^i \bar{p}_A x_A + \bar{p}_B{}^i x_B \geqslant \bar{\lambda}^i \bar{p}_A \bar{x}_A + \bar{p}_B{}^i x_B$. It is not hard to show that $\bar{\lambda}^i \bar{p}_A \bar{x}_A + \bar{p}_B{}^i \bar{x}_B = W_i(\bar{p})$ for all $i \in I$. Applying the same procedure used in the final step of Theorem 2 one can show that $\bar{x}$ maximizes R_i subject to $\bar{\lambda}^i \bar{p}_A x_A + \bar{p}_B{}^i x_B \leqslant W_i(\bar{p})$ for each $i \in I$. This completes the proof.   q.e.d.

This theorem could be given the following interpretation for decentralized governmental administration. If preferences of all consumers are identical on A_k for $k = 1, \ldots, r$, one could delegate the responsibility for providing commodities in each A_k to a separate bureau. Each bureau would be given a budget b_k and instructed to maximize the commonly held projection $\gtrsim A_k$, of preferences on A_k subject to $\Sigma_{j \in A_k} \bar{p}_j x_j \leqslant b_k$. A share $\lambda_k{}^i$ of the budget b_k is assigned to be paid by each consumer i. Equilibrium cost shares $\bar{\lambda}_k{}^i$ and budgets $\bar{b}_k$ are found so that, knowing how each bureau will spend its budget, each consumer agrees that so long as his cost share is $\bar{\lambda}_k{}^i$, the proper size for the budget of the bureau is $\bar{b}_k$.

Another application of Theorem 3 concerns the problem of Pareto efficient income redistribution among benevolent consumers. This problem is discussed in Bergstrom [4]. Theorem 5 provides an alternative proof of the main theorem of that paper.

IV.

A. Generalized Lindahl Equilibrium is Pareto Optimal

Theorem 7   *If $(\bar{p}, \bar{z})$ is a generalized Lindahl equilibrium and if preferences of all consumers are locally nonsatiated at $\bar{z}$, then the allocation $\bar{z}$ is Pareto optimal.*

Proof As in the traditional proofs of the optimality of competitive equilibrium it can be shown that for all $i \in I$, if $z P_i \bar{z}$, then $\bar{p}^i z > \bar{p}^i \bar{z} = W_i(\bar{p})$ and if $z R_i \bar{z}$, then $\bar{p}^i z \geqslant \bar{p}^i \bar{z} = W_i(\bar{p})$. Therefore if the allocation z' is Pareto superior to $\bar{z}$, it must be that $\Sigma_{i \in I} \bar{p}^i z' > \Sigma_{i \in I} W_i(\bar{p})$. But by assumption, $\Sigma_{i \in I} W_i(\bar{p}) \geqslant \Sigma_{i \in I} \bar{p}^i z$ for all $z \in Z$. Therefore $z' \notin Z$. It follows that $\bar{z}$ is Pareto optimal.   q.e.d.

B. Pareto Optimal Allocations Can Be Sustained as Generalized Lindahl Equilibria

Theorem 8 *If assumptions* A, B, D, *and* E *of Theorem 2 are true and if $\bar{z}$ is a Pareto optimal allocation such that:*

(F$'$) *For all $h \in I$, there exists a $\bar{z} \in \cap_{i \in I} C_{i \cap} Z$ such that $\hat{z} P_i \bar{z}$ for all $i \neq h$, $i \in I$, then there exists a wealth distribution vector $W = (W_1, \ldots, W_n)$ and a Lindahl price vector $\bar{p}$ such that $(\bar{p}, \bar{z})$ is a generalized Lindahl equilibrium under the income distribution function $W(p) = \overline{W}$.*

Proof Consider the sets R^* and Z^* where $R^* = \Pi_{i \in I} R_i(\bar{z})$ and $Z^* = \{(z, \ldots, z) \mid z \in Z\}$. Assumptions A–II and B ensure that R^* and Z^* are convex sets. Local nonsatiation implies that R^* does not intersect the interior Z. According to the separation theorem for convex sets, there exists a vector $\bar{p} = (\bar{p}^1, \ldots, \bar{p}^n) \in E^{mn}$ that separates R^* and Z^*. Since $\bar{z} \in R^* \cap Z^*$, the following results follow:

  (i)   For all $i \in I$, if $z \in R_i(\bar{z})$, then $\bar{p}^i z \geqslant \bar{p}^i \bar{z}$.

  (ii) For all $z \in Z$, $\Sigma_{i \in I} \bar{p}^i z \leqslant \Sigma_{i \in I} \bar{p}^i \bar{z}$.

It remains to be shown for all $i \in I$ that if $z P_i \bar{z}$, then $\bar{p}^i z > \bar{p}^i \bar{z}$. Assumption A–III and result (i) of the previous paragraph can be used to show that this is the case for i such that $\min_{z \in C_i} \bar{p}^i z < \bar{p}^i \bar{z}$. It will be demonstrated that in fact $\min_{z \in C_i} \bar{p}^i z < \bar{p}^i z$ for all $i \in I$. Suppose that for some $h \in I$, $\min_{z \in C_i} \bar{p}^i z = \bar{p}^i \bar{z}$. By assumption F$'$ there is an allocation $\hat{z} \in \cap_{i \in I} C_i$ such that $\hat{z} P_i \bar{z}$ for all $i \in I$ where $i \neq h$. Result (i) above implies that $\bar{p}^i \hat{z} \geqslant \bar{p}^i \bar{z}$ for all $i \in I$. As demonstrated in footnote 6, assumption D implies that $\min_{z \in C_i} \bar{p}^k z < \bar{p}^k \bar{z}$ for some $k \in I$. Therefore $\bar{p}^k \hat{z} > \bar{p}^k \bar{z}$. Hence $\Sigma_{i \in I} \bar{p}^i \hat{z} > \Sigma_{i \in I} \bar{p}^k \bar{z}$. But this contradicts result (ii) of the previous paragraph. Therefore for all $i \in I$, $\min_{z \in C_i} \bar{p}^i z < \bar{p}^i z$. It follows that $\bar{z}$ maximizes R_i on $\{z \mid \bar{p}^i z \leqslant \bar{p}^i \bar{z}\}$ for all $i \in I$. Therefore the Lindahl price vector $\bar{p}$ and the wealth distribution vector $(\overline{W}_1, \ldots, \overline{W}_n) = (\bar{p}^1 \bar{z}, \ldots, p^n \bar{z})$ satisfy the conditions of Theorem 4.   q.e.d.

V.

A. Units of Measurement and Convexity

The assumption that specific private commodities are freely exchangeable puts a restriction on the choice of units of measurement. In particular, suppose that a nonspecific private commodity k can be measured in two different choices of units such that $y_k = f(x_k)$ where x_k is the quantity of k measured in one choice of unit and y_k in the other. If specific private commodities in k are to be freely exchangeable under either choice of unit, then it must be that $f(\Sigma_{i \in I} x_{ki}) = \Sigma_{i \in I} f(x_{ki})$. But this implies that $f(x) = cx$ for some scalar x. Thus the choice of units of measurement is determined up to a multiplicative constant if the property of free exchange ability is to hold.

One has more freedom of choice of units in measuring quantities of communal commodities that are not freely exchangeable. If some method of measurement provides a sufficiently fine partition of states of the world as discussed in Section 1.A, then any choice of units that are strictly monotonic functions of the initially chosen units will also allow a sufficient amount of disaggregation. If, however, one wishes to satisfy the assumptions of Theorem 2, care must be taken to choose units so that preferences are weakly convex *and* the set of feasible allocations is convex.

The following example illustrates this principle. Consider a village in which there is one nonspecific private commodity, bread, and one nonprivate communal commodity, a church tower. Preferences of consumers are represented by $u_i = x_i + a_i h^2$ where x_i is bread consumed by i and h is the height of the church tower measured in feet. Where $a_i \geqslant 0$, preferences are nonconvex in terms of these units. The community initially holds a fixed stock w of bread. Bread may be converted into church tower by means of a production function of the form $h = \sqrt{x_h}$ where x_h is the quantity of bread used to build the tower. The set of feasible allocations is then $\Omega^{n+1} \cap \{(x_1, \ldots, x_n, h) \mid \Sigma_{i=1}^n x_i + h^2 = w\}$. If one chooses to measure units of church tower by the square root of height, one can write the utility functions as $u_i = x_i + a_i z$ and the set of feasible allocations as $\Omega^{n+1} \cap \{(x_1, \ldots, x_n, z) \mid \Sigma_{i=1}^n x_i + z = w\}$ where z is the square of the height of the tower measured in feet. Under this choice of units, preferences are weakly convex and the set of feasible allocations is convex.

B. Further Implications of Convexity

An argument due to Starrett [24] suggests that the aggregate production possibility set is unlikely to be convex in the presence of external diseconomies in production. Starrett's results suggest that some care must be taken in employing negative Lindahl prices to guide production decisions. Other discussions of nonconvex externalities in production are found in Bradford and Baumol [9] and Bergstrom [7].

The assumption of convex preferences also limits the admissable kinds of disagreement about the utility of communal commodities. For example, the following remark is true.

Remark *Suppose that preferences of two consumers are similar on $A \subset J$ and* *are represented by* $U_1(v(x_A), x_B)$ *and* $U_2(v(x_A), x_B)$ *where* U_1 is an increasing and U_2 a decreasing function of v. *Then either (a) preferences of at least one consumer are nonconvex, or (b) all isoquants of* v *are linear.*

Proof Consider any x_A and x_A' such that $v(x_A) = v(x_A',)$. If $v(\lambda x_A + (1 - \lambda) x_A') < v(x_A)$, then $(x_A, x_B) I_1 (x_A', x_B)$ but $(x_A, x_B) P_1 (\lambda x_A + (1 - \lambda)x_A', x_B)$. In this case, preferences of consumer 1 are nonconvex. But if $v(\lambda x_A + (1 - \lambda)x_A') > v(x_A)$, then $(x_A, x_B) P_2 (\lambda x_A + (1 - \lambda)x_A', x_B)$ so that preferences of consumer 2 are nonconvex. The only case in which preferences of both consumers are convex is where $v(\lambda x_A + (1 - \lambda)x_A') = v(x_A)$. q.e.d.

Consider an economy in which some communal commodity is liked by some consumers and disliked by others. In Lindahl equilibrium consumers who like the commodity must pay those who dislike the commodity to induce them to accept it. Suppose the controversial commodity is produced according to a concave production function. If one wished to further disaggregate the commodity space, he could define preferences on the inputs used to produce the controversial commodity instead of on the commodity itself. But if this is done, preferences of the consumers who dislike the commodity will be nonconvex in terms of the inputs. In general, no Lindahl equilibrium will exist on the disaggregated commodity space. At any Lindahl prices on the factors, it would always be in the interest of those who liked the commodity to maximize output for any given factor cost while those who dislike the commodity would wish to sabotage production by minimizing output given the total factor cost.

VI. CONCLUSION

Theorems on the existence of competitive equilibrium make no explicit claims for the possibility or stability of institutions that would enforce competitive behavior. The tatônnement paradigm and the result that the core of an economy shrinks to the set of competitive equilibria as the economy becomes large each suggest some plausibility for the notion that nearly competitive behavior might actually occur in a world relatively innocent of nonconvexity and coercion.

All that has been demonstrated in this paper is that for seemingly reasonable economies, the conditions required for Lindahl equilibrium are not in themselves logically contradictory. The question remains open whether there are workable institutional arrangements that would sustain Lindahl equilibrium.

One approach to this problem would be to consider a central authority that acquired information about tastes and technology and used this information to compute a system of taxes and subsidies that approximate a Lindahl solution. Aside from computational difficulties, there remains the so-called "free rider problem." If an individual's stated preferences influence the prices that he pays for communal commodities, it may be in his interest to misrepresent his preferences. A discussion of the free rider problem and references to the literature are found in Bergstrom [8].

A second line of approach is the study of the relation of the Lindahl equilibrium to the core. As demonstrated by Foley [14], if all communal commodities are desirable for all consumers, a Lindahl equilibrium is in the core. The relation between Lindahl equilibrium and the core when some commodities are disliked by some consumers is studied by Bergstrom [5]. If benefits from some communal commodities are diffused to all consumers, the core remains larger than the set of Lindahl equilibria even if the economy becomes large (see Muench [20]). Where the nonprivate communal commodities are (as police, parks, or streets) of a spatially localized nature, consumers may be interested only in the quantities of services made available in their home communities. Suppose blocking coalitions can be formed as alternative communities with different local services and tax structures. There may then be some hope that when the number of possible communities becomes large, the core approaches the set of Lindahl equilibria. As yet this remains an unsolved problem. An interesting attempt along these lines is made by Rader [22].

REFERENCES

1. Arrow, K. J., "The Organization of Economic Activity: Issues Pertinent to the Choice of Market Versus Nonmarket Allocation," in Joint Economic Committee, *Analysis and Evaluation of Public Expenditures: The PPB System*, Washington, D.C.: U.S. Govt. Printing Office, 1969, 47–64.
2. Arrow, K. J., and G. Debreu, "Existence of Equilibrium for a Competitive Economy," *Econometrica*, July 1954, **22**, 265–290.
3. Bergstrom, T. C., "On the Existence and Optimality of Competitive Equilibrium for a Slave Economy," *Review of Economic Studies*, January 1971, **38**, 23–36.
4. Bergstrom, T. C., "A 'Scandinavian Consensus' Solution for Efficient Income Distribution Among Nonmalevolent Consumers," *Journal of Economic Theory*, December 1970, **2**, 383–397.
5. Bergstrom, T. C., "The Core When Strategies are Restricted by Law," *Review of Economic Studies*, April 1975, **42**, 249–257.
6. Bergstrom, T. C., "Regulation of Externalities," *Journal of Public Economics*, 1976, **5**, 1–8.
7. Bergstrom, T. C., "On Efficient Provision of Social Overhead Goods," *Yearbook of East-European Economics*, 1973, **4**.
8. Bergstrom, T. C., "On the Free Rider Problem," Mimeo.
9. Bradford, D., and W. Baumol, "Detrimental Externalities and Non-Convexity of the Production Set," *Economica*, May 1972, **39**, 160–176.
10. Debreu, G. "Market Equilibrium," *Proceedings of the National Academy of Sciences*, 1956, **42**, 876–878.

11. Debreu, G., "New Concepts and Techniques for General Equilibrium Analysis," *International Economic Review*, September 1962, **3**, 257–273.
12. Debreu, G., *Theory of Value*, New York: Wiley, 1959.
13. Dreze, J., and D. Poussin, "A Tatônnement Process for Public Goods," *Review of Economic Studies*, April 1971, **38**, 133–150.
14. Foley, D. K., "Lindahl's Solution and the Core of an Economy with Collective Goods," *Econometrica*, January 1970, **38**, 66–73.
15. Gorman, W. M., "The Structure of Utility Functions," *Review of Economic Studies*, October 1968, **35**, 367–390.
16. Lindahl, E., "Just Taxation – A Positive Solution," in R. Musgrave and A. Peacock, eds., *Classics in the Theory of Public Finance*, London: Macmillan, 1958, 168–176.
17. Malinvaud, E., "Prices for Individual Consumption, Quality Indicators for Collective Consumption," *Review of Economic Studies*, October 1972, **39**, 385–406.
18. McKenzie, L. W., "On the Existence of General Equilibrium," *Econometrica*, January 1959, **27**, 54–57.
19. Milleron, J., "Theory of Value with Public Goods – A Survey Article," *Journal of Economic Theory*, December 1972, **5**, 419–477.
20. Muench, T., "The Core and the Lindahl Equilibrium of an Economy with Public Goods: An Example," *Journal of Economic Theory*, April 1972, **4**, 241–255.
21. Rader, J. T., "Edgeworth Exchange and General Economic Equilibrium," *Yale Econ. Essays*, 1964, **4**, 132–180.
22. Rader, J. T., "An Economic Approach to Social Choice," *Public Choice*, Summer 1973, **15**, 49–75.
23. Samuelson, P. A., "The Pure Theory of Public Expenditure," *Review of Economics and Statistics*, November 1954, **36**, 387–389.
24. Starrett, D., "Fundamental Nonconvexities in the Theory of Externalities," *Journal of Economic Theory*, April 1972, **4**, 180–199.
25. Wicksell, K., "A New Principle of Just Taxation," in R. Musgrave and A. Peacock, eds., *Classics in the Theory of Public Finance*, New York: Macmillan Co., 1958, 72–118.

Discussion

DAVID A. STARRETT

Stanford University

This paper makes basically two contributions. First, the author extends the proofs of existence of Lindahl equilibria from the case of external economies only (as presented by Bergstrom [1]) to the case of general externalities. Secondly, he shows that the resulting price system will take on special simple structures if certain special assumptions are made on the behavioral model.

The main existence theorem is proved by employing Debreu's methods [2] which can handle negative prices, in place of the Arrow–Debreu methods which are restricted to economic "goods." All that needs to be assumed about the nature of economic commodities is that there is some direction in the commodity space representing a desirable direction of movement for all agents. With this assumption, prices can be restricted to a half-space, and Debreu's theorems are applicable.

Bergstrom goes on to exploit the special structure of the externalities problem. For example, he shows that whenever externalities are impersonal (so that if I am jealous of my neighbor's cars, I care only about the total number of cars, and not which neighbors own them), then Lindahl payments should be the same for all affected parties.

The general theorems presented in this paper are very useful ones. They will provide a valuable source of reference for others working in the field. Up until now, everyone has found it necessary to prove his own version of the Lindahl equilibrium theorem because no sufficiently general version is available. The result is a serious waste of paper in the associated literature. Bergstrom's paper should put a stop to this practice.

As to the practical usefulness of the Lindahl method in solving externalities, I think we are all (including Bergstrom) aware of the limitations. There are serious incentive problems associated with getting people to behave according to the Lindahl rules. To overcome these, we may have to pass to more complicated methods such as those presented by Groves [3] at this conference. Unfortunately, the general equilibrium nature of the Groves procedure is as yet unknown, but at least there is hope in this direction.

Furthermore (as Bergstrom notes), externality problems are very likely to involve nonconvexities, and with nonconvexities inherent in the problem, Lindahl equilibria may not exist even if there is no incentive problem. However, the issues involved in nonconvexities should not be laid at Bergstrom's feet, but rather on the doorstep of the entire profession.

REFERENCES

1. Bergstrom, T. C., "A 'Scandinavian Consensus' Solution for Efficient Income Distribution among Nonmalevolent Consumers," *Journal of Economic Theory*, December 1970, **2**, 383–397.
2. Debreu, G., "New Concepts and Techniques for Equilibrium Analysis," *International Economic Review*, September 1962, **3**, 257–273.
3. Groves, T., "Information, Incentives and the Internalization of Production Externalities," this volume.

Pairwise Optimality, Multilateral Optimality, and Efficiency with and without Externalities

J. TROUT RADER, III

Washington University
St. Louis

I. INTRODUCTION

When each pair of traders exploits all mutual gains given their position with respect to other, we say that there is pairwise optimality. In Rader [12, Chapter 2] we have formulated this notion for an exchange economy and shown its equivalence with economic efficiency under certain convexity and smoothness conditions on preferences. This approach to efficiency has considerable computational advantage over the usual competitive equilibrium approach.

It is easy to design trading systems that attain pairwise optimality. Furthermore, many economists and anthropologists regard pairwise trading as the epitome of social decentralization. We show that on the margin transactions follow a competitive price system. However, it is not necessary for transactions to be competitive on the average. That is to say, the final positions may not be the same as the competitive equilibrium for the given wealth distribution. One or

The author has benefitted from conversations and/or correspondence will Allan Feldman of Brown University, Theodore Bergstrom, Arthur Denzau, James Little, and Robert Parks of Washington University, S. Q. Lemche of The University of Kentucky, Lloyd Shapley of The Rand Corporation, and David Starrett of Stanford University.

another traders may get the better bargain. Competition results when large numbers of similar traders eliminate all special bargains.

A similar approach to that in Rader [12, Chapter 2] has been made by Feldman [4]. In addition to a related result on the equivalence of pairwise optimality and efficiency, he also proves that a special sequence of bilateral trades will lead to a pairwise optimal final position. We say no more of this adjustment system except to recommend it to the interested reader.

Of course pairwise optimality does not have the fine properties shown by Debreu and Scarf [3] for competitive equilibrium. A pairwise optimal choice need not be equitable nor in the core.

Our basic purpose is to see what is a minimal degree of cooperation or centralization necessary for economic efficiency. By centralization we do not mean just that decisions are made by a central authority as in the Soviet Union. Instead we mean that each centralized group, ideally small, makes a decision optimal for itself given its position vis-à-vis others. Quite possibly this could result from some bargaining that involved both small and large groups. It is just that only bargaining among smaller groups will be absolutely required to solve our problem. Then the question is, When will the outcome be Pareto optimal for the whole economy?

Our purpose here is threefold. First, we seek a general theorem for exchange economies that contains both the Rader [12, Chapter 2] and the Feldman [4] equivalence theorems as special cases. In addition many other cases will be covered and the number of possible applications will be increased. Naturally, we wish to make the application as broad as possible. It will be argued that our conditions are fairly close to the weakest possible ones.

Secondly, we wish to make applications to economic systems related to but different from trade in pure exchange economies. The power of the theory of exchange is enhanced by its equivalence with other important social systems. The author has studied such transformations of other systems into pure exchange economies.

Production—exchange economies can be transformed into pure exchange economies (Rader [11, Chapter 9]). This has a particular case of some empirical importance, namely where the household is a unit of production. More or less independent versions of this view appear in Grilliches [6], Lancaster [7], Muth [10], Mincer [9], and Becker [2].

Interindustry production can be transformed into economies of pure exchange of factors among the industries (Rader, [11, chapter 4]).

General social systems can be transformed into economies of pure exchange as in Rader [13] (following a suggestion of Shapley and Shubik [15] and Arrow [1]). However, the framework, developed here will be seen to be not applicable to this case. Indeed, in Section VI we shall see that generally speaking the equivalence theorem does not hold.

The first two applications will be considered in detail in Sections III and IV. An example of exchange without the equivalence theorem is given in Section V.

Thirdly, in Sections VI and VII we aim to analyze efficiency from a decentralized viewpoint in social systems with externalities. There we shall have to replace pairwise optimality with more general decision systems. For bilateral externalities only, efficient exchange between every triple of agents will suffice. For multilateral externalities, we will also need to have an efficient operation of the so-called public externalities, namely those affecting two or more individuals.

Sections II and III are logically quite independent from Sections VI and VII. Depending on the reader's taste, he may consider one or the other or both groups of sections. He who is interested only in externalities will greatly shorten his reading time by turning now to sections VI and VII. Then perhaps he might read the example in Section V to see how pairwise optimality can fail to ensure Pareto optimality.

As a matter of further information we point out that Sections II–V are relatively more difficult mathematically. The rather tenuous reason for presenting them first is that they set a standard of generality that ideally the later sections should meet. Unfortunately, we have not yet seen so deeply into the problem of optimality under multilateral externalities.

II. THE GENERAL EQUIVALENCE THEOREM FOR EXCHANGE WITHOUT EXTERNALITIES

In terms of previous work we wish to generalize in two directions. First, preferences will be more general and not necessarily representable by utility nor even complete. Second, there will not necessarily be a good used by all traders as in Rader [12, Chapter 2] and in Feldman [4]. Neither will there necessarily be a trader with so-called directional dense preferences as in Rader [12]. This trader is one who has smooth preferences and who uses all goods to change his preference levels. Both the Feldman and Rader cases are highly restrictive in many applications, e.g., regional economics and international trade.

Each trader evaluates trades $x \in X^k$ by a preference relation $R_k \subset X^k \times X^k$ that is independent of the position of others. As usual, $x\, R_k\, y$ reads x is at least as good as y. Ordinarily, $X^k \subset E^R$, where R is the number of commodities. The upper contour sets

$$R_k(x) = \{y \mid y\, R_k\, x\}$$

are convex (desire for variety) and contain x in their boundaries (local unsaturation).

In pairwise trading, there is a competitive price system normal to a hyperplane separating the upper contour sets of the two traders. (The situation is that of a point on the contract curve in an Edgeworth box.)

Recently, Madden [8] has stated the problem as follows. When will the sets of normals Q_k for each individual, have a nonempty intersection: $\cap_{k=1}^{N} Q_k \neq \phi$? Note that the Q_k are convex cones and therefore we can restrict our attention to prices in an $(R-1)$-dimensional subspace, for instance the simplex. As Madden notes, we can then apply Helly's theorem. If every group of R consumers has a common price, then there is a price common to all of $\cap_{k=1}^{N} Q_k$. In turn, a common price for R is equivalent to optimality for the group of R given their position with respect to the others. Thus we have that the amount of cooperation need not exceed that in groups of R individuals. However, if the number of commodities is large, as when there is an infinite time horizon, this information is not too valuable. Therefore other methods seem preferable. All of these methods require some kind of smoothness of preferences.

For a directional dense trader, there must be the same unique price system normal to the unique hyperplane bounding his upper contour set in final trade. That price system is the set of normals for all with whom he trades. Thus, this price is in $\cap_{k=1}^{N} Q_k$ and all traders "as-if" maximize with respect to that price system. There is competitive behavior and this then implies efficiency as already shown in Rader [12].

Another idea is due to Feldman [4] who requires that utility instead be differentiable, which in turn implies that preferences are directional dense only for a subset I_k of goods. Other goods are then assumed to yield no utility. In Feldman, these subsets I_k are tied together by a common element, the money good. We shall not make such a strict assumption, but nevertheless we shall need smoothness on preferences.

In our definition of smoothness, parenthetical verbal explanations appear after the formal language. At the point x, the preferences R_k are *smooth* if there are commodities I_k such that we have the following:

(i) For all $x, y \, R_k \, x$, $\hat{y}_j = y_j$, $j \in I_k$ implies $\hat{y} \, R_k \, x$ (only goods in I_k affect preference levels).

(ii) There is an *intrinsic price system* p^k, $\Sigma_{j \in I_k} p_j^{\,k} y_j \geqslant \Sigma_{j \in I_k} p_j^{\,k} x_j$ whenever $y \, R_k \, x$ (weak convexity of preferences in goods that count).

Let π_I *project* onto the components k in I.

(iii) The intrinsic price system $\pi_{I_k} p^k$ is unique up to multiplication by a positive constant. Thus the cone

$$Q^k = \{t \pi_{I_k} p^k \mid t > 0, p^k \text{ an intrinsic price system at } x\}$$

when projected into its I_k coordinate is a ray through the origin (directional density in the goods that count).

(iv) $p_j^k \neq 0$ for all $j \in I_k$ (monotonicity of preferences, either increasing or decreasing, in the goods that count).

Note the (iii) implies that goods consumed in zero quantities must not affect preferences.

To be pairwise optimal between individuals i and j we must have common prices

$$\pi_{I_i \cap I_j}(Q_i) = \pi_{I_i \cap I_j}(Q_j).$$

A *listing* is a $1-1$ function on the set of individual traders, $i = 1, \ldots, N$, onto itself.

Feldman's [4] version of equivalence can be characterized as follows. List the traders in order of their names. Assign p^1 to be the price vector for Mr. A but with components only for the goods in I_A, namely, those goods that affect Mr. A's preferences. Inductively construct p^{n+1} from p^n as follows. If i is in I_n and m is the money good and i is not in $\cup_{k<n} I_k$, set p_i/p_m equal to n's marginal rate of substitution between i and m. If i is in I_n and i is in $\cup_{k<n} I_k$, then i is in say I_k. Now both k and n use the goods i and m. The $i-m$ marginal rate of substitution for k is equal to p_i^{n-1}/p_m^{n-1} and by pairwise optimality between k and n, it is equal to the $i-m$ marginal rate of substitution for n. No further adjustment of p^{n-1} is needed for such goods. The resulting p^n by adding the prices for goods in I_n and $\cup_{k<n} I_k$ is a price system p^n both for I_n and for all I_k, $k < n$. By induction, we have a price system p^N for all traders. It is this method of proof that we generalize by introducing condition (c) below.

Our result derives a common price system that is intrinsic to each individual.

Theorem 1 *Suppose a pure exchange economy with independent preferences R_i such that:*

(a) *the R_i are smooth;*

(b) $\pi_{I_i \cap I_j}(Q_i) = \pi_{I_i \cap I_j}(Q_j)$ *for all i and j (pairwise optimality price condition);*

(c) *there is a listing $f(i)$ such that for any n and any $i, j, \in I_n \cap (\cup_{f(k)<f(n)} I_k)$, $f(n) > 1$ there exist r_m and k_m, $m = 1, \ldots, M$, such that*

(i) $r_m, r_{m+1} \in I_{k_m} \cap I_n$, $m < M, f(k_m) < f(n)$,
(ii) $r_1 = i$,
(iii) $r_M = j$.

Then there is a common price system p such that $\pi_{I_i}(p) \in Q_i$ for all i.

Hypothesis (c) is a noncyclicity assumption that will be discussed in the corollaries to the theorem. Note that condition (c) is *decomposable*. That is, suppose there are two or more disjoint collections of traders who used no goods in common and in each economy there is condition (c). Then condition (c) holds for all the traders taken together.

Proof   Without loss of generality, take $f(k) = k$. The proof is in numbered steps.

1. Choose $p^1 \in Q_1$.
2. We define p^n inductively for $n > 1$. Suppose $n - 1$ has been shown such that for all $k < n$, $\pi_{I_k} p^{n-1} \in Q_k$.
3. Consider $q \in Q_n$. We must have

$$q_i/q_j = p_i^{n-1}/p_j^{n-1}$$

for all $i, j \in \cup_{k<n} I_k$. To see this, consider only i, j also is I_n. Hypothesis (c) gives that there are goods r_m, $m = 1, \ldots, M$, and individuals $k_m < n$ such that

(i) $r_m, r_{m+1} \in I_{k_m}$,
(ii) $r_1 = i$,
(iii) $r_M = j$.

Hypothesis (b) implies that for all $m < M$,

$$\frac{q_{r_m}}{q_{r_{m+1}}} = \frac{p_{r_m}^{n-1}}{p_{r_{m+1}}^{n-1}} = \frac{(\pi_{I_{k_m}} p^{n-1})_{r_m}}{(\pi_{I_{k_m}} p^{n-1})_{r_{m+1}}}.$$

Thus

$$\frac{q_i}{q_j} = \prod_{m=1}^{M-1} \frac{q_{r_m}}{q_{r_{m+1}}} = \prod_{m=1}^{M-1} \frac{p_{r_m}^{n-1}}{p_{r_{m+1}}^{n-1}} = \frac{p_i}{p_j}.$$

4. There exists a $t > 0$ such that $\pi_{I_k \cap I_n} tq = \pi_{I_k \cap I_n} q^{n-1}$, $k < n$, namely $t = p_i^{n-1}/p_i$ for any $i \in I_n \cap (\cup_{k<n} I_k)$ (if $I_n \cap (\cup_{k<n} I_k) = \phi$, set $t = 1$).
5. Choose

$$p^n = (p_i^{n-1} \, i \in \bigcup_{k<n} I_k, \, tq_i, \, i \in I_n \bigcup_{k<n} I_k)$$

and note that $\pi_{I_k}(p^n) \in Q^k$ for all $k < n$. This completes the induction process.
6. Letting $n = N$, we have a price system $p = p^N$ such that $\pi_{I_k} p^N \in Q^k$. This is the required price system.   q.e.d.

We now discuss conditions that ensure hypothesis (c) of the theorem.

Corollary 1   (Rader [12, Chapter 2]). *The conclusion of the theorem holds if hypothesis* (c) *is replaced by* (c_1) *for some* $\bar{k}$, $I_{\bar{k}}$ *is the set of all goods.*

(This new version is somewhat less general than the original.)

Proof   Choose $f(\bar{k}) = 1$, $f(n)$ arbitrary for $n \neq k$. Then for any $f(n) > 1$, i,

$j \in I_n \cap I_k$, we have $M = 2$, $r_1 = i$, $r_2 = j$ and $\bar{k} = k$ gives (c) of the theorem. q.e.d.

Corollary 2   (Feldman [4]).   *The conclusion of the theorem holds if hypothesis* (c) *is replaced by*

$$(c_2) \quad \bigcap_{i=1}^{N} I_i \neq \phi.$$

The result is not as general as Feldman's inasmuch as Feldman allows some nonconsumed goods that nevertheless could generate positive utility but at a small marginal gain.

Proof   For all k, choose $f(k) = k$. Then let $i, j \in I_n \cap \cup_{k<n} I_k$, or $i \in I_n \cap I_k$, $j \in I_n \cap I_e$, $k, e < n$. Then choose $\bar{r} \in \cap_{i=1}^{N} I_i$ and set $M = 3, r_1 = i, r_2 = \bar{r}, r_3 = j$, $k_1 = k, k_2 = e$. This gives hypothesis (c).   q.e.d.

Feldman calls (c_1) the case of a broker and (c_2) the case of a money good. Other cases not previously considered are as follows.

Corollary 3   *The conclusion of the theorem holds if hypothesis* (c) *is replaced by*

(c$_3$) $I_k \cap I_e \neq \phi$ for all k, e.

Condition (c_3) says that every pair of consumers shares a taste in at least one good.

Proof   For all k, choose $f(k) = k$. Then let $r \in I_n \cap I_k$, $j \in I_n \cap I_e$, $k, e < n$. Choose $\bar{r} \in I_k \cap I_j$, $M = 3$, $r_1 = i$, $r_2 = \bar{r}$, $r_3 = j$, $k_1 = k$, $k_2 = e$. This gives hypothesis (c).   q.e.d.

Corollary 4   *The conclusion of the theorem holds if hypothesis* (c) *is replaced by*

(c$_4$) *for every k, I_k contains all but at most one good.*

Condition (c_4) is the case where every consumer consumes all but possibly one good.

Proof   If there are three or more goods, (c_4) implies (c_3). For one good only, we have (c_1). For two goods only, we either have (c_1) or else two distinct sets of traders, one containing traders k that use only one good and the other containing traders e that use only the other good. In the latter case, the price system p is easily constructed directly. Take any vector (p_1, p_2), $p_1 \in Q_k$, $p_2 \in Q_e$.   q.e.d.

Now we are ready to show that pairwise optimality implies Pareto optimality. The result that Pareto optimality implies pairwise optimally is a trivial consequence of the definitions and the fact that a trader's preference depends only upon what the trader receives (Rader [12, pp. 84–85]).

Preferences are (strongly) *quasi transferable* if there is a listing of all traders $f(i)$, $i = 1, \ldots, N$, such that $f(i)$, $f(i) + 1$ can, by transferring foods among them, increase the preference level of any one or the other trader (see Rader [12, pp. 74–80] for a more detailed discussion).

Strict preference is written $x P_k y$ if $x R_k y$ but not $y P_k x$. The upper contour set is

$$P_k(x) = \{y \mid y P_k x\}.$$

Of course, $x I_k y$ if both $x R_k y$ and $y R_k x$. We speak of $I_k(x) = \{y \mid y I_k x\}$ as preference levels and a natural relation on the $I_k(x)$ is induced by P_k if only R_k is reflexive and complete.

Theorem 2   (Pairwise optimality implies Pareto optimality)   *Suppose*

(a′) *The R_i are smooth and locally unsaturated and quasi transferable and the $R_i(x^i)$ are convex.*

(b′) $R_i(x) \cap \sim P_j(x) = \phi$ *for all i, j (pairwise optimality).*

(c) *There is a listing $f(i)$ such that for any i, $j \in I_{n\cap} (\cup_{f(k)} <_{f(n)} I_k)$, $f(n) > 1$, there exist r_m and k_m, $m = 1, \ldots, M$ such that $f(k_m) < f(n)$:*

(i) $r_m, r_{m+1} \in I_{k_m} \cap I_{k_n}$,

(ii) $r_1 = i$,

(iii) $r_M = j$.

(d) $\Sigma_{k=1}^{N} x^k = 0$ *(Pure exchange).*

Then there is Pareto optimality, i.e. "$y^k R_k x^k$ for all k, $\Sigma y^k = 0$" implies "$x^k R_k y^k$ for all k."

Proof   Condition (a) is included in condition (a′).

From condition (b′) and (a′), we deduce condition (b) by applying Minkowski's theorem to separate convex sets.

Thus we have the conclusion of Theorem 1. Using the p derived there, we need only show $p R_i(x^i) \geqslant p x^i$ for all i. Theorem 2 will then follow as in Rader [12, pp. 83–84].

Suppose to the contrary that $p y^k = p_1 y_1{}^k + p_2 y_2{}^k < p_1 x_1{}^k + p_2 x_2{}^k$ where $y^k \in R_k(x^k)$ and $p_2 = \pi_{I_k}(p)$. Since $p_2 y_2{}^k \geqslant p_2 x_2{}^k$, we have

$$p_1 y_1{}^k < p_1 x_1{}^k.$$

Then

$$\sum_{j \notin I_k} (y_j{}^k - x_j{}^k) p_j < 0,$$

and thus for some j, $p_j(y_j{}^k - x_j{}^k) < 0$. Let $j \in I_n$. Then $p_j(x_j{}^k - y_j{}^k) > 0$, and thus by giving to n the quantity $\epsilon(x_i{}^k - y_i{}^k)$ for some $\epsilon > 0$ we will improve n's position (Rader [11, pp. 32, 129], applied to smoothness of k's preference). By convexity of $R_k(x^k)$, k is no worse off than x^k. Evidently, this change can be made by taking $\epsilon(y_j{}^k - x_j{}^k)$ from k without hurting k. Thus x^{kj} could not be pairwise optimal (b'). q.e.d.

The next two sections give applications of Theorem 2.

III. PRODUCTION—EXCHANGE ECONOMICS

In view of Rader [11, Chapter 9], all we have to do is interpret our conditions for production and exchange. The preferences in Theorem 2 are then the preference induced on trade by production and consumption.

First, production technology is assumed to be known and thus controlled by individual consumers. The production sets are convex and closed. The consumers have closed and convex upper contour sets $R_i(x)$. It follows that induced preferences are defined and convex.

Local unsaturation can be obtained if preference levels increase monotonically in a good that can be traded.

Smoothness has not been studied for this transformation. If every traded good can be consumed, that is, can be rated by individual consumer preferences without any production, and if preferences are smooth before production, then they can be shown to be smooth after production.

Let $R_i'(x)$ be the point at least as good as x if no change in production by the consumer is possible. Then $R_i'(x) \subset R_i(x)$. Furthermore, if x were associated with a preference maximizer production, then x can be expected (under local unsaturation) to be in the boundary of both $R_i'(x)$ and $R_i(x)$. Restricting attention to the coordinates I_i, smoothness says that preferences are directional dense (Rader [11, pp. 32, 129]) and the intrinsic price system is nonzero. It can be easily shown that A is directional dense at x and $A \subset B$ implies B is directional dense at x. Furthermore, if $x \in \partial A \cap \partial B$ and $A \subset B$, then the intrinsic price system at x for A and B are the same (where ∂A is the boundary of A). Thus smoothness follows for $R_i(x)$ if it is true for $R_i'(x)$. The very interesting case where some traded goods are not consumed remains unknown.

The interpretation of quasitransferability is that after accounting for production, there is a way of transferring benefit from one consumer to others. Hypothesis (b') is just pairwise optimally where consumers make trades for consumption, directly or indirectly through production. Hypothesis (c) is best interpreted in the various corollaries to Theorem 1. If one consumer can consume directly or use productively each good, then I_k is the set of all goods.

This consumer is then a very ingenious person. If instead there is one good (a Renoir good) consumed by all or one factor (labor services) used productively by all, then the Renoir good or labor good is in $\cap_{i=1}^{N} I_i \neq \phi$. This is Feldman's money good. If every consumer pair has in common at least one good that is used productively or directly consumed by both, we have $I_k \cap I_l \neq \phi$ for all $k \neq l$.

IV. INTERINDUSTRY PRODUCTION

With interindustry production, industry or producer preferences are determined by the levels of output of the given industry. The production functions must be quasiconcave, whereupon the preference relations automatically have convex upper contour sets. Preference smoothness and local unsaturation follow from differentiability of the production function and nonzero marginal products of factors. Quasitransferability is simply the factor connectivity discussed in Rader [11, Chapter 4].

Hypothesis (b′) refers to the fact that industries equate marginal rates of substitution between factors used in positive quantities and exploit any mutual gains by trades of factors between pairs of industries. Hypothesis (c) is a condition on the pattern of use of factors that implies factor connectivity. Under (c_1), one industry uses all factors. Under (c_2), all industries use, say, raw labor services. Under (c_3) every pair of industries uses at least one factor in common.

Pareto optimality is then efficiency in gross outputs. Efficiency in gross outputs is shown to be equivalent to efficiency in net outputs in Rader [11, Chapter 4].

V. AN EXAMPLE OF NONEQUIVALENCE

Consider four farmers located on a lake as in Figure 1 who can use fields at or contiguous to their house (indicated by $\otimes$). Then we shall see that pairwise optimality is not equivalent to Pareto optimality.

Let there be five goods and four traders with utilities:

$$u_A = x_1{}^A x_2{}^A x_3{}^A$$
$$u_B = x_2{}^B x_3{}^B x_4{}^B$$
$$u_C = x_3{}^C x_4{}^C x_5{}^C$$
$$u_D = x_1{}^D x_4{}^D x_5{}^D.$$

Table of Positive Marginal
Utilities

Traders	Goods				
	1	2	3	4	5
A	x	x	x		
B		x	x	x	
C			x	x	x
D	x			x	x

With positive endowments, pairwise optimality is assured if the following marginal rates of substitution are equated:

$$\frac{\partial u_k/\partial x_j}{\partial u_k/\partial x_i} = \frac{\partial u_l/\partial x_j}{\partial u_l/\partial x_i} \qquad \text{for} \quad i, j \text{ used by both } k \text{ and } l.$$

This gives

$$\frac{\partial u_A/\partial x_2}{\partial u_A/\partial x_3} = \frac{x_1^A x_3^A}{x_1^A x_2^A} = \frac{x_3^A}{x_2^A} = \frac{x_3^B}{x_2^B} = \frac{x_3^B x_4^B}{x_2^B x_4^B} = \frac{\partial u_2/\partial x_2}{\partial u_2/\partial x_3}$$

and similarly

$$\frac{x_4^B}{x_2^B} = \frac{x_4^C}{x_2^C}, \qquad \frac{x_5^C}{x_4^C} = \frac{x_5^B}{x_4^B}.$$

and that is all, as is evident from the table of positive marginal utilities. To obtain a Pareto optimal allocation, we must have a competitive price system.

$$\frac{p_j}{p_i} = \frac{\partial u_k/\partial x_j^k}{\partial u_k/\partial x_i^k} \qquad \text{for all} \quad x_j^k > 0, \quad x_i^k > 0.$$

Set all x_j^k equal to one except for x_1^D. Let $x_1^D = 2$. Then there is pairwise optimality and

$$\frac{p_2}{p_3} = \frac{x_3^A}{x_2^A} = 1, \qquad \frac{p_4}{p_5} = \frac{x_5^C}{x_4^C} = 1.$$

Also,

$$\frac{p_1}{p_2} = \frac{\partial u_A/\partial x_1}{\partial u_A/\partial x_2} = \frac{x_2^A}{x_1^A} = 1 \qquad \text{and} \qquad \frac{p_1}{p_5} = \frac{\partial u_D/\partial x_1}{\partial u_D/\partial x_5} = \frac{x_5^D}{x_1^D} = \frac{1}{2}.$$

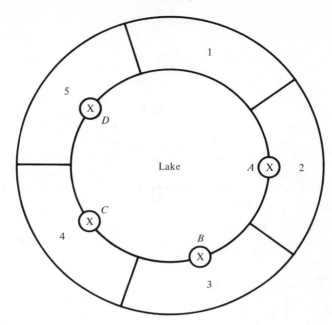

Figure 1

This gives

$$\frac{p_1}{p_2} = \frac{p_1}{p_5} \cdot \frac{p_5}{p_4} \cdot \frac{p_4}{p_3} \cdot \frac{p_3}{p_2} \cdot \frac{p_2}{p_1} = \frac{1}{2} \times 1 \times 1 \times 1 \times 1$$

contrary to $p_1/p_2 = 1$.

To see that the example does not satisfy the hypothesis of Theorem 1, we note first that traders D and A have in common no two goods and thus no common marginal rate of substitution for two goods. Second, $1,5 \in I_A \cup I_B \cup I_C$. Thus condition (c) requires r_m, $r_{m+1} \in I_{X_m} \cup I_D$ with $r_1 = 1$, $r_M = 5$. An examination of the table of positive marginal utilities shows this to be impossible. Only for $X_m = A$ do we have $1 \in I_A$, but also $j \notin I_A \cap I_D$ for any $j \neq 1$.

VI. PARETO OPTIMALITY FOR SOCIETIES WITH BILATERAL EXTERNALITIES

We now consider a general social framework where all transactions are between pairs of agents. It will be seen essentially that exchange of private goods is required for pairwise optimality to imply efficiency.

Let X^{kj} denote the set of feasible transactions between k and j with typical elements x^{kj}. By convention, $x^{kj} = -x^{jk}$. Then set $u_k = u_k(\Sigma_{j \neq k} x^{kj})$. Assume that the sets X^{kj} are convex and the u_k are concave. We adopt the convention that a "good" specific to i does not affect the utility of others. Presumably others will have a minimum amount of it after trade. Thus we could as well write $u_k = u_k(x^{kj}, j \neq k)$.

We note that under our assumptions Scarf's theorem [14] shows the existence of efficient points and implies the existence of one weak version of the core.

We can regard $(u_k, k = 1, \ldots, N)$ as a mapping from $X \equiv \mathsf{X}_{j,k} X^{kj}$ into N space. Then an allocation is *Pareto optimal* if it is a maximal point of the set

$$u(X) = \{u(x) \mid x \in X\}.$$

The set

$$U = \{v \mid v \leqslant u(x) \text{ for some } x \in X\}$$

has upper boundary equal to the maximal points of $u(X)$. The set U is convex by concavity of u. For a point u in the upper boundary of U, we have, by Minkowski's theorem, $c_k \geqslant 0$, not all zero, such that $\Sigma c_k u_k$ is maximized at u. There is more or less equivalence between a maximal u and u maximizing $\Sigma c_k u_k$ for arbitrary $c_k > 0$. (More or less because some c_i can be zero at extremities of the u_i and no longer will maximization of $\Sigma c_k u_k$ necessarily imply Pareto optimality.)

Since $\Sigma c_k u_k$ is concave, it is maximized if and only if the first order conditions for maximization hold:

$$\frac{\partial \Sigma c_k u_k}{\partial x_i^{ki}} \begin{cases} = 0 & \text{if } x_i^{kj} \text{ can be increased and decreased} \\ \geqslant 0 & \text{if } x_i^{kj} \text{ can be further decreased} \\ \leqslant 0 & \text{if } x_i^{kj} \text{ can be further increased.} \end{cases}$$

Note that x_i^{ki} can be increased and decreased for all i if and only if both x^{kj} is internal to the domain of u_k and $-x^{kj}$ is internal to the domain of u_j. Then we evaluate the derivative:

$$\frac{\partial \Sigma c_k u_k}{\partial x_i^{kj}} = c_k \frac{\partial u_k}{\partial x_i^{kj}} + c_j \frac{\partial u_j}{\partial x_i^{jk}} \frac{dx_i^{jk}}{dx_i^{kj}} = c_k \frac{\partial u_k}{\partial x_i^{kj}} - c_j \frac{\partial u_j}{\partial x_i^{jk}}.$$

Setting the derivatives equal to zero, as for an internal solution of x^{kj}, we have

$$c_k \frac{\partial u_k}{\partial x_i^{kj}} = c_j \frac{\partial u_j}{\partial x_i^{jk}}.$$

Also,

$$c_k \frac{\partial u_k}{\partial x_i^{kj}} \leqslant c_j \frac{\partial u_j}{\partial x_i^{jk}}$$

if x_i^{kj} can be further increased, and

$$c_k \frac{\partial u_k}{\partial x_i^{kj}} \geqslant c_j \frac{\partial u_j}{\partial x_i^{jk}}$$

if x_i^{kj} can be further decreased. The collection of all such relationships is necessary and sufficient for maximization of $\Sigma c_k u_k$ at $(x^{jk}, j, k = 1, \ldots, N, j \neq k)$.

Let each pair of agents k, j optimize given its transactions with others. By concavity of u_k and u_j we have that $u_k + \lambda_{kj} u_j$ is maximized by the pair given the transactions with other. Here the first order condition for pairwise optimality is

$$\frac{\partial u_k}{\partial x_i^{kj}} = \lambda_{kj} \frac{\partial u_j}{\partial x_i^{jk}}$$

for x_i^{kj} an internal solution, and

$$\frac{\partial u_k}{\partial x_i^{kj}} \stackrel{<}{>} \lambda_{kj} \frac{\partial u_j}{\partial x_i^{jk}}$$

according as x_i^{kj} can be further increased or further decreased. To obtain the condition for Pareto optimality, we must additionally have c_is such that for k, j,

$$\frac{\partial u_k}{\partial x_i^{kj}} = \frac{c_k}{c_j} \frac{\partial u_j}{\partial x_i^{jk}} \tag{+}$$

for x_i^{jk} and internal solution, and

$$c_k \frac{\partial u_k}{\partial x_i^{kj}} \stackrel{<}{>} c_j \frac{\partial u_j}{\partial x_i^{jk}}$$

according as to whether x_i^{kj} can be further increased or decreased.

Lemma 1 *A necessary and sufficient condition for $\lambda_{jk} = c_k/c_j$ for $c_j \neq 0$ for all j is that $\lambda_{jk} \neq 0$ for all j, k and $\lambda_{kj}\lambda_{je} = \lambda_{ke}$.*

Proof First observe that $\lambda_{jk}\lambda_{kk} = \lambda_{jk}$ so that $\lambda_{kk} = 1$ since $\lambda_{jk} \neq 0$. Now set $c_j = \lambda_{1j}$ for all j. Also, $\lambda_{jk}\lambda_{kj} = \lambda_{jj} = 1$ so that $\lambda_{jk} = 1/\lambda_{kj}$. Then

$$\lambda_{jk} = \lambda_{1j}\lambda_{jk}\lambda_{j1} = \lambda_{1k}\lambda_{j1} = \frac{\lambda_{1k}}{\lambda_{1j}} \equiv \frac{c_k}{c_j}.$$

Thus the conditions $\lambda_{jk}\lambda_{ke} = \lambda_{je}$ are sufficient. Necessity is immediate.   q.e.d.

The condition in Lemma 1 can be weakened somewhat to the case where only some λ_{jk} are nonzero or, equivalently, only some pairs of traders pairwise optimize with nonzero weights for both parties' utilities.

Lemma 2 *A sufficient condition for* $\lambda_{jk} = c_k/c_j$ *whenever* $\lambda_{jk} \neq 0$ *is that:*

(i) $\lambda_{kj}\lambda_{je} = \lambda_{ke}$ *if* $\lambda_{kj}\lambda_{je}\lambda_{ke} \neq 0$, *and*

(ii) *for all* λ_{jk}, *there exist* $k_m, m = 1, \ldots, M$ *such that*

$$k_1 = j, \qquad k_M = k, \qquad \text{and} \qquad \lambda_{k_m k_{m+1}} \neq 0 \qquad \text{for} \quad 1 \leqslant m < M.$$

Proof If $\lambda_{jk} = 0$, we change λ_{jk} to

$$\lambda_{jk} = \prod_{m=1}^{M-1} \lambda_{k_m k_{m+1}}$$

where k_m is as in (ii) of the lemma. It is easy to verify the rule $\lambda_{jk}\lambda_{ke} = \lambda_{je}$:

$$\lambda_{jk}\lambda_{ke} = \prod_{m=1}^{M} \lambda_{k_m k_{m+1}} \prod_{m=1}^{\widetilde{M}} \lambda_{\widetilde{k}_m \widetilde{k}_{m+1}}$$

where $k_m = k$, $\widetilde{k}_1 = k$, $k_1 = j$, $\widetilde{k}_m = e$. Then from rule (i) and mathematical induction we have $\lambda_{jk}\lambda_{ke} = \lambda_{je}$. Now apply Lemma 1.   q.e.d.

The condition $\lambda_{kj}\lambda_{je} = \lambda_{ke}$ will hold if and only if

$$\lambda_{kj}\lambda_{je} = \frac{\partial u_k/\partial x_i^{kj}}{\partial u_j/\partial x_i^{jk}} \frac{\partial u_j/\partial x_i^{je}}{\partial u_e/\partial x_i^{ej}} = \frac{\partial u_k/\partial x_i^{ke}}{\partial u_e/\partial x_i^{ek}} = \lambda_{ke}. \qquad (*)$$

Thus (*) is the necessary and sufficient condition for efficiency given that we have λ_{kj} derived from pairwise optimality. (Notice that, to define λ_{kj}, the pair of consumers kj must have one good in common use after trade.) Condition (*) together with the interpretation of λ_{kj} and λ_{je} is exactly that the members of the triple k, j, e trade efficiently among themselves given their obligations to others. Thus we have that *tripartite optimality* is equivalent to efficiency.

Condition (ii) is a chain condition analogous to condition (c) of Theorems 1 and 2. Whenever there is an internal solution both in x^{kj} and x^{jk} for enough pairs for (ii) to hold under tripartite optimality, we say that the *generalized chain condition* holds. Formally, the chain condition holds if for every j, k, there are $k_m, m = 1, \ldots, M, k_1 = j, k_M = k$, such that $x^{k_m k_{m+1}}x^{k_{m+1}k_m} \neq 0$.

Our analysis so far is subsumed under Theorem 4 in the next section. (We put off a formal statement until later, when multilateral externalities are added to the model.) This still leaves open the question as to when pairwise optimality implies tripartite optimality.

One case where (*) is implied by pairwise optimality only is that of exchange where x gives utility regardless of where it originated. Then

$$\partial u_k/\partial x_i^{kj} = \partial u_k/\partial x_i^{ke} \qquad \text{for all} \quad k, j, e,$$

and the condition (*) holds provided only that there is one good i consumed by all (Feldman's money good, presumably). In turn, this implies condition (+) which implies that $\Sigma c_i u_i$ is maximized and the resulting u_i are Pareto optimal.

Somewhat more generally, it suffices to assume that for every triple of traders j, k, e such that $\lambda_{jk} \neq 0$, $\lambda_{ke} \neq 0$, some good is consumed by all three in positive quantities.

Theorem 3   *If there are bilateral externalities with concave utility functions having nonzero derivatives and the generalized chain condition holds, then tripartite optimality is equivalent to Pareto optimality. If also every triple of consumers j, k, e with $x^{jk}x^{kj} \neq 0$ and $x^{ke}x^{ek} \neq 0$ consumes a common private good as well, then pairwise optimality is equivalent to Pareto optimality.*

Proof   Apply the generalized chain condition to show (i) and (ii) in Lemma 2 for $\lambda_{kj} = (\partial u_k / \partial x_i^{kj})/(\partial u_j / \partial x_i^{jk})$. This gives that tripartite optimality implies Pareto optimality. The converse is immediate; Pareto optimality implies tripartite optimality. The case of a common private good reduces tripartite optimality to pairwise optimality, as already explained.   q.e.d.

Possibly there are other important cases satisfying (*). However, we can easily imagine situations where (*) is not satisfied. For instance, let agents be distinguished as male and female and let x_i be affection. Then

$$\partial u_k / \partial x_i^{kj} < \partial u_k / \partial x_i^{ke}$$

if k and j are male and e is female. Condition (*) can be rewritten as

$$\frac{\partial u_k / \partial x_i^{kj}}{\partial u_k / \partial x_i^{ke}} \frac{\partial u_j / \partial x_i^{je}}{\partial u_j / \partial x_i^{jk}} = \frac{\partial u_e / \partial x_i^{ej}}{\partial u_e / \partial x_i^{ek}}$$

On the left-hand side, the first ratio is less than one, the second greater than one. The right-hand side is indeterminant and thus equality (*) would not be implied by only the equations

$$\frac{\partial u_k / \partial x_i^{kj}}{\partial u_j / \partial x_i^{jk}} = \lambda_{kj}.$$

For example, suppose each male regarded the affection of the one female as yielding equal incremental utility relative to incremental utility yielded by affection of the other male. Optimality would result from pairwise optimality only if the female regarded affection from either of the two males as equally good at the margin! This could happen if goods can substitute for affection as shown in Theorem 3. Otherwise further rules of exchange would have to supplement pairwise optimality in order to ensure Pareto optimality. It therefore appears that the equivalence of pairwise optimality and efficiency is restricted to more or less the cases that include classical economic exchange in private commodities.

The above example should not be confused with the marriage game (Gale and Shapley [5]) which is a game with indivisibilities. It happens that the equivalence of pairwise optimality and efficiency holds in the marriage game, and thus there is still some small hope for extending the equivalence theorem vis-à-vis general social systems.

VII. PARETO OPTIMALITY WITH MULTILATERAL EXTERNALITIES

To model *multilateral externalities*, we supplement the transactions x^{kj} with "public externalities" $y_i{}^k$, produced by individual k. These influence exactly the people in the group $J(k, i)$. For instance, $y_i{}^k$ could be smoke produced by individual k and blown in the direction of k's northward neighbors, namely those in the group $J(k, i)$. Presumably, the south blown smoke would be another good i_0.

As before, Pareto optimality is equivalent to maximizing "social" utility, $\Sigma c_j u^j(x^{kj}, y^k, \ k = 1, \ldots, m)$ subject to $x^{kj} = -x^{jk}$, $x^{kk} = 0$. The first order conditions are necessary and sufficient for maximization:

(1) $\Sigma_j c_j \ \partial u^j / \partial y_i{}^k = 0$ for $y_i{}^k$ an internal solution, and

(2) $c_j \ \partial u_j / \partial x_i^{jk} \lesseqgtr c_k \ \partial u_k / \partial x_i^{kj}$ according as x_i^{jk} can be further increased or further decreased. All other coordinates may be governed by inequality first order conditions without detracting from our argument.

As explained in Section VI, tripartite optimality on nonpublic externalities assumes the fulfillment of Eq. (2). Assuming tripartite optimality, Eq. (1) are now

$$\sum_j \frac{\partial u_k / \partial x_{i_0}^{kj}}{{}_j \partial u_j / \partial x_{i_0}^{jk}} \frac{\partial u^j}{\partial y_i{}^k} = 0. \tag{1a}$$

A typical equation in (1a) is equivalent to the first order condition on the Pareto optimality in the group $J(k, i)$ which consists of those individuals affected by k's externality of type i. Thus Eqs. (1a) are equivalent to each group $J(k, i)$ obtaining Pareto optimality given the level of public externalities other than i. In this case, where $J(k, i)$ has more than two members and the group $J(k, i)$ is in a Pareto optimal position given its position with respect to all others, we say that a public utility *manages the externality* in a Pareto optimal manner. What we have shown is the following theorem.

Theorem 4   *Let utility functions be concave and have nonzero derivatives.*

Suppose both tripartite optimality with respect to nonpublic goods (or else pairwise optimality with each triple consuming in positive quantities a common private good) and Pareto optimality for each public utility that manages the public externalities. Furthermore, suppose the generalized chain condition and interior solutions for the externalities affecting more than two individuals so that the first order conditions for optimization of the utility functions hold with equality. Then the social system is in a Pareto optimal position.

The conditions for Theorem 4 are admittedly strict. It would be worthwhile to try to release them, especially with regard to the requirement of concave, differentiable utility.

REFERENCES

1. Arrow, K. J., "The Organization of Economic Activity," in Joint Economic Committee, *Analysis and Evaluation of Public Expenditures: The PPB System*, Washington, D.C.: Govt. Printing Office, 1969, 47–64.
2. Becker, G., "A Theory of the Allocation of Time," *Economic Journal*, September 1965, 75, 493–517.
3. Debreu, G., and H. Scarf, "A Limit Theorem on the Core of an Economy," *International Economic Review*, September 1963, 4, 235–246.
4. Feldman, A., "Bilateral Trading Processes, Pairwise Optimality and Pareto Optimality," *Review of Economic Studies*, October 1973, 40, 463–474.
5. Gale, D., and L. S. Shapley, "College Admissions and the Stability of Marriage," *American Mathematical Monthly*, January 1962, 69, 9–15.
6. Grilliches, Z., "Hedonic Price Indexes for Automobiles," in Price Statistics Review Committee, *The Price Statistics of the Federal Government*, New York: Nat. Bur. of Econ. Res., 1961, 173–196.
7. Lancaster, K., "A New Approach to Consumer Theory," *Journal of Political Economy*, April 1966, 74, 132–157.
8. Madden, P., "Efficient Sequence of Non-Monetary Exchange," *Review of Economic Studies*, October 1975, 62, 581–596.
9. Mincer, J., "Market Prices, Opportunity Costs, and Income Effects," in C. Christ, et.al., *Measurement in Economics*, Stanford, California: Stanford Univ. Press, 1963, 67–82.
10. Muth, R., "Household Production and Consumer Demand Function," *Econometrica*, July 1966, 34, 699–708.
11. Rader, T., *Theory of Microeconomics*, New York: Academic Press, 1972.
12. Rader, T., *Theory of General Economic Equilibrium*, New York: Academic Press, 1972.
13. Rader, T., "An Economic Approach to Social Choice," *Public Choice*, Summer 1973, 15, 49–75.
14. Scarf, H., "On the Existence of a Cooperative Solution for a General Class of N-Person Games," *Journal of Economic Theory*, March 1971, 3, 167–181.
15. Shapley, L. S., and M. Shubik, "On the Core of an Economic System with Externalities," *American Economic Review*, September 1969, 59, 678–684.

Discussion

DAVID A. STARRETT

Stanford University

The first part of this paper presents a very interesting result on the efficiency of bilateral trade. To explain the result it is perhaps useful to look at an example in which bilateral trade is not efficient. The simplest such example involves three persons (A, B, C) and three commodities (X, Y, Z); suppose that A owns X and desires *only* Y, while B owns Y and desires *only* Z and C has Z and desires *only* X. Then it is clear that no pair of individuals has any incentive to trade, so that bilateral trade as described by Rader will lead to no trade at all. On the other hand, the no-trade outcome is clearly inefficient since a cyclic trade makes everyone better off.

Obviously one of the special features of this example is that there is no overlap in the collection of goods that the various consumers want. Rader shows that one can restore the efficiency of bilateral trade by assuming a sufficient degree of overlap in tastes. His condition would appear to be the weakest one that will do for this purpose.

The second part of the paper deals with the same set of questions in the presence of externalities. The main proposition states that if each externality involves at most n different people, then as long as all groups of size $n + 1$ or smaller trade efficiently among themselves, the outcome will be efficient.

The first thing to note about this proposition is that the concept of externalities used is somewhat nonstandard. Externalities are not on final outcomes, but on with whom one trades. Rader uses the example of affection: males will prefer to get affection from females than from other males, and vice versa. This type of phenomena is certainly present in social relationships but I would suggest that it is rarely important in relationships that are economic in nature (with all apologies to Gary Becker).

Thus, I found it interesting to ask whether the above proposition was still true for the more traditional definition of externalities on outcomes. The answer appears to be no as the following example illustrates:

There are four individuals and a single consumption good to be exchanged among them. Let externalities be such that utility functions take the form:

$$U^1 = c_1 - 2(c_2)^2, \qquad U^2 = c_2 - 2(c_3)^2, \qquad U^3 = c_3 - 2(c_1)^2, \qquad U^4 = c_4$$

where c_i is the consumption of individual i, and U^i his utility. The intuition of the example is that the first three individuals jointly pollute each other unless they can dispose of goods on the fourth person. Note that each externality involves at most two people.

Suppose that there are four units of the good available. Then we argue that the allocation $(1,1,1,1)$ cannot be improved on by any triple of traders. Clearly, the coalition $(1,2,3)$ cannot find an improvement as long as they must absorb their three units. Consider the coalition $(2,3,4)$. If c' is an improving allocation for them, then we must have $c_4' \geqslant c_4$. Since individual 1 is outside the coalition, $c_1 = 1$ whatever the coalition does, so that we must have $c_3' \geqslant c_3$ in order that individual 3 be at least as well off under the prime allocation as before. But then, $c_2' \geqslant c_2$ must hold in order that individual 2 be at least as well off. Hence, the prime program can be feasible only if $c' = c$ and there can be no Pareto improving plan for coalition $(2,3,4)$. Since the remaining coalitions are isomorphic to $(2,3,4)$, no triple of traders can improve on $(1,1,1,1)$.

On the other hand, there are certainly allocations preferred to $(1,1,1,1)$ by everyone. For example, if

$$c_1 = c_2 = c_3 = {}^1\!/_4 , c_4 = 3{}^1\!/_4$$

then $U = ({}^1\!/_8 , {}^1\!/_8 , {}^1\!/_8 , 3{}^1\!/_4)$ as compared to $U = (0,0,0,1)$ for the allocation $(1,1,1,1)$. Thus, Rader's theorem is invalid for the standard definition of externalities.

Noncooperative General Exchange

LLOYD S. SHAPLEY

The Rand Corporation
Santa Monica, California

I. BACKGROUND

It is commonly recognized that the classical Walrasian model of pure competitive exchange is not well suited to applications in which the markets for some commodities may be "thin," in the sense that the number of traders interested in buying or selling those commodities is very small. The mathematical representation of the model gives no hint of this weakness; indeed, the formal equilibrium theory goes through beautifully regardless of the number of traders. But when we cross the indistinct watershed between the worlds of "many" and "few," we begin to encounter individual entrepreneurs who are "big" enough to be able to influence marketwide prices, and so find that the implicit behavioral assumptions on which the competitive model rests are no longer met.

In the 1960s, the theory of games had reached a stage of development where it could begin to throw some light into this shadowy transition zone between "many" and "few." As it happens, the classical model of an exchange economy

The models presented in this paper are the result of an extended collaboration between the author and Martin Shubik; a more detailed joint paper will appear elsewhere. The author wishes to thank the National Science Foundation for its support under Grant GS-31253.

fits very neatly into the format of a multiperson cooperative game. This makes it quite easy to bring to bear a number of different game-theoretic solution concepts and to compare them with the Walrasian competitive equilibrium. Best known of these game solutions, to economists, is the *core* – the set of coalitionally unimprovable outcomes. The core has been shown to yield substantial agreement with the set of competitive equilibria in suitably large and homogeneous economies, but to yield qualitatively different results in the presence of "big" traders. A similar situation exists with respect to several other cooperative solution concepts.[1] Since each of them can be defined in an economically plausible way, the possibility is open that the core, or one of the others, might more faithfully describe the "true state of affairs," with the competitive equilibrium standing merely as a convenient approximation when the situation approaches the limiting ideal of "perfect" competition. At the very least, it seems worthwhile to try to use game theory to build a bridge between that asymptotic ideal, on the one side, and the "imperfections" of oligopolistic behavior and small-group bargaining, on the other.[2]

These developments may hold great promise of explaining deviations from pure competition that are attributable to coalitional activity in thin markets. But they hardly seem to touch the more inherent and longer recognized weakness of the classical model, which has little to do with coalitions, namely, the need to assume that *entrepreneurs cannot single-handedly influence the price structure.* Walrasian prices are given *ex machina* and by definition are not responsive to the traders' buy/sell decisions. The Walrasian equilibrium is tested by conjectural variation of individual bids for goods, but without allowing for any price fluctuation in response to the changed bids. The rigid-price assumption cannot be allowed to stand if we hope to build a theoretical bridge between general equilibrium and, say, Cournot oligopoly. The game model that we construct must somehow permit the traders to participate in the formation of prices, and hence must differ radically from the "cooperative game" models that have been offered to date, which virtually ignore the price mechanism while concentrating on coalitional phenomena.

---

[1] For example, the "value" of a game; see Aumann [2], Aumann and Shapley [3], and Shapley and Shubik [15]. The von Neumann–Morgenstern solution behaves rather differently; see Hart [8, 9].

[2] We feel that the core may have been oversold in this regard. Though "collusive" in a certain sense, the core has little to do with the characteristic tactics of economic collusion: boycotts, strikes, price manipulation, insincere bidding, and restraint of trade (see Aumann [1], Drèze *et al.* [5], Gabszewicz and Drèze [6], Gabszewicz and Mertens [7], Shapley [14], Shapley and Shubik [15, 18], and Shitovitz [19]). Moreover, like the other cooperative solution concepts, the core is by definition Pareto optimal, precluding the social inefficiency that is almost the hallmark of monopolistic competition.

II. A NEW APPROACH WITH APPLICATIONS TO EXTERNALITIES

In this paper we shall describe a new method of "making a game" out of general equilibrium, which we have recently been exploring in collaboration with Martin Shubik. It is based on the "noncooperative" side of game theory, in the spirit of Nash and Cournot. Our traders do not collude, but they do influence prices through their buy and sell orders. The noncooperative equilibria (NE) of the game are conceptually not too far removed from the classical competitive equilibria (CE), the relationship between the two being especially close when there are many traders of each type and hence relatively stable prices. But when there are "thin" markets, we shall typically find substantial Pareto inefficiency in the NE, with trading sharply reduced in volume or otherwise displaced from the competitive pattern.

Our previous attempts in this vein had been hampered by the fact that the classical model of an exchange economy does *not* fit neatly into the *non*cooperative game format. The noncooperative theory requires a game in "strategic form" rather than "coalitional form." Many ad hoc assumptions were apparently necessary to specify the range of choices for the traders and the rules for price formation in the market; these led to a series of special models of special situations, often interesting in themselves, but with little claim to generality (see Shubik *et al.* [10–12, 16, 20, 21, 24]). Our current approach offers new hope. The decisive step was to meet the problem of money head on – to accept the proposition that, in the world of buying and selling, money is "real." Granting this, the rest falls into place, with remarkably few other generality-restricting assumptions. While some special rules on the handling of money must be made for definiteness (corresponding, indeed, to actual constraints on methods of payment, credit, bankruptcy, etc.), they can be varied widely without upsetting the basic mechanisms of the model or the general method of analysis. Thus, what we present here is not a single model of noncooperative general exchange, but a sampling from a class of related models, suitable both for general-purpose microeconomic theory and for studying the phenomena of money and financial institutions (see Shubik *et al.* [22, 23, 25]).

There are two ways in which these noncooperative game models may be of service in the study of *externalities*.[3] First, most mathematical theories in this area rely upon some kind of competitive pricing mechanism, both for their negative results (e.g., nonexistence or nonoptimality of Walrasian prices) and for their positive results (e.g., existence or other properties of Lindahlian prices). But most applications of these models must confront "thin" markets.[4] It would

---

[3] For a "cooperative game" approach to externalities, see Shapley and Shubik [17].

[4] This occurs automatically when artificially differentiated goods are interjected into the model, each applicable to only one or a few individuals.

seem prudent, in the light of the above discussion, to consider whether competitive pricing is really suitable in such applications, or whether it would be better (even leaving aside any questions of collusion) that we recognize the ability of the traders to influence price levels.

It might be added that our one major restrictive condition — the requirement of an explicit "money" to serve as a medium of exchange — will not be an added burden in many studies in the field of externalities since "money" will have to be brought into the model anyway, say as a vehicle for taxation, subsidy, or interpersonal compensation — or even as a metric for social value.

To avoid potential misunderstanding, we would stress that the NE characteristically "breaks down" in the presence of externalities in much the same way and for much the same reasons as does the classical CE.[5] An important difference, however, is that when the NE fails to exist, we are still left with a well-defined game, for which other types of solution may be attempted.[6] But it is difficult to see how to salvage anything from the wreckage when the CE fails to exist.

The second point at which our approach relates to the question of externalities has to do with the way the market operates. So-called "pecuniary externalities" arising out of the economic system itself can have significant impact, even in the absence of the more familiar and better-understood externalities of production and consumption. Consider, for example, the effect on the fortunes of the small suppliers of a commodity when a large producer "dumps" his surplus on the market. If we choose to regard the rules by which prices are determined as "laws of nature," i.e., as part of the physical or technological environment, then this effect is as much an externality as, say, the lowering of the underground water table by a thirsty industrial plant. The analogy is not perfect; economics is not physics. There is perhaps a semantic question here, but our approach does give one a theoretical grip on these pecuniary externalities, however they may fit into the general scheme of things.

Another "systemic" externality that we are able to study is the evaluation of the market itself as a public good, or perhaps, a public "bad." As we have already mentioned, the NE typically yields outcomes that are Pareto-inefficient, in the manner of a Cournot oligopoly. Some of this social loss might be rationalized as a kind of social transactions cost, to be compared with costs that might be associated with other possible methods of price determination. But when the loss is great, most of it would better be charged directly to the account of monopolistic concentration, which is another kind of public "bad." The use of noncooperative game models may prove to be the key to successful analysis of these questions.

---

[5] See Professor Rosenthal's comments following this paper.
[6] Including the "Nash equilibrium in mixed strategies," which will exist under very general conditions, though it may be hard to justify in economic terms.

III. THE BASIC MODEL

Let there be n *traders* and $m + 1$ *commodities*. The $(m + 1)$th commodity might be called "gold," because it both has intrinsic utility (possibly) and plays a special monetary role in the market. The traders have nonnegative *initial bundles*:

$$a^i = (a^i_1, \ldots, a^i_m, a^i_{m+1}), \qquad i = 1, \ldots, n, \tag{1}$$

and concave, nondecreasing *utility functions*:

$$u^i(x^i) = u^i(x^i_1, \ldots, x^i_m, x^i_{m+1}), \qquad i = 1, \ldots, n. \tag{2}$$

(We do not exclude the possibility that u^i is independent of x^i_{m+1}.) Horizontal bars will denote summation over the traders; for example, $\bar{a}_{m+1}$ is the total amount of "gold." We assume that all commodities are present somewhere in the economy, i.e., that

$$\bar{a} > 0. \tag{3}$$

Unlike the usual general equilibrium game, goods in our model are *not* freely transferable among consenting traders, but are subject to specific marketing rules. For the present exposition we shall focus first on one version of these rules, pointing out later some possible variations. Also, in this account, we shall confine ourselves to the one-period case, although several aspects of our approach (for example, the treatment of fiat money or of loans and interest rates) can only be done justice to in a multiperiod setting.

Given just the one period, each trader has a single strategic decision to make. This will be represented by a pair (b^i, s^i) of nonnegative m-vectors, subject to

$$s_j^i \leqslant a_j^i, \qquad j = 1, \ldots, m, \tag{4}$$

and

$$\sum_{j=1}^m b_j^i \leqslant a^i_{m+1}. \tag{5}$$

The letters b and s are meant to connote buy and sell. To interpret this, imagine that there are m different markets or "trading posts," $M_1, \ldots, M_m$. Trader i sends the amount s_j^i of good j to M_j, to be sold "on consignment," and he sends the amount b_j^i of "gold" to M_j toward the purchase of good j. We could add the constraint $b_j^i s_j^i = 0$, forbidding a trader to enter a market on both sides, but we shall save that for later (see Section V).

Once all traders have made their choices, the outcome is readily determined. In fact, if neither $\bar{b}_j$ nor $\bar{s}_j$ are zero, then the *price*

$$p_j = \bar{b}_j / \bar{s}_j > 0 \tag{6}$$

will obviously clear the market M_j. If it happens that $\bar{b}_j = 0$ (no "gold" sent to M_j), then we arbitrarily remove the goods $\bar{s}_j$ from the system. Similarly, if $\bar{s}_j = 0$ (no goods sent to M_j), then the "gold" $\bar{b}_j$ disappears.[7] Carrying out the indicated transfers, we calculate the *final bundles* as follows:

$$
x_j^i = \begin{cases} a_j^i - s_j^i + (\bar{s}_j/\bar{b}_j)b_j^i & \text{if} \quad \bar{b}_j > 0, \\ a_j^i - s_j^i & \text{if} \quad \bar{b}_j = 0 \end{cases} \tag{7}
$$

if $j \neq m + 1$, and

$$
x_{m+1}^i = a_{m+1}^i - \sum_{j=1}^{m} b_j^i + \sum_{j:\bar{s}_j>0} (\bar{b}_j/\bar{s}_j)s_j^i. \tag{8}
$$

The ith trader's *payoff*, as a function of all the traders' strategies, is then given by

$$
P^i = P^i((b^1, s^1), \ldots, (b^n, s^n)) = u^i(x^{,i}). \tag{9}
$$

However, note that this can be reduced to a function of two variables (each a $2m$-dimensional vector):

$$
p^i = \Pi^i((b^i, s^i), (\bar{b} - b^i, \bar{s} - s^i)) \tag{10}
$$

since the other players' strategies affect i's payoff only in the aggregate.

The definition of the noncooperative equilibrium[8] is now easily stated using (10): it is a pair of matrices $b^{\#}, s^{\#}$, such that for each i the expression

$$
\Pi^i((b^i, s^i), (\bar{b}^{\#} - b^{\#i}, \bar{s}^{\#} - s^{\#i})) \tag{11}
$$

is maximized, subject to (4) and (5), at $b^i = b^{\#i}$, $s^i = s^{\#i}$. In other words, no trader, given the bids of the others, can improve.

We would like to observe that it is part of the peculiar discipline of game theory that there be *players* and *rules*. The players are independent decision

---

[7] This proves to be the best way to handle the very real (and realistic) discontinuity in the mechanics of our system, occasioned by the failure to form a market for good j. From the individual trader's point of view, it is reasonable to expect (1) that he never gets something for nothing, but (2) that he does get nothing for something, when the price of the "something" goes to zero. From the global point of view, it is reasonable to expect that an equilibrium solution will avoid outcomes where goods or money disappear from the system in accordance with this rule.

The reader disturbed by our toying with the law of conservation of matter may be reassured if we postulate an extra trader, or "scavenger," who makes an infinitesimal bid on both sides of every market. Ordinarily, his effect on the system is also infinitesimal, but he can take home a substantial windfall if it happens that one of his infinitesimal bids is not outmatched by a positive bid from one of the regular traders.

[8] Robert Wilson has suggested the term "best-response equilibrium." The concept was introduced to game theory by John Nash, who however admitted the possibility of randomized or "mixed" strategies. Thus, our NE is a "Nash equilibrium in pure strategies."

makers, explicitly constrained, while the rules associate a definite outcome with every set of legal strategy choices. The *description* of the game (i.e., what can happen) is kept conceptually separate from the *solution* of the game (i.e., what will or should happen). This contrasts sharply with the classical model, in which prices appear mysteriously out of the air and in which the overall outcome is undefined in the event any trader "irrationally" steps out of line and fails to conform to the preordained behavior pattern. The contrast fades, however, if one merges description and solution, i.e., considers the equilibrium conditions (NE or CE) as an integral part of the model. But there will be important applications, especially in the study of externalities, in which the NE does not exist or is heuristically inappropriate as a solution concept. We wish to stress that our game model, unlike the competitive model, remains well defined in such situations.

IV. THE EDGEWORTH BOX

The case $n = 2$, $m = 1$ lends itself to diagrammatic analysis. In the figures that follow, the vertical coordinate is the money commodity, $j = 2$, and the horizontal coordinate is the other commodity, $j = 1$. The first trader measures his holdings from O^1, the second from O^2. The point R represents the initial allocation, with coordinates $(a_1{}^1, a_2{}^1)$ measured from O^1. A typical strategy for trader 1 is the point S^1 in Figure 1; it is constrained to lie in the rectangle "southwest" of R. Similarly, S^2 for trader 2. Here, the vectors RS^1 and RS^2 represent what goes to market and $O^1 S^1$ and $O^2 S^2$ what stays home; thus the actual O^1-coordinates of S^1 are $(a_1{}^1 - s_1{}^1, a_2{}^1 - b_1{}^1)$.

The price p_1 is easily visualized. In fact, it is just the slope $(b_1{}^1 + b_1{}^2)/(s_1{}^1 + s_1{}^2)$ of the line $S^1 S^2$. The intercepts of this line with the perpendiculars through R determine the coordinates of the final allocation, which is represented by the point X. Note that X must lie either "northwest" or "southeast" of R.

The line RX corresponds to the "price ray" of the familiar Edgeworth construction; its slope is of course $-p_1$. But in our present model it does not represent a "budget set" from which the trader selects his preferred outcome. Instead, the set of outcomes from which trader 1 chooses is the curve $A^1 B^1$. This is the trace of the point X, as S^1 varies over its permitted rectangle with S^2 held fixed. Algebraically it is a segment of a hyperbola, the asymptotes being the perpendiculars through S^2. The analogous set for trader 2, given S^1 fixed, is the curve $A^2 B^2$.

Observe the contrast between the *marginal* prices, which are different for the two traders, and the *average* price p_1. Trader 1's marginal is the (absolute) slope of $A^1 B^1$ at X; it is greater than p_1 in the case illustrated because he is a net buyer of the commodity when X is in the southeast quadrant. Should he try to

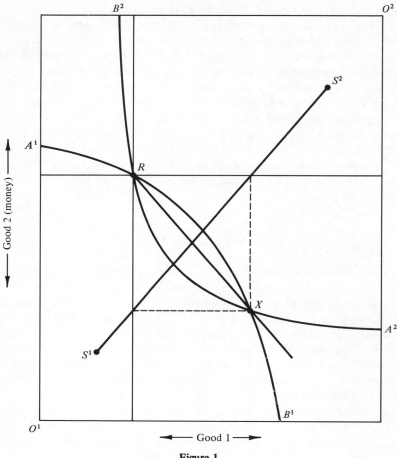

Figure 1

increase his order, he would drive up the demand and would have to pay a higher market price not merely on the increment, but on his entire purchase. Similarly, trader 2's marginal, the absolute slope of A^2B^2 at X, is less than p_1 because he happens to be a net seller.

So far we have just considered the machinery of exchange. In Figure 2 we show trader 1's utility maximization problem. Note that a unique optimum M exists because of the convexity of the indifference curves and the opposite curvature of A^1B^1. This optimum is achieved by any legal choice of S^1 on the slanting line through S^2. Note also that M is a continuous function of S^2, so long as the vector RS^2 is strictly positive. These properties of uniqueness and continuity continue to hold quite generally in our model, under certain weak nonsaturation assumptions, when there are more traders and/or commodities.

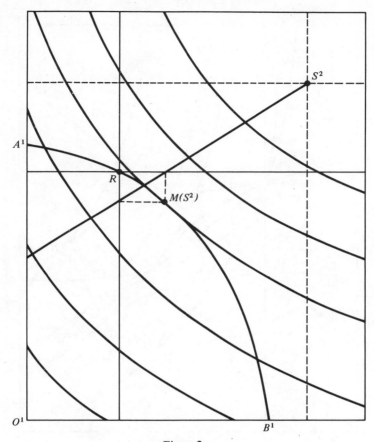

Figure 2

Figure 3 shows typical indifference curves for both traders, as in the usual Edgeworth diagram, but illustrates a *noncooperative* equilibrium, with each trader optimizing against the other's strategy. Note that the NE allocation X is *not* Pareto efficient. The difference between the two marginal prices leaves room for joint improvement, as indicated by the shaded region.

The Edgeworth "contract curve" of common tangents CD passes through this shaded region, as it must. It might appear at first glance that there must always be a CE allocation in this region, i.e., a point at which the common tangent, extended back, passes through the point R. A CE so situated would not only represent a higher volume of trade than the NE, but would actually raise the utility of both traders. But matters are not always so straightforward. In Figure 4 we show how the contract curve, given that there is a NE at X, can still twist in such a way that it enters the rectangle *between* R and X; moreover the unique

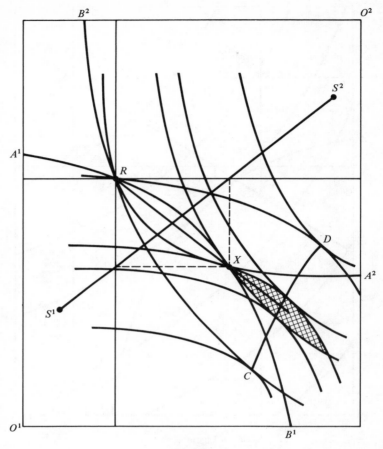

Figure 3

CE can lie in that rectangle, as shown at *W*. This perverse "twist" is not unrelated to the phenomenon of inferior goods and Giffen's paradox.

On the other hand, given any CE allocation *W*, we can show that there is always a NE in the rectangle determined by *W* and *R*. (This is not true for the variants in the next section, however.) In fact, we can show something stronger. Take any line through *R* that contains jointly profitable points, for example, the price ray through a CE allocation like *W* in Figure 4. Then if *R* is interior to the box, there will be a whole interval of NE allocations on this line in the neighborhood of *R*.

To see why this is so, consider the problem of trying to construct a NE that will yield an allocation on such a ray (Figure 5). Start with the jointly

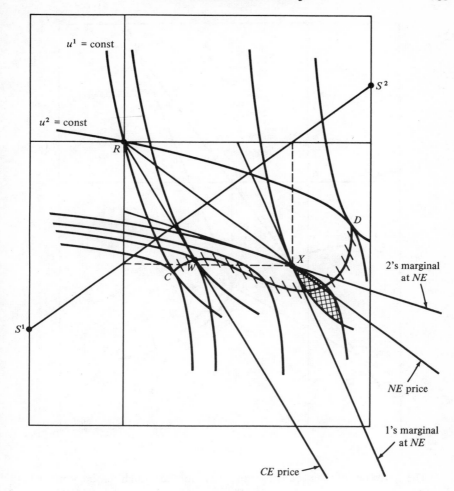

Figure 4

profitable point X, sufficiently close to R so that both utilities increase monotonically from R to X. Then determine G and H as shown, and draw the line through G and H. Then draw XS^2 through X with positive slope matching the negative slope of the u^1 indifference curve through X; this slope will be steeper than XR, and so S^2 will lie in the northeast quadrant from R, as shown. Similarly draw XS^1. If S^1 and S^2 happen to lie within the Edgeworth box, then they are allowable strategies and constitute a NE yielding X, as desired. If not, move X toward R, along the ray RX, and ultimately this will bring the points S^1 and S^2 so close to R that they will be allowable strategies.

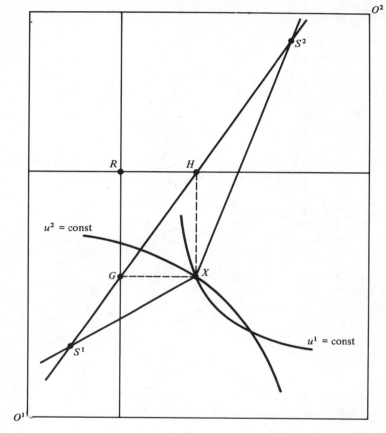

Figure 5

The purpose of this construction was not so much to demonstrate an economic theorem, since the result will disappear under the tighter definitions of strategy in the next section; rather, we wish to highlight the nonuniqueness of the NE solution in our basic, expository model and to suggest the desirability of the sharper variants to come.

Much of the foregoing diagrammatic analysis applies when there are more traders and/or more goods. As far as traders are concerned, the model has the "aggregation" property. Thus, from trader 1's point of view, the point S^2 can be regarded as the *sum* of the strategies of traders 2 through n. His personal optimization problem does not depend on the number n, but only on the magnitude and position of the vector RS^2.[9] As far as goods are concerned, each

---

[9] Note that if RS^2 is very large, then trader 1's choice set $A^1 B^1$ approaches a straight line, approximating what it would be in a fixed-price "competitive" market.

trading post M_j operates independently of the others. The only links are through the budget constraint (5), whereby the set of allowable choices in any one post depends on how much the trader spends in the others, and through complementarities, etc. in the preferences for different goods, whereby the indifference map for each trading post may depend on what happens at the other posts.

These remarks illustrate vividly the function of money as a *decoupler*, enabling independent centers of economic initiative (the traders) and independent centers of exchange and price formation (the trading posts) to operate smoothly within a single system without inconsistency or indeterminateness.

V. VARIANTS

In our basic formulation, a trader does not usually have a unique "best response." This may be seen, e.g., in Figure 2. Trader 1 is indifferent in his choice of S^1 along any given line through S^2 since the outcome $M(S^2)$ is not affected. All that he accomplishes by moving S^1 along such a line is to change the marginal prices that confront the *other* trader or traders. The further S^1 is from R, the more stable the price is for them.[10] While this nonuniqueness of response does not directly account for the nonuniqueness of the NE (cf. the construction in the preceding section), it does illustrate the presence of an unnecessary degree of strategic freedom. One would expect that the prospects for a sharp solution concept would be enhanced with that freedom eliminated. Two variants that do this will now be discussed.

In variant I we insist that the traders not bid on both sides of a trading post simultaneously; in other words, we require

$$b_j{}^i s_j{}^i = 0, \qquad j = 1, \ldots, m, \quad i = 1, \ldots, n. \tag{12}$$

In our Edgeworth diagram this means that each S^i is now restricted to the two edges of the previously allowed rectangle that meet at the point R. Under this trading rule, the two-trader case collapses into a triviality: either the traders just exchange goods for money directly, if they happen to choose opposite sides of the market, or they both lose their goods or money outright, if they happen to choose the same side. But with more traders in the market, a given trader will more likely find both sides active, so that the *combined* bids of his opponents will not satisfy (12), but rather yield a point like S^2 in Figure 2, in the interior of the northeast quadrant. Thus, variant I does not have the aggregation property.

It is of course true that any NE for variant I is also a NE for the original

---

[10] It is accepted practice for a company issuing additional shares of its stock to simultaneously buy or sell in the open market in order to stabilize the price.

model since in restricting the strategy spaces we have not materially reduced the response capabilities of the traders, even considering the budget constraint (5). Conversely, a solution of the original version that happens to satisfy (12) will also be a solution of variant I, a fortiori.

In variant II, we insist that *all* goods pass through the market before they are consumed; nothing (except money) may be held back. In other words, we require

$$s_j{}^i = a_j{}^i, \qquad j = 1, \ldots, m, \quad i = 1, \ldots, n. \tag{13}$$

This eliminates the $s_j{}^i$ as strategic variables. Geometrically, the permitted strategies in the Edgeworth box are restricted to the edges $O^i G^i$ (Figure 6). The market price now has an upper bound, as it can never exceed the slope of the diagonal $O^1 O^2$. Certain outcomes are therefore unattainable, and the "response

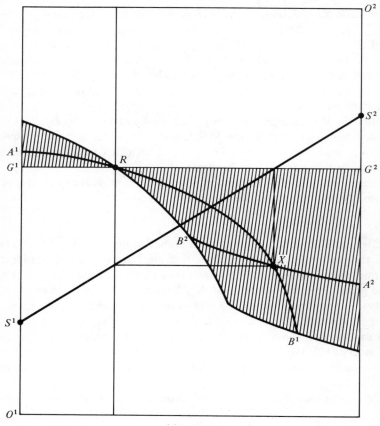

Figure 6

curves" $A^i B^i$ of the previous diagrams are shortened at the B end. The shaded area in Figure 6 indicates the full range of outcomes that remain feasible in variant II, as compared with the two complete quadrants that were possible before. The intuitive reason for this curtailment of the feasible set is that we are requiring the traders to sell all their goods, but are not allowing them to hypothecate the receipts. The terms of trade are "cash in advance."

It is entirely possible that the Edgeworth contract curve will now fail to intersect the feasible set. This raises an interesting point about social efficiency. We have been using the term *Pareto efficient* in the customary way, i.e., with reference to the set of all allocations that could be reached by *unrestricted transfers* of goods among the traders. If the market rules are regarded as "laws of nature," however, many transfers will be impossible, and a different Pareto set will result, inferior to the first. In variant II it may even be strictly inferior; that is, it may have no points in common with the original. That would be exemplified by the contract curve missing the feasible set in the two-trader Edgeworth market.

But even in our basic model (and in variant I) it will not ordinarily be possible, when there are more than two traders, to reach most of the points on the unrestricted-transfer Pareto surface. This is easy to see if we observe that each feasible point has associated with it a particular marketwide price schedule. Once we have decided, say, what we want trader 1's final bundle to be, we are burdened with a linear-equation condition on the prices, which will limit the possible ways in which the others traders can redistribute the complementary bundle among themselves. Some of the Pareto-efficient outcomes will always be feasible under fixed-price trading, for example, the CE allocations, but most of the unrestricted-transfer Pareto surface will in general be inaccessible if $n > 2$. We should emphasize, however, that exactly the same situation prevails with respect to the Walras model.

These matters may be important from the cooperative-game viewpoint: they mean that the several different "strategic forms" that we consider have different characteristic functions, and hence may have different cores, values, bargaining sets, etc.[11] From the noncooperative viewpoint they are less important. Two points deserve mention however. First, in all our variants, the NE are usually socially inefficient, even with respect to the restricted Pareto set. It usually still pays to collude. Second, the more drastic curtailment possible in variant II, where the entire original Pareto set becomes infeasible, is most likely to be associated with shortages or maldistribution or near worthlessness of the "money"

---

[11] It might surprise some people to learn that the core of the cooperative game that most closely resembles the Walrasian model of exchange (the game in which the players negotiate a marketwide price schedule to govern all transactions) is different from the core usually studied. We do not know of any treatment of this core in the literature.

commodity. This observation is a sample of the sort of heuristic commentary on the phenomenology of money that we can expect our theory to produce as the analysis proceeds.

The third variant to be discussed points in a different direction; it is an extension rather than a restriction, and may be applied equally well to any of the three versions discussed heretofore. The idea is to introduce *credit* into the model, i.e., to modify or eliminate the constraint (5). But we wish to avoid (at least at first) any detailed consideration of special rules for repayment, security, interest, bankruptcy, etc. This can be accomplished by the simple expedient of eliminating (5) entirely and extending the consumption set for each trader to include negative as well as positive values of x_{m+1}. "Cash in advance" is out, but suitable disutility for being caught without sufficient funds at the close of trading is built into the extended utility functions, without any specific modeling of the machinery of insolvency or bankruptcy. Considering the nature of this negative commodity, "debt," it would not be unreasonable to demand concavity of the utility functions over the extended domain. If the disutility of debt is made steep enough,[12] we can expect the actual NE *solutions* to lie within the positive orthant for each trader, although the spending limit (5) may well be violated in the process of getting there. But, as remarked before, we insist that our game model provide a well-defined "payoff" (final utility vector) for *any* choice of strategies, in or out of equilibrium.

The effect of this extension is easily described in the Edgeworth diagram: simply knock out the top and bottom ends of the box. Among other things, this enlarges the feasible set for variant II, making it coextensive with that for the other models, since arbitrarily high prices can now be generated, not by withholding goods from market but by simultaneous overbidding by both traders.

VI. TWO THEOREMS

An existence theorem for NE is of course a sine qua non of the theory, but it is not easy to prove and we have thus far obtained a satisfactory result only for variant II. The other cases, however, involve an interesting auxiliary concept, called *virtual price*, and it is worth taking some space to describe it even though we cannot yet assert a theorem.

We have already alluded to the discontinuity in the system when "no market

---

[12] The extreme case would be to make the penalty for being caught short essentially infinite. The opposite, "easy credit" extreme would be to use the maximal concave extension of the concave utility function originally defined on the positive orthant — such an extension exists and is unique if we adopt the useful viewpoint of Rockafellar [13] wherein convex and concave functions can assume the values $\pm\infty$.

forms" for some good. Suppose it happens that no bids are received, say, on the money side of M_j, though a positive quantity of good j is offered for sale.[13] An arbitrarily small increase in any of the zero bids $b_j{}^i$ would then suffice to buy up the full supply $\bar{s}_j$, which otherwise disappears from the system. This type of situation is therefore quite unstable if we suppose there is at least one trader with money and with a desire for good j. Intuitively, one would hardly expect this sort of unstable situation to have much bearing on the existence of an equilibrium.

It is quite another matter, however, when nothing is offered on *either* side of a trading post. In this case, the situation is highly *stable*. A bid by any one person is futile: either he just loses it outright or (if the rules permit) he may find himself selling his own goods to himself. It takes joint action on the part of two or more individuals to start up a profitable market in a good previously untraded. This is surely not just a technical defect in the model — the world is full of "latent" markets awaiting discovery and exploitation. But it has the strange effect of making our existence theorem too easy! There is always the trivial, "null" equilibrium, at which nothing is bought or sold. There will be numerous other equilibria (usually) that are almost as trivial: one or two trading posts "open for business" and all others arbitrarily shut down.

While these trivial solutions may not be totally unrealistic, one would hope that there would be at least one full-fledged, "robust" NE in which all posts M_j are *active* in the sense that $\bar{b}_j > 0$ and/or $\bar{s}_j > 0$. This, however, is too much to demand. Some markets may be "legitimately" inactive, the existing distribution being exactly what it "should" be. For example, if the initial allocation of all goods happens to be Pareto optimal, then even the "null" solution will be legitimate in this sense.

The following definition points a way through the difficulty. If (b, s) is a NE and if M_j is inactive, i.e., if $\bar{b}_j = \bar{s}_j = 0$, then we define the number v_j to be a *virtual price* for M_j if all the individual strategies (b^i, s^i) would remain "best responses" for their users in the presence of added "external" bids $b_j{}^0 = \epsilon v_j$ and $s_j{}^0 = \epsilon$, for any $\epsilon > 0$. There may be one or many virtual prices, or none, for any given inactive M_j. Intuitively, a virtual price means that a trading post, if it were "open for business" at that price, would attract no business. Our goal is a theorem that asserts (for variant I, say, and under suitable conditions on the utilities, etc.) that a NE exists in which each commodity has either an actual price p_j, if actively traded, or a virtual price v_j, if not.

In variant II all markets are automatically stocked, so virtual prices do not arise. The possibility of no money being bid for a good still does present a technical problem since the fixed-point theorems that we rely on require continuity of the mapping from strategies to "best responses." The problem is

---

[13] There is a similar discontinuity if money but no goods are offered to a trading post.

resolved in our proof by approximating the economy by continuous models having small "external" bids in all markets, and we can report the following theorem:

Theorem 1 *In variant II, assume that the u^i are continuous, concave, and nondecreasing; that $\bar{a} > 0$, and that for each good $j = 1, \ldots, m$, there are at least two traders i such that $a^i_{m+1} > 0$ and u^i is strictly increasing in x_j. Then a NE exists.*

The "two traders" condition in this theorem makes sense: if only one moneyed trader desired good j, then he would have no competition in the bidding and hence no "best" bid $b_j{}^i > 0$.

Note that we do not require that money have any utility for anyone. But if money is intrinsically worthless (i.e., valuable only strategically), then the variant II solution is independent of who owns the initial endowments since no one would care what his goods bring in the marketplace.[14] The case of "paper" or "fiat" money becomes distinctly more interesting in a multiperiod setting (see Shubik [22] and Shubik and Whitt [25]).

The other theorem that we shall discuss expresses a relationship between the two equilibrium concepts — NE and CE — when there are many traders, each "small" relative to the whole. Our setting will be a "replication sequence" of economies $\Gamma_1, \Gamma_2, \ldots, \Gamma_k, \ldots$, in the manner of Scarf and Debreu [4]. That is, there are a fixed number t of *types* of traders, characterized by their utilities u^i and endowments a^i, $i = 1, \ldots, t$. The economy Γ_k then has $n = kt$ traders, k of each type. Of course, while traders of the same type have identical descriptions we cannot constrain them to behave identically in the game since each is a free agent. But a NE in which traders of the same type do choose the same strategies is called *symmetric*, and such a NE can be represented in a space whose dimension does not depend on the replication number k. Specifically, in variant II, any symmetric NE of Γ_k can be represented by an $m \times t$ matrix $b(k)$ of bids b_j^i (rather than an $m \times kt$ matrix). Thus, symmetry permits a straightforward comparison of $b(k)$ for different values of k.

One final concept of interest must be introduced before we can state the theorem. At any NE a price if defined for each good, by (6). There is also defined, for each trader, a *marginal utility for spending money*, associated with the constraint

$$\sum_{j=1}^{m} b_j{}^i \leqslant a^i_{m+1}. \qquad (14) = (5)$$

In fact, let $\lambda^i \geqslant 0$ be the Lagrangian multiplier for (14), i.e., the number

---

[14] If credit is allowed, we would need to impose a negative utility for negative holdings of this "paper" money, or else the bidding would become unbounded.

(perhaps not unique) such that the choice of b^i would remain optimal for i if the constraint (14) were dropped and the maximand $u^i(x^i)$ replaced by[15]

$$u^i(x^i) + \lambda^i \left(a^i_{m+1} - \sum_{j=1}^m b_j^i \right).$$

Thus, λ^i is a kind of "shadow price" for cash; it is in general different for each trader, and different for the same trader at different NEs. Of course, when the constraint (14) is slack, as it may well be if money has some value of its own, the corresponding λ^i will be zero. We note that in a symmetric NE the shadow prices for cash can be taken to be the same for all members of the same type, so we can use a t-vector $\lambda(k)$ to denote them all (rather than a tk-vector).

Theorem 2   *Let $b(k)$ represent a symmetric NE for the variant II economy Γ_k, as described above, and let $p(k)$ and $\lambda(k)$ represent the associated price and shadow price vectors. Suppose that for some increasing subsequence $\{k_v\}$ we have $p(k_v) \to p^*$ and $\lambda(k_v) \to 0$. Then the prices $(p^*, 1)$ are competitive for Γ_1, and indeed for each Γ_k. That is, an allocation $x = \{x_j^i\}$ exists such that $x \geqslant 0$, $\bar{x} = \bar{a}$ and, for each i, $u^i(x^i)$ is maximal subject to the constraint*

$$\sum_{j=1}^m p_j^*(x_j^i - a_j^i) + x^i_{m+1} - a^i_{m+1} \leqslant 0.$$

The condition $\lambda \to 0$ in this theorem means that the spending limits (14) are not binding in the limit — everyone eventually has "enough" money. This means in turn that money must have had some intrinsic value for every trader, except that there might be totally saturated individuals who no longer care whether they spend or save.[16] Thus, we can begin to address the larger question of how to *select* a suitable commodity to serve as a medium of exchange, with the social aim of achieving or approaching a competitive and hence Pareto-efficient solution. Other properties of the money commodity, like separability and additivity, appear to have some bearing on the uniqueness of the NE; we intend to pursue these questions.

[15] When (14) is dropped, it is possible for x^i_{m+1} to go negative; to prevent this from confusing the definition of λ^i (in the no-credit models), it suffices to impose the extra constraint $x^i_{m+1} \geqslant 0$, noting that the strategies b^h for $h \neq i$, on which x^i_{m+1} in part depends, are for the time being considered to be fixed.

[16] In the "credit" version of variant II, there is a similar theorem with the condition $\lambda(k_v) \to 0$ replaced by one that states that in the limit no trader is "in the red."

REFERENCES

1. Aumann, R. J., "Disadvantageous Monopolies," *Journal of Economic Theory*, February 1973, **6**, 1–11.
2. Aumann, R. J., "Values of Markets with a Continuum of Traders," *Econometrica*, July 1975, **43**, 611–646.
3. Aumann, R. J., and L. S. Shapley, *Values of Non-Atomic Games*, Princeton, New Jersey: Princeton Univ. Press, 1974.
4. Debreu, G., and H. E. Scarf, "A Limit Theorem on the Core of an Economy," *International Economic Review*, September 1963, **4**, 235–246.
5. Drèze, J., J. J. Gabszewicz, D. Schmeidler, and K. Vind, "Cores and Prices in an Exchange Economy with an Atomless Sector," *Econometrica*, November 1972, **40**, 1091–1108.
6. Gabszewicz, J. J., and J. H. Drèze, "Syndicates of Traders in an Exchange Economy," in H. W. Kuhn and G. P. Szegö, eds., *Differential Games and Related Topics*, Amsterdam: North-Holland Publ., 1971, 399–414.
7. Gabszewicz, J. J., and J. F. Mertens, "An Equivalence Theorem for the Core of an Economy whose Atoms are not 'Too' Big," *Econometrica*, September 1971, **39**, 713–721.
8. Hart, S., "Symmetric Solutions of Some Production Economies," *International Journal of Game Theory*, 1973, **2**, 53–62.
9. Hart, S., "Formation of Cartels in Large Markets," *Journal of Economic Theory*, April 1974, **7**, 453–466.
10. Levitan, R. E., and M. Shubik, "Noncooperative Equilibria and Strategy Spaces in an Oligopolistic Market," in H. W. Kuhn and G. P. Szegö, eds., *Differential Games and Related Topics*, Amsterdam: North-Holland Publ., 1971, 429–447.
11. Levitan, R. E., and M. Shubik, "Price Duopoly and Capacity Constraints," *International Economic Review*, February 1972, **13**, 111–122.
12. Mayberry, J. P., J. F. Nash, and M. Shubik, "A Comparison of Treatments of a Duopoly Situation," *Econometrica*, January 1953, **21**, 141–154.
13. Rockafellar, R. T., *Convex Analysis*, Princeton, New Jersey: Princeton Univ. Press, 1970.
14. Shapley, L. S., "Let's Block 'Block'," *Econometrica*, November 1973, **41**, 1201–1202.
15. Shapley, L. S., and M. Shubik, "Pure Competition, Coalitional Power, and Fair Division," *International Economic Review*, October 1969, **10**, 337–362.
16. Shapley, L. S., and M. Shubik, "Price Strategy Oligopoly with Product Variation," *Kyklos*, 1969, **22**, 30–44.
17. Shapley, L. S., and M. Shubik, "On the Core of an Economic System with Externalities," *American Economic Review*, September 1969, **59**, 678–684.
18. Shapley, L. S., and M. Shubik, "The Assignment Game I: The Core," *International Journal of Game Theory*, 1972, **1**, 111–130.
19. Shitovitz, B. "Oligopoly in Markets with a Continuum of Traders," *Econometrica*, May 1973, **41**, 467–501.
20. Shubik, M., *Strategy and Market Structure*, New York: Wiley, 1959.
21. Shubik, M., "A Further Comparison of Some Models of Duopoly," *Western Economic Journal*, September 1968, **6**, 260–276.
22. Shubik, M., "A Theory of Money and Financial Institutions: Fiat Money and Noncooperative Equilibrium in a Closed Economy," *International Journal of Game Theory*, 1972, **1**, 243–268.

23. Shubik, M., "A Theory of Money and Financial Institutions: Commodity Money, Oligopology, Credit and Bankruptcy in a General Equilibrium Model," *Western Economic Journal*, March 1973, 11, 24–38.
24. Shubik, M., and G. L. Thompson, "Games of Economic Survival," *Naval Research Logistics Quarterly*, 1959, 6, 111–123.
25. Shubik, M., and W. Whitt, "Fiat Money in an Economy with One Non-durable Good and No Credit," in A. Blaquiere, ed., *Topics in Differential Games*, Amsterdam: North-Holland Publ., 1973, 401–448.

Discussion

ROBERT W. ROSENTHAL

Northwestern University

Dr. Shapley has presented us with a tantalizing glimpse of a rich new approach to microeconomic modeling, which, from all appearances, will provide the basis for many economist-hours of study. His and Professor Shubik's criticisms of the Walrasian model (see also Professor Shubik's series of Cowles Foundation papers concerning money and financial institutions) are compelling, and this new approach promises insights into areas previously inaccessible through the Walrasian model. (That something new can still be done with Edgeworth boxes is in itself a surprise for me.) Of most interest, in my opinion, is the potential through multiperiod extensions of this approach for improvements in our understanding of the complex roles of financial intermediaries in economic systems.

A brief word is perhaps in order regarding the seemingly unrealistic nature of bids in this class of models, in which players offer a stated amount of "gold" in a market without being able to specify a lower bound on the number of units of the commodity that they will accept in return (and similarly on the supply side). One should keep in mind that in adopting the NE solution concept, no player wishes to alter his bids given what he does receive for his gold. In that regard, at least equilibrium strategies resemble more traditional demand schedules. In addition, one could conceive of variations in the model in which disequilibrium strategies would also resemble supply and demand schedules, but this would seem to lead back to the Walrasian equilibrium idea.

Turning to externalities, I take some issue with Dr. Shapley on his apparent view that the economic system itself may be viewed as a kind of externality. While this is indeed a semantic point, it seems to me that it is useful to separate the phenomenon of an individual's preferences depending on more than just his own consumption or of the production possibilities of a firm being altered through the activities of others on the one hand from the influence of an individual's supply or demand decisions on the terms of trade in the economy on the other hand. "Pecuniary externalities" look a lot like imperfect competition.

Finally, I should like to point out that the presence of externalities of the traditional variety may cause additional problems in these models. Consider the following example. There are two goods and three individuals in an economy under the rules of variant II. The endowments of the three individuals are $a^1 = (1, 0)$, $a^2 = (0, 1)$, and $a^3 = (1, 1)$. The externalities arise in that individuals' preferences may depend on the consumption of others. Specifically,

$$u^1 = x_2^{\,1},$$
$$u^2 = (x_1^{\,2} + x_1^{\,1})^{1/2}(x_2^{\,2} + x_2^{\,1})^{1/2},$$
$$u^3 = (x_1^{\,3} + x_1^{\,2})^{1/2}(x_2^{\,3} + x_2^{\,2})^{1/2}.$$

Although these functions are seemingly well behaved, no NE exist. To see this, note that player 1 is a strategic dummy, having no gold to bid and being compelled to offer up all of his endowment of good 1.

Case 1 $b^2 = b^3 = 0$. Good 1 disappears from the market. Player 3 can do better by bidding any positive amount less than 1.

Case 2 $b^2 > 0$, $b^3 > 0$. Player 3 can improve his position by bidding zero. He thereby loses good 1 to player 2, which does not affect his utility level, and gains gold from player 1, which improves his position.

Case 3 $b^2 = 0$. $b^3 > 0$. Player 3 can improve his position by bidding a smaller positive amount.

Case 4 $b^2 > 0$, $b^3 = 0$. Player 2 can improve his position by bidding a smaller positive amount.

The lack of existence of NE in this example does not appear to be merely a technical problem. The utility functions seem to be well behaved (indeed, can be changed quite a bit with no NE appearing) and the kinds of assumptions needed in Theorem 1 do not appear to be violated.

V

Measurements of Externalities

Possible interdependencies of consumption and production functions are so various and empirically so difficult to uncover that many models of economic processes involving externalities assume simply that they do not exist or that the externality is identifiable in simple terms. This simple and unrealistic assumption most often impairs the operationality and normative prescriptive value of economic models involved with policy recommendation for efficient resource allocation. At the conference, the problems involving measurement of externalities are not taken lightly. Eleven participants are involved in this aspect of discussion either as speakers or as discussants.

Cicchetti and Smith propose a general methodology for accommodating and measuring congestion costs related to quality deterioration so that the costs associated with it might be accounted for in public allocation decisions. The general model is applied to a specific example: low density or wilderness recreation.

In the general methodology of Cicchetti and Smith, each individual is assumed to have a utility function expressed in terms of attributes or characteristics. Each good or service is assumed to provide some or all of these attributes in various proportions, and the consumer's choice problem is to maximize utility subject to an income constraint and the attributes' relationships to these goods and services. The value of the good to the individual is directly related to the attributes it possesses. Accordingly, congestion and attendant quality deterioration of a particular service flow will inevitably reduce the individual's willingness to pay for the good or service. Such reductions are reflections of marginal congestion costs.

In the experimental design, ordinary and Aitken generalized least squares are used to evaluate their model and to estimate the individual willingness to pay functions. The overall findings of the paper suggest that it is possible to measure nontime congestion effects. Moreover, it would seem that such measures are essential for the analysis of the management and allocation of "open access" environmental resources.

De Vany investigates the reaction of individuals to airport noise. He views the attempt of psychoaccousticians to devise a measure of noise as basically one of devising a utility indicator that will rank noises in terms of their disutility. Using this as a starting point, he then investigates the properties of a number of noise measures currently in use in terms of utility theory. Several models are used in an attempt to explain the evaluation of noise by individuals as revealed by their actions in the real estate market.

The data consist of the 1970 Census Survey of Housing in Dallas, Texas. These data include the census block average of owner estimated value of housing, and such characteristics of the census blocks as the average age of housing, number of rooms, percentage of homes that are air conditioned, and so on. To these data have been added distance to the central business district, distance to the airport, the NEF value for the block, information regarding the occurrence of direct overflights and the altitudes at which they occur, and the zone of the block.

The only region where the airport exerts a net positive effect on value is from six to eight miles away. At lesser distances the positive effect is either neutralized or more than offset. There are real benefits of reducing noise. Reducing noise may be worth more than it costs, in which case it should be done irrespective of the fact that some persons gain more than they lose because of the presence of the airport.

Haurin and Tolley present the Alonso—Muth—Wingo model which explains movement of households to the suburbs due to such factors as a rising real income level or falling transportation costs. Implications of the model with the changes in property taxes are also presented.

Another application of the model presented is the question of the efficiency of metropolitan governments. In the empirical work, the welfare cost of a metropolitan government that provides all services and allows no "escape" is compared to the welfare cost of the city—suburban model. Chicago and its suburbs are used as an example in the empirical estimates of social costs.

The example taken to be the public good in the model is education where national external effects are ignored. Thus, there are two distortions, the property tax in the city where full Tiebout adjustment will not occur, and a legal constraint creating a distortion in consumption of public services.

Sudit and Whitcomb present a general framework for the estimation of externality production functions. They consider specifications of alternative generalized joint product processes, and the possibilities of input allocation among salable commodities and externalities.

Apart from estimation techniques for multivariate models, the issue of specification of proper functional forms is discussed. It is shown that for joint product externality models "conventional" production function forms (such as Cobb—Douglas, CES, Homothetic, and CRES) may be even more restrictive than in ordinary cases. The highly nonrestrictive forms (e.g., additive and multiplicative nonhomogenous types) are thus recommended.

Two methods for the empirical estimation of profit maximization and socially optimal solutions are suggested. The data requirements for the respective methods and their relative merits for policy-making purposes are also reviewed.

The Measurement of Individual Congestion Costs: An Economic Application to Wilderness Recreation

CHARLES J. CICCHETTI

University of Wisconsin

V. KERRY SMITH

State University of New York, Binghamton

I. INTRODUCTION

Increasing professional and popular attention is being devoted to a variety of externalities, including pollution of the air and water, and urban congestion. As Rothenberg [13] notes, highway traffic jams, airport crowding, and public transit overcrowding are all forms of social congestion, although their effects are felt in a variety of ways. Many such examples of congestion externalities can be described in terms of the quality deterioration of the services involved. While many of the measures of this deterioration have been related to time in some respect, there are a large array of cases in which increases in waiting time or total

The research reported in this chapter was conducted as a part of the National Environments Program at Resources for the Future. Thanks are due Robert Lucas and George Stankey for providing the names of users of the area. Thanks are also due Anthony C. Fisher, John V. Krutilla and Joseph J. Seneca, Eugene Smolensky, and Charles Metcalf for helpful comments on earlier drafts of this work. We would also like to thank David Bradford for most constructive comments on our paper during the SIU Conference. A detailed account of the use of this research for management problems is available in C. J. Cicchetti and V. K. Smith, *The Costs of Congestion: An Econometric Analysis of Wilderness Recreation* (Cambridge, Mass: Ballinger, 1976).

servicing time will not provide reasonable proxies for this quality deterioration.

The purpose of this paper is to propose a general methodology for accommodating and measuring congestion-related quality deterioration. Our model is a straightforward extension of Lancaster's [9] framework. In this scheme an individual is assumed to have a utility function expressed in terms of attributes or characteristics. Each good or service is assumed to provide some or all of these attributes in various proportions, and the consumer's choice problem is to maximize utility subject to an income constraint and the attributes' relationships to these goods and services. Within this model, congestion and the attendant quality deterioration of a particular service flow becomes a reduction (perhaps elimination) of the service's attributes. The value of the good to the individual is directly related to which attributes it possesses.

Accordingly with quality deterioration there is an inevitable reduction in the individual's willingness to pay for the good or service. Such reductions are reflections of marginal congestion costs.[1]

In some cases a model has been developed in which congestion costs add to the marginal private costs of providing the good or service. However, this approach can lead one to conclude that congestion for a given good or service has the same effect on each individual. Such a conclusion would be erroneous. Quality deteriorations associated with congestion are dependent on the preferences of each individual. Some consumers will have greater (or less) preference for a subset of their attributes. In such cases the effects of congestion measured though reduced prices will, *ceteris paribus*, be perceptibly greater than others. Therefore, a definition that treats congestion as serving to increase the costs of obtaining constant quality services flows, while analytically correct may not be operationally useful. In some cases, it may be misleading.

The analysis that follows will discuss the effects of congestion in terms of the reductions of each individual's willingness to pay. This general model is applied to a specific example: low-density or wilderness recreation. The activities that fall within this framework are primarily hiking and camping with the associated activities of fishing and viewing wildlife and scenery in a primeval setting. Such activities require a combination of solitude and a sizeable amount of underdeveloped lands (largely of the character mandated under the terms of the Wilderness Act of 1964). While the methodology we propose is general and therefore can be applied to a variety of problems, it is also the case that the problem of congestion in low-density recreation is one of the most important of current environmental concerns.

Use data for the National Forest Wilderness Areas suggest that use of these facilities increased by more than 350% over the 12-year period from 1947 to

---

[1] Note that there are two components of congestion costs, those imposed by other users on the marginal user and those imposed by the marginal user on inframarginal users. The reduction referred to in the text is an example for the former.

1959 (see Fisher and Krutilla [8] for more discussion). Moreover there is additional evidence to believe that this pattern of growth in low-density recreation will continue for some time. The Cicchetti *et al.*, [5] study of outdoor recreation participation patterns suggests that remote camping (one type of low-density recreational activity) is a luxury good over certain high income ranges. With growing income as well as growth in complementary forms of outdoor recreation rapid growth in the demand for low-density recreation is expected. In a more recent study of the preferences of wilderness users, Cicchetti notes that "the strength of the 'associations' presented in this analysis should make rational and sober planners and policy makers realize that recent increases in wilderness use are very likely to continue into the future" [3, p. 170].

The pressure of increased demands raises inevitable questions associated with the allocation of resources to this form of low-density recreation. There are presently about ten million acres of land within the National Wilderness System and about another forty million that are suitable for inclusion under some low-density status. Thus the problem is now and will likely continue to be an important one.

Section II develops the Lancaster model for our case and discusses the characteristics of low-density recreation that are most important to users. In Section III we outline the experimental design and sampling procedure for evaluating our model. Section IV presents the ordinary least squares and Aitken generalized least squares estimates of individual willingness to pay functions. The final section discusses the conclusions from the analysis and the role of further research.

II. A GENERALIZED MODEL FOR THE MEASUREMENT OF CONGESTION EFFECTS

As we have indicated above economists have traditionally treated the congestion problem as one associated with waiting times or queues at public facilities. Hence a natural measure of the effects of congestion is available in the amount of time spent in waiting or the addition to the total time required to engage in a particular activity. An example of such analysis is Nichols, Smolensky, and Tideman who not that [11, p. 312]:

> Waiting time does allocate public services, rationing them, as would money prices, according to the tastes, income and opportunity costs of consumers.

More generally congestion affects the quality of a service flow and that quality deterioration can be evidenced in any number of ways. Recent adaptions to consumer theory (summarized by Cicchetti and Smith [6]) suggest that there are a variety of ways in which we might include the congestion externality into the model of individual choice. We should note at the outset that all of these approaches are observationally equivalent in terms of the restrictions they imply for the willingness to pay functions we estimate. Accordingly the selection of any one from this set will ultimately be made on the basis of convenience and simplicity.

It is also reasonable to inquire into the need for the explicit statement of one model if all possible selections imply the same general willingness to pay relationship. The response here is simply that it forces the analyst specifically to take account of the decision making process involved. We have selected the Lancaster [10] model for its inuitive appeal and ability to utilize the behavioral research of Stankey [18].

Consider the following formalization of this model in which the individual seeks to maximize utility stated in Eq. (1) subject to a budget constraint and a set of technical relationships relating goods to attributes as in (2) and (3) respectively:

$$U = U(A_1, A_2, A_3, \ldots, A_K) \tag{1}$$

$$Y = P^T X \tag{2}$$

$$A = BX \tag{3}$$

where U is the utility, $A^T = [A_1, A_2, \ldots, A_K]$, a $1 \times K$ vector of values of the K attributes important to individual utility, X is an $N \times 1$ vector of quantities of each of N goods and services, P an $N \times 1$ vector of prices for each of the N goods and services, B a $K \times N$ matrix of technical coefficients describing the relationship between attributes and goods, and Y individual income. In order to illustrate how the model can be used for the congestion problem, assume we have a case with two characteristics and three goods. Then eqs. (1)–(3) could be rewritten as

$$U = U(A_1, A_2) \tag{4a}$$

$$Y = P_1 x_1 + P_2 x_2 + P_3 x_3 \tag{4b}$$

$$\begin{bmatrix} A_1 \\ A_2 \end{bmatrix} = \begin{bmatrix} b_{11} & b_{12} & b_{13} \\ b_{21} & b_{22} & b_{23} \end{bmatrix} \begin{bmatrix} x_1 \\ x_2 \\ x_3 \end{bmatrix} \tag{4c}$$

Graphically we can represent the individual's maximization problem as in Figure 1. Each ray from the origin describes the mix of characteristics provided by each good. The efficiency frontier BCD is defined by the goods' prices (i.e., P_1, P_2, and P_3 respectively) and the individual's income. That is, if all of Y were spent on x_1, then the individual would necessarily receive $b_{11}(Y/P_1)$ of A_1 and $b_{21}(Y/P_1)$ of A_2. These points designate the vertical and horizontal coordinates

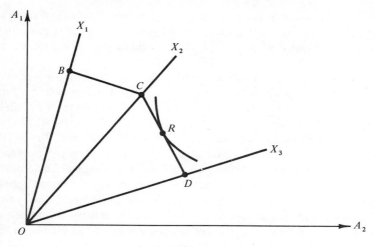

Figure 1

of the point B in Figure 1. Similarly the coordinates of C and D are $(b_{22}(Y/P_2)$, $b_{12}(Y/P_2))$ and $(b_{23}(Y/P_3)$, $b_{13}(Y/P_3))$. The nature of individual preferences will determine which point on this efficient locus will be selected. In order to illustrate simply the relationship between the price an individual would be willing to pay for either of these goods and the attributes they provide, assume the individual's equilibirum point is a facet optimum, such as R in Figure 1. Since each facet is a convex linear sum of the two extreme points in attribute space (Lancaster [10, pp. 37–47]), individual equilibrium involving the tangency of the indifference curve to the facet implies that we can directly relate the goods' prices and the attributes' shadow prices. Let (5) describe the facet CD, on which the individual selects his equilibrium mix of attributes at R; then we can use this information to define P_1 and P_2 in terms of the technical coefficients, measures of attributes' value, and income as follows:

$$\lambda_1 A_1 + \lambda_2 A_2 = c \qquad \text{where} \quad c = \text{constant.} \tag{5}$$

Substituting for A_1 and A_2 using the coordinates of points C and D two expressions for the facet are derived:

$$\lambda_1 b_{12} + \lambda_2 b_{22} = (c/Y)P_2 \tag{6}$$

$$\lambda_1 b_{13} + \lambda_2 b_{23} = (c/Y)P_3; \tag{7}$$

if (6) and (7) are solved λ_1 and λ_2 the "shadow prices" of the characteristics A_1 and A_2 are determined. Alternatively, one can solve for P_2 and P_3 in terms of the extent to which each provides the attributes of interest (A_1 and A_2). Equations (6) and (7) illustrate how an individual's valuation of the attributes relates to income and the prices of the goods involved. Similarly, if these prices were not given, then the individual's demand price (willingness to pay) could be related to the amounts of each attribute a single unit of each good or service provided.

This simple case demonstrates as we have already noted that it is reasonable to define the individual willingness to pay for a wilderness recreational experience as a function of the amounts of each attribute provided. Consequently measurements of the effects of variations in these attributes on individual willingness to pay and the relationship between the levels of congestion and the relevant attributes provides the information necessary to measure a congestion cost for individuals. Before proceeding we should note that Rosen's [12] recent work noting the importance of identification in hedonic pricing relationships is not strictly relevant to our problem. His case refers to prices resulting from the actions of demanders and suppliers, determined in the market place. Our direct solicitation of the preferences of users (to be explained in more detail in Section III) records the preferences of only one of these groups. Consequently the relationships we estimate are to be distinguished from reduced-form hedonic price indexes, which reflect both demand and supply influences.

Operationalizing this result requires that we define the characteristics or attributes of wilderness recreation that are important for individual satisfaction and are affected by the level of use or a given recreational area. Wilderness recreation is an activity in which the individual seeks the interaction he has with others. That is, each individual generally engages in the activity with a group he may select (e.g., family or friends) but does not wish to interact with others. Solitude, which can approximately be measured in terms of avoiding interaction with individuals outside your control, has been found to be an important attribute of wildnerness or low-density recreation.

In 1969 Stankey surveyed the users of four wilderness areas: the Bob Marshall Wilderness in Montana, the Bridger's Wilderness in Wyoming, the High Uintas Primitive Area in Utah, and the Boundary Waters Canoe Area in Minnesota. Of all the users in his sample, 82% felt that "solitude — not seeing many other people except those in your own party" was desirable [18, pp. 100—101]. Moreover, Stankey's data suggest that encounters with other parties provide an operational means of measuring disruptions to solitude.

While it is true that the impact depends on which parties were met and where, a disaggregated measure of such meetings performs reasonably well as an indicator of intrusion on solitude. We shall hypothesize that encounters on the trail and in camp affect an individual's willingness to pay for a given wilderness experience. This hypothesis follows from the Lancaster model previously developed. Consider a change in the amount of solitude provided to a recreationist in a given trip to a wilderness area. Such a change will be measured in terms of the number of encounters experienced during the trip. If A_1 represents solitude, then increased use of any wilderness area in a given time interval will increase the likelihood of encounters experienced by a particular party (Stankey [18], pp. 106–108]) and thereby reduce the perceived solitude. In terms of Figure 1, if X_3 measures the amount of wilderness recreation consumed, then such increases in use intensity and attendant effects on solitude can be represented by a clockwise pivoting of OX_3. In terms of Equation (7) the quantity of A_1 provided by a unit of X_3 (i.e., b_{13}) is reduced. Hence the demand price or willingness to pay (P_3) for wilderness recreation will also be less than before the change in the attribute (solitude) provided.

Accordingly, an individual's willingness to pay for wilderness recreation can be specified as a function of income, the quantity of the good consumed, and the attributes or characteristics of that recreational experience, as

$$wp_i = wp_i(q_i, y_i, A_{1i}, \ldots, A_{ni}) \tag{8}$$

where wp_i is the individual's willingness to pay, q_i the quantity of wilderness recreation, y_i the ith individual's income, and $A_{1i}, \ldots, A_{ni}$ the attributes of q_i's service flow.

III. EXPERIMENTAL DESIGN AND SAMPLING

Our research strategy employed a questionnaire distributed to wilderness users to obtain their willingness to pay for a variety of hypothetical experiences. Some consideration must be given the general issue that any attempt to determine directly an individual's preferences is likely to be confronted with biases. Samuelson has noted that "it is in the selfish interest of each person to give *false* signs to pretend to have less interest" [14, p. 389] when he feels that he will have to pay for the good or service according to his revelations.

Equally important, if the individual believes that his answers will not be used as a basis of pricing, there may be incentives for him to overstate his enjoyment so that more of the good or service will be provided.

More recently Bohm has expressed an alternative view. He suggests that [1, pp. 59–60]:

> Once it is clear that there is no open-and-shut case for the individual when considering under- or over-statement of his preferences, the choice of strategy may well seem so complicated to him that he prefers to state his true maximum willingness to pay. Only an actual test of alternative approaches to estimating the demand for public goods could reveal the true state of affairs in this respect. But one important argument in favor of the hypothesis that people will abstain from the complicated calculations

of optimal strategy inherent in our approach is that most people simply won't find such calculations worthwhile, considering the small individual sums usually involved.

In a series of follow-up experiments Bohm [2] examined five approaches for determination of willingness to pay for public goods. The schemes of interest range from soliciting individual willingness to pay with knowledge that payments will then be based upon the response to soliciting the information without tying payments to them. Bohm's findings indicate that none of the approaches (each applied to a random sample of consumers) exhibited significantly different average maximum willingnesses to pay.

The approach we have used for questioning in our study corresponds to one of those examined by Bohm in that each respondent was assured that his revealed maximum willingness to pay would not be used to alter existing pricing practices. While Bohn's findings would seem to indicate that our method does not provide significantly different responses than several alternative approaches, there remains no definitive assurance that the revealed willingness to pay reflects the actual level of satisfaction of each individual repondent.

Finally, the primary concern of our work is with the change in the level of willingness to pay in response to congestion. Hence the absolute level can be biased and our objectives accomplished if individual respondents react without bias to the attributes changes that congestion will precipitate. Thus the traditional nonrevelation problem may not be as serious for our application as it would be for others.

Turning to the experimental design, approximately 600 questionnaires were mailed to a sample of present users of the Spanish Peaks Primitive Area in Montana. The sample was compiled by Robert Lucas and George Stankey of the Inermountain Forest and Range and Experiment Station and is representative of the actual users of the area in the summer of 1970. Each individual in the sample was asked to respond to a set of hypothetical recreational experiences in the area.

The primary question that had to be answered in the design of this survey consisted of the selection of a set of recreational experiences that would permit the estimation of an individual willingness to pay function. Assume that the model may be written as

$$Y = X\beta + Z\gamma + U \tag{9}$$

where Y is a $T \times 1$ vector of observations on the regressand (i.e., willingness to pay or some transformation of it); X a $T \times K$ matrix of values for each K factors under the control of the experinenter; Z a $T \times L$ matrix of observations for those factors, L, in number which are not subject to experimental control; β a $K \times 1$ coefficient vector; γ a $L \times 1$ coefficient vector; and U a $T \times 1$ vector of stochastic errors. The ordinary least squares (hereafter OLS) estimator of this model is given by

$$\begin{bmatrix} \beta \\ \gamma \end{bmatrix}_{OLS} = \begin{bmatrix} X^T X & X^T Z \\ Z^T X & Z^T Z \end{bmatrix}^{-1} \begin{bmatrix} X^T Y \\ Z^T Y \end{bmatrix} \tag{10}$$

Assuming that the two sets of regressors are orthogonal, the variance—covariance matrix for the OLS estimates of β may be written as

$$\underset{\beta_{OLS}}{\Sigma} = \sigma^2 (X^T X)^{-1} \tag{11}$$

where $\sigma^2 = E(u_i^2)$ and u_i is the ith element of U with $E(u_i) = 0$.

Experimental design addresses the issue of how to select the design points (in our case the wilderness experiences) from the set of feasible values. If we assume that there are t such admissible values, with a_t the ith of them, then $X^T X$ may be written as

$$X^T X = \sum_{i=1}^{t} n_i a_i^T a_i \tag{12}$$

where n_i is the number of times a_i is asked and $\Sigma_{i=1}^{t} n_i = N$ (sample size). Thus the problem is one of selecting the n_i so as to optimize some objective function subject to constraints. Conlisk and Watts [7] spell out the primary considerations in this selection process. The objective function is usually expressed in terms of the estimated coefficients' covariance structure (given in (11) in our case), and the constraint in terms of the cost of each design point (a_i).

For the present problem the unit costs are equal for each design point. Therefore, our objective function may be expressed as minimizing the variance of the estimated β. Finally the range of values for each of the factors of interest has been bounded by experience with wilderness recreation patterns. As a result of previous work of Stankey, we shall specify the control factors for our experimental design as the average number of trail encounters per day in the wilderness, the number of nights in which there was at least one camp encounter, and finally the length of stay of the wilderness visit. In order to restrict the number of possible combinations of these three variables, the range of values for the number of trail encounters was selected to be from zero to three. For the nights of camp encounters, it was zero to four, and the length of stay ranged from one to five days.

Consistency in the construction of these hypothetical wilderness experiments required that the nights of camp encounters be bounded by the value implied by the length of stay variable. Consequently, there were 60 possible combinations or design points. These combinations were randomly assigned to each individual in the sample, with each respondent required to answer five independent possibilities.

The rationale for this assignment pattern stems from several considerations. First we do not know the precise form of the willingness to pay relationship, hence a priori selection between first-order and second-order models cannot be made. In addition, our design points must reflect consistency between the length-of-trip variable and the nights-of-camp-encounter variable. Finally, it was not possible to anticipate the response pattern to the mailed questionnaires.

Five independent responses were solicited from each individual for several reasons. It is reasonable to suspect that each error term u_i will not have constant variance for all individuals within our survey. Consequently ordinary least squares estimation of the willingness to pay functions will not be the most efficient estimator. A more efficient technique would make use of the differences in the variance of the error across observations in the estimation process. This statement, of course, assumes that the variance of each u_i is known, which is not the case. These must be estimated. The five observations upon each respondent are used to do so.

IV. ESTIMATED WILLINGNESS TO PAY FUNCTIONS

Over 40% of the questionnaires were returned after two mailings. A number of these were necessarily omitted from our final sample because the individual respondents did not or could not answer the questions.[2] The remainder (195 individuals, each with five responses) were used to estimate the above mentioned willingness to pay relationship. Several functional forms and a variety of

[2] Over 40% of those sampled responded to our mailings. However, of these respondents, approximately one-third did not answer our questions concerning their willingness to pay for certain wilderness experiences. Many indicated that they were incapable of quantifying their value for wilderness recreation. Others did not answer and did not indicate reasons. However, for the most part, all respondents indicated their economic and demographic characterisitics.

Consequently, in order to examine whether there are economic and demographic characteristics that affect an individual wilderness user's ability to quantify his or her willingness to pay, we estimated a linear probability function, coding all those who answered the *WP* question with a one and a zero otherwise.

Our estimated equation indicates that while none of the characteristics are strong causal factors, age and weeks of paid vacation do seem to influence this probability.

$$\text{Prob} = \quad .574 \quad +.013Eds \quad -.004Ag \quad -.002Fy \quad +.017Wv \quad +.067Sx$$
$$(3.426) \quad (1.201) \quad (-1.881) \quad (-.569) \quad (1.989) \quad (1.125)$$

where Eds = years of schooling, Ag = age in years, Fy = income in thousands of dollars, Wv = weeks of paid vacation, Sx = sex (1 = male, 0 = female), and $\bar{R}^2$ = .0210. The numbers in parentheses are t-ratios, testing the null hypothesis of no association. The low $\bar{R}^2$ cannot be interpreted in the usual fashion since it does not have a maximum value of 1 in models containing dichotomous dependent variables (see Smith and Cicchetti [15]).

TABLE 1

Definition of Variables

Name	Description
WBP	Individual willingness to pay per trip when the encounters are with backpacker (hiker) parties, measured in dollars
WHP	Individual willingness to pay per trip when the encounters are with horse parties, measured in dollars
LN	Length of stay of the trip in days
TN	Number of encounters on the trail per day
CN	Number of nights of camp encounters
FY	Income of the household in thousands of dollars
WV	Weeks of paid vacation of the individual
SX	Sex of the individual, dichotomous variable (i.e., 1 = male, 0 = female)
ED	Education of the individual in years of schooling
AG	Age of the individual in years

variables were pretested using ordinary least squares estimation. In what follows we shall summarize our results with linear and semilog specifications of the willingness to pay functions.

Table 1 defines the variables used in this analysis. Table 2 provides a sample of the linear specifications considered in evaluating the relationship between willingness to pay and encounters with backpacking parties. The first equation (2.1) in the table presents the relationship with all variables entered. Through a sequential process we have examined alternative combinations of omitted variables and interactions of the variables noted. Equations (2.2)–(2.5) are a sample of these. Equation (2.6) is considered our "best" equation for this specification.

Recent research examining the properties of sequential estimation procedures, such as the one we have used, suggests that the question of whether one should rely on statistical testing to discriminate between specifications of a model (in terms of the inclusion or exclusion of variables) is as yet unresolved (see Wallace and Ashar [20] for a discussion of these issues). Suffice it to say that this is not the place to debate this topic and our results do not depend appreciably on this decision.

For our final equation with the linear specification, all variables have the signs we anticipated, and with the exception of income are significantly different from zero at the 95% level. It would appear from our estimates that camp encounters have a greater deleterious effect upon individual willingness to pay for wilderness recreation at the Spanish Peaks than do trail encounters. However statistical testing of this proposition (i.e., $H_0 : \alpha_{CN} - \alpha_{TN} = 0$) failed to reject the null hypothesis.

TABLE 2
Linear Willingness to Pay for Encounters with Backpacking Parties (OLS)[a]

Variable	Equations					
	(2.1)	(2.2)	(2.3)	(2.4)	(2.5)	(2.6)
LN	5.646	5.130	4.511	4.303	5.016	5.163
	(1.167)	(5.297)	(0.980)	(0.933)	(5.180)	(5.309)
LN^2	−0.079	−	0.091	0.131	−	−
	(−0.109)		(0.133)	(0.190)		
TN	−2.297	−2.299	−1.809	−1.797	−1.862	−1.804
	(−0.676)	(−0.677)	(−1.864)	(−1.849)	(−1.925)	(−1.856)
TN^2	0.161	0.162	−	−	−	−
	(0.151)	(0.152)				
CN	−4.136	−4.043	−2.342	−2.338	−2.283	−2.350
	(−1.492)	(−1.534)	(−2.321)	(−2.313)	(−2.272)	(−2.326)
CN^2	0.521	0.495	−	−	−	−
	(0.685)	(1.304)				
FY	−1.290	−1.290	0.211	0.262	0.106	0.256
	(−1.977)	(−1.977)	(1.251)	(1.567)	(0.635)	(1.575)
FY^2	0.043	0.043	−	−	−	−
	(2.239)	(2.240)				
SX	5.615	5.611	6.423	7.321	5.867	7.287
	(2.360)	(2.360)	(2.721)	(3.122)	(2.469)	(3.110)
ED	0.582	0.581	0.895	−	0.672	−
	(1.305)	(1.304)	(2.036)		(1.507)	
AG	0.263	0.263	−	−	0.250	−
	(3.028)	(3.029)			(2.875)	
WV	1.055	1.056	1.018	1.078	1.020	1.073
	(3.642)	(3.647)	(3.502)	(3.723)	(3.522)	(3.708)
Int.	−10.866	−10.171	0.501	−5.598	−20.930	−6.609
	(−0.994)	(−1.145)	(0.051)	(−0.714)	(−2.844)	(−1.435)
$\bar{R}^2$	0.064	0.065	0.040	0.051	0.062	0.052
F	6.50	0.710	0.603	0.848	9.04	9.90

[a]The numbers in parentheses are student t-ratios for the null hypothesis H_0: $\alpha_i = 0$. $\bar{R}^2$ is the coefficient of determination adjusted for degrees of freedom. F is the F-statistic for the test of the overall relationship.

Table 3 reports the estimated willingness to pay functions using the semilog specification for encounters with hikers and riders with the logarithm of willingness to pay as the dependent variable. Once again we have included a sample from the trial equations, indicating the pretesting and sequential process utilized to derive final equations. In this case the final specification is numbered as (3.7) in the table. The variables that enter these final equations are essentially the same as with the linear form. The length of trip variable (LN) admits a quadratic effect upon the logarithm of willingness to pay.

TABLE 3
Semilog Willingness to Pay Functions for Encounters with Backpacking Parties (OLS)[a]

	Equations						
Variable	(3.1)	(3.2)	(3.3)	(3.4)	(3.5)	(3.6)	(3.7)
LN	0.899	0.954	0.890	0.279	0.935	0.945	0.934
	(3.519)	(3.983)	(3.522)	(5.497)	(3.886)	(3.952)	(3.887)
LN^2	−0.092	−0.102	−0.093	—	−0.099	−0.101	−0.099
	(−2.466)	(−2.872)	(−2.464)		(−2.765)	(−2.848)	(−2.763)
TN	0.026	0.025	−0.144	0.024	0.114	−0.111	−0.114
	(0.145)	(0.142)	(−2.247)	(0.132)	(−2.255)	(−2.211)	(−2.249)
TN^2	−0.046	−0.045	—	−0.045	—	—	—
	(−0.818)	(−0.815)		(−0.810)			
CN	−0.106	−0.211	−0.108	0.005	−0.211	−0.211	−0.211
	(−0.728)	(−4.021)	(−0.745)	(0.034)	(−4.001)	(−4.019)	(−4.011)
CN^2	−0.031	—	−0.031	−0.063	—	—	—
	(−0.785)		(−0.782)	(−1.664)			
FY	−0.014	−0.015	−0.014	−0.013	0.013	—	0.013
	(−0.400)	(−0.432)	(−0.395)	(−0.382)	(1.420)		(1.513)
FY^2	0.001	0.001	0.001	0.001	—	—	—
	(0.711)	(0.730)	(0.703)	(0.689)			
SX	0.236	0.236	0.234	0.231	0.302	0.229	0.307
	(1.901)	(1.895)	(1.880)	(1.855)	(2.457)	(1.854)	(2.513)
ED	0.078	0.077	0.077	0.077	—	0.080	—
	(3.328)	(3.309)	(3.312)	(3.278)		(3.560)	
AG	−0.001	−0.001	−0.001	−0.001	0.001	—	—
	(−0.179)	(−0.163)	(−0.228)	(−0.208)	(0.319)		
WV	0.040	0.040	0.041	0.041	0.045	0.041	0.045
	(2.663)	(2.662)	(2.687)	(2.702)	(2.990)	(2.696)	(2.987)
$Int.$	−1.093	−1.128	−1.028	−0.271	−0.248	−1.162	−0.214
	(−1.912)	(−1.980)	(−1.816)	(−0.582)	(−0.587)	(−2.314)	(−0.524)
$\bar{R}^2$	0.064	0.064	0.064	0.059	0.055	0.066	0.056
F	6.53	7.07	7.07	6.54	8.08	10.81	9.23

[a]The numbers in parentheses are student t-ratios for the null hypothesis H_0: $\alpha_i = 0$. $\bar{R}^2$ is the coefficient of determination adjusted for degrees of freedom. F is the F-statistic for the test of the overall relationship.

The Student t-ratios for the null hypothesis of no association are somewhat higher using this form than with the linear specifications for most of the independent variables. The coefficients of determination should not be directly compared since the dependent variables are not measured in the same scale in the linear and semilog forms.

Both functional forms appear to perform reasonably well, so that the ultimate choice between them must be made on the basis of a priori reasoning. While it is true that there is no explicit functional form for individual willingness to pay schedules from economic theory, it is possible to derive some tentative guidelines. For example, there is good reason to suspect that encounters will have a diminishing marginal effect. Thus the fifth encounter on the trail in some fixed time interval is likely to have a smaller effect upon willingness to pay than the first. The linear specification implies that each encounter has the same effect upon willingness to pay, therefore it cannot capture this kind of behavior.

Cross-sectional data characteristically exhibit a problem of heteroscedasticity with the disturbances of the linear regression model. That is, the assumption of constant variance (i.e., $E(u_i^2) = \sigma^2$, where u_i is the stochastic error) is not satisfied. There are any number of reasons that may underlie such nonspherical errors. Since the data used in our analysis represent a survey of wilderness users' responses to hypothetical wilderness experiences, the problem can arise from either the characteristics of the individuals or the nature of the questions. The second possibility can be dismissed fairly readily. Each individual has an equal probability of receiving any particular question, thus there should be nothing in common about the first or second or fifth questions addressed to each of our respondents. Moreover our specification accounts for those factors that distinguish one experience from another. Thus the other possibility, namely respondents characteristics that we have not accounted for, seems to be a potentially important source for difference in the errors' variance.

As we noted the design of our experiment anticipated this possibility by soliciting five independent, hypothetical wilderness experiences from each sampled individual. It is possible to use the ordinary least squares (OLS) residuals to (1) determine whether or not heteroscedasticity is a problem, and (2) construct an estimate of the error covariance matrix in order to adjust for it. We shall assume that each individual's error's variance is proportional to the sum of squared OLS residuals across the five responses as in

$$\sigma_i^2 = \sigma^2 \left[\sum_{i=1}^{5} \epsilon_{ij}^2 \right] \tag{13}$$

where ϵ_{ij} is the OLS residual for the ith question posed to the jth respondent.

The ratio of the largest sum of squared residuals for a given individual to the smallest within our sample respondents using the semilog specification and the willingness to pay derived for encounters with hikers is over 600. Thus there are substantial discrepancies in the "informational content" of each respondent's replies, and heteroscedasticity appears to be a significant problem. Generalized least squares estimation will take these differences into account in the estimation process, and thereby yield a more efficient set of estimates. This conclusion is, of course, conditioned on our estimate of the error's covariance matrix. A priori we do not know the exact nature of the error's structure. We are assuming that an estimate of the conditional sum of squared residuals for each individual respondent will provide a reasonably good approximation.

TABLE 4

Generalized Least Squares Estimates of
Willingness to Pay Functions: Encounters
with Backpacking Parties[a]

Variable	Linear	Semilog
LN	4.141	0.780
	(19.249)	(8.750)
LN²	−	−0.069
		(−5.127)
TN	−1.211	−0.083
	(−5.345)	(−4.601)
CN	−1.723	−0.152
	(−7.685)	(−8.044)
FY	0.140	0.020
	(3.432)	(6.189)
WV	1.123	0.057
	(14.838)	(8.308)
SX	5.188	0.362
	(10.703)	(8.258)
Int.	−5.048	−0.354
	(−5.388)	(−2.322)
$\bar{R}^{*2}$	0.694	0.756

[a]The numbers in parentheses are student
t-ratios for the null hypothesis H_0: $\alpha_i = 0$.
$\bar{R}^{*2}$ is the coefficient of determination
adjusted for degrees of freedom.

Table 4 provides the Aitken (GLS) estimates for each of the final equations
from the preceding tables (i.e., Eqs. (2.6) and (3.7)). It should be noted that
corresponding to each of these equations is a different estimated variance—
covariance matrix. That is, the GLS estimates of the linear willingness to pay
schedule for encounters with backpackers is based on the OLS residuals from its
counterpart. In all cases the improvement in the efficiency of estimation is
implied by the increase in t-ratios. The estimated standard errors for our
coefficient estimates are one-half or less the values of the OLS estimates that
were based upon the variance—covariance matrix $(\sigma^2 (X^T X)^{-1})$ which presumes
the errors to be homoscedastic.

The coefficient of determination $(\bar{R}^2)$ for Aitken estimates does not in
general permit the same interpretation as when it is used with ordinary least
squares estimates. In the case of the latter the total sum of squares of the
residuals may be partitioned into two components. Such a partitioning is not

possible with Aitken residuals.[3] Consequently, we report an alternative measure of goodness of fit. Aitken estimation may be constructed by transforming the data to reflect the weights heteroscedasticity requires and then estimating the relationships using the transformed data. $\bar{R}^{*2}$ is the estimated coefficient of determination, adjusted for degrees of freedom, when the predictions of each of the above equations are compared with transformed dependent variables to estimate the residuals. In this case the sum of squared residuals will partition orthogonally and $\bar{R}^{*2}$ will be confined to the interval from zero to one. It should be noted that the heteroscedasticity adjustment reduces the total variation in the transformed dependent variables. Consequently $\bar{R}^2$ and $\bar{R}^{*2}$ are not comparable statistics. Nevertheless, it would appear that GLS estimation has provided a rather dramatic increase in the efficiency of the estimates and improved our ability to perceive the effects of congestion on individual willingness to pay.

V. CONCLUSIONS

The economic analysis of externalities has developed from the study of largely irrelevant whimsical examples such as the bees and nectar fable to become the focal point of the literature comprising environmental economics. The problem of pollution and congestion are recognized as among the most challenging to the efficient allocation of resources. The purpose of this paper has been to develop a methodology for measuring the effects of congestion so that the costs associated with it might be accounted for in public allocation decisions.

Conventional economic analysis of the consumer choice problem largely assumes the congestion effects away by postulating a model in which the

[3] If we define the Aitken residuals as

$$e = Y - W(W^T \hat{\Omega}^{-1} W)^{-1} W^T \hat{\Omega}^{-1} Y$$

then the total sum of squared errors is

$$e^T e = Y^T Y + Y^T \hat{\Omega}^{-1} W(W^T \hat{\Omega}^{-1} W)^{-1} W^T W(W^T \hat{\Omega}^{-1} W)^{-1} W^T \hat{\Omega}^{-1} Y$$
$$-2Y^T W(W^T \hat{\Omega}^{-1} W)^{-1} W^T \hat{\Omega}^{-1} Y.$$

Assume that $\hat{\Omega}^{-1} = R^T R$, then the residuals V may be written as

$$V = RY - RW(W^T R^T R W)^{-1} W^T R^T R Y$$
$$V^T V = Y^T \hat{\Omega}^{-1} Y - Y^T \hat{\Omega}^{-1} W(W^T \hat{\Omega}^{-1} W)^{-1} W^T \hat{\Omega}^{-1} Y.$$

Consequently, the coefficient of determination defined in terms of e is not constrained to the interval zero to one. Alternatively, the coefficient of determination defined in terms of V is bound to this interval and, therefore, permits interpretation as the percent of $Y^T \hat{\Omega}^{-1} Y$ "explained."

individual consumes goods and services of given quality. It has often been considered difficult to integrate the effects of congestion into this framework. The use of the time costs associated with waiting as a result of congestion is one attempt to reflect the implications of high use intensity patterns. However, crowding can have a variety of effects that will not be associated with time. They range from the litter and available space for sunbathing on a public beach to the ecological damage to a natural habitat.

In order to account for all the dimensions of the congestion problem we have selected Lancaster's [9] model of consumer behavior. The individual selects goods and services because of their characteristics, and it is these characteristics that enter his utility function. Congestion alters the mix of attributes or characteristics available from a good or service and hence can reduce its value to the individual. The measurement of the effects of crowding must therefore proceed to: (1) define the attributes of the goods and services of interest; (2) measure the relevant quantities of these attributes provided by the goods and services; (3) evaluate the effects of crowding on this attribute configuration; and (4) convert these changes into value terms.

The overall findings of our research suggest that it is possible to measure non-time-related congestion effects. Moreover, it would seem that such measures are essential for the analysis of the management and allocation of "open access" environmental resources. These conclusions, while encouraging, also serve to indicate the need for continued research in this area.

There are several areas that require more extensive research effort. The first of these is the modeling and measurement of the effects of total use on those attributes that indicate disruptions to solitude. We would suggest that informed judgment and conventional statistical techniques are not likely to be very successful in addressing this problem. It amounts to modeling an extremely complex production process; in the economist's jargon, a process in which both quality and quantity must be noted. There are no global controls on the system, but rather the process is one in which the open access facility is used by a variety of individuals at each one's discretion. Continued research by Smith *et al.* [17] and Smith and Krutilla [16] has resulted in the development of a large-scale traffic simulation model of the process which may serve to provide the required technical data on use patterns and the associated expected levels of encounters. Consequently it will be possible to define the carrying capacity of low-density recreational areas and to examine the ability of alternative rationing policies to maintain use levels at this limit.

REFERENCES

1. Bohm, P., "An Approach of the Problem of Estimating Demand for Public Goods," *Swedish Journal of Economics*, March 1971, 73, 55–66.

2. Bohm, P., "Estimating Demand for Public Goods: An Experiment," *European Economic Review*, 1972, 3, 111–130.

3. Cicchetti, C. J., "A Multivariate Statistical Analysis of Wilderness Users," in *Natural Environments: Studies in Theoretical and Applied Analysis*, Ed. J. V. Krutilla, Baltimore, Maryland: Resources for the Future, Inc. (Johns Hopkins Univ. Press), 1972, 142–170.

4. Cicchetti, C. J., A. C. Fisher, and V. K. Smith, "Economic Models and Planning Outdoor Recreation," *Operations Research*, September/October 1973, 21, 1104–1113.

5. Cicchetti, C. J., J. J. Seneca, and P. Davidson, *The Demand and Supply of Outdoor Recreation*, New Brunswick, New Jersey: Bur. of Econ. Res., Rutgers Univ., 1969.

6. Cicchetti, C. J., and V. K. Smith, "Interdependent Consumer Decisions: A Production Function Approach," *Australian Economic Papers*, December 1973, 12, 239–252.

7. Conlisk, J., and H. Watts, "A Model for Optimizing Experimental Designs for Estimating Response Surfaces," *Proceedings of the American Statistical Association*, 1969, Social Statistics Section, 150–156.

8. Fisher, A. C., and J. V. Krutilla, "Determination of Optimal Capacity of Resource-Based Recreation Facilities," *Natural Resources Journal*, July 1972, 12, 417–444.

9. Lancaster, K. J., "A New Approach to Consumer Theory," *Journal of Political Economy*, April 1966, 74, 132–157.

10. Lancaster, K. J., *Consumer Demands: A New Approach*, New York: Columbia Univ. Press, 1971.

11. Nichols, D., E. Smolensky, and N. Tideman, "Discrimination by Waiting Time in Merit Goods," *American Economic Review*, June 1971, 61, 312–323.

12. Rosen, S., "Hedonic Prices and Implicit Markets: Product Differentiation in Pure Competition," *Journal of Political Economy*, January/February 1974, 82, 34–55.

13. Rothenberg, J., "The Economics of Congestion and Pollution: An Integrated View," *American Economic Review*, May 1970, 60, 114–121.

14. Samuelson, P. A., "The Pure Theory of Public Expenditures," *Review of Economics and Statistics*, November 1954, 36, 387–389.

15. Smith, V. K., and C. J. Cicchetti, "Regression Analysis with Dichotomous Dependent Variables," presented to 1972 Econometric Society Meetings.

16. Smith, V. K., and J. V. Krutilla, *Structure and Properties of a Wilderness Travel Simulator: An Application to the Spanish Peaks Area*, (Baltimore: Johns Hopkins Press, 1976).

17. Smith, V. K., D. Webster, and N. Heck, "A Prototype Simulation Model For a Wilderness Area," *Operational Research Quarterly*, December 1974, 25, 529–539.

18. Stankey, G. H., "A Strategy for the Definition and Management of Wilderness Quality," in *Natural Environments: Studies in Theoretical and Applied Analysis*, ed. J. V. Krutilla, Baltimore, Maryland: Resources for the Future, Inc. (Johns Hopkins Univ. Press), 1972, 88–114.

19. Tocher, K. D., "A Note on the Design Problem," *Biometrika*, 1952, 39, 189.

20. Wallace, T. D., and V. Ashar, "Sequential Methods in Model Construction," *Review of Economics and Statistics*, May 1972, 54, 172–178.

Discussion

DAVID F. BRADFORD

Princeton University

Since my comments as discussant will tend to focus on what I view as weaker points in their paper, I would like to emphasize at the outset that Cicchetti and Smith have given us a highly useful example of quantitative analysis of a significant class of externalities. In sophistication of design and execution their work marks a distinct advance over any I have seen on this topic. Their study indicates the potential, noted by Bergstrom in his paper on the free rider problem, for exploiting relatively expensive methods on relatively small random samples to reach quantitative conclusions about these elusive effects.

My first point concerns the theoretical framework within which Cicchetti and Smith have chosen to cast their analysis, namely the Lancaster attribute model. It would be more accurate, I think, to say that they have *not* cast their analysis within this model, and I do not think that there is any need for them to do so. Although they assert that their hypothesis that encounters on the trail, etc., affect the amount an individual would be willing to pay to enjoy a certain wilderness experience "follows from the Lancaster model," I can see no sense in which this is the case. Rather, to suggest that the Lancaster model represents the situation under study would require a careful specification of the dimensions of the A's and X's, along with unwelcome linearity assumptions, which the authors have not undertaken. In my view they could perfectly well omit the discussion

201

of the Lancaster model and start their own analysis with expression (8), or perhaps with some such slight variation on (8) as $wp = wp(Z_i, A)$, where Z_i is a vector of characteristics of the ith household (including such things as income, age, education, etc.) and A is a vector of characteristics of the wilderness experience being described (number of days, number of camp encounters, etc.). None of the remainder of the paper would need to be altered if this were taken as the starting point.

My second point concerns the interpretation of the coefficients of the two versions, linear and semilog, of the empirical model. (Incidentally, I am not sure it is in general clear whether a "semilog" model is of the form $y = f(\log x)$ or $\log y = f(x)$. I, at least, had to infer from the fact that the independent variables included zero values, as well as from the numerical magnitudes of the coefficients, that the latter is intended here.) Once one is satisfied that the general level of "willingness to pay" is reasonable, a matter of inspection of the data, attention should be focused on determining the effect on this magnitude of changes in the congestion variables. (As the authors point out, even the general level of willingness to pay need not be plausible since it is the latter effects that are of interest here.) Except as variables such as household income, sex, education, etc., interact with the externality variables they should be viewed here purely as taste controls. This is not to say that the bearing of these characteristics on willingness to pay could not be itself a matter of study, but that here the authors should keep at the center of attention the discovery of the determinants of the value placed by a household on congestion phenomena. This is so not only because that is the immediate subject of the paper, but because it is of some interest for policy. Will rising incomes and levels of education tend to raise the relative value of solitude? By how much? Do younger individuals, having grown up in a more crowded society, value solitude less than older people? For making long-term, difficult-to-reverse resource allocation choices, the interactions here seem to me of great relevance, and I would gladly sacrifice goodness of fit for information about them.

Unless interaction terms (e.g., the product of income and camp encounters) are explicitly included, the linear form of the model implicitly hypothesizes that changes in household characteristics have no effect on the evaluation of congestion. The semilog form of the model incorporates another hypothesis about interactions, namely, that the elasticity with respect to an independent variable of the marginal willingness to pay for externalities is the same as the elasticity of the willingness to pay with respect to that variable:

$$\log y = \alpha x; \qquad \frac{x_i}{y} \frac{\partial y}{\partial x_i} = \alpha_i x_i.$$

In the case of income, from Table 4, $\alpha_i = .02$. Thus the elasticity of the premium for solitude with respect to family income for a household with an income of

$10,000 is implicitly estimated to be 0.2, a result of the (my) a priori expected direction, but (to me) unexpectedly low. This sketchy discussion is merely illustrative, but I hope sufficient to induce someone, perhaps Cicchetti and Smith, to pursue the question further.

A final subpoint concerning the interpretation of the results: it would be of interest, I suspect, to many readers to have some of the implications of the results for wilderness management (at least for the Spanish Peaks Primitive Area) calculated. How, for example, might congestion-sensitive pricing look? What sorts of trade-offs would be profitable between the extra costs of more numerous but smaller campsites and the reduced frequency of camp encounters? I pose the questions with due humulity, for the answers no doubt involve complications beyond the reach of this study, but some indication of how the results might be applied would be very welcome.

An Economic Model
of Airport Noise Pollution
in an Urban Environment

ARTHUR S. DE VANY

Texas A & M University

Spurred by the Airport and Airway Development Act, the United States is building or expanding airports at an unprecedented rate. This program is taking place amid great uncertainty concerning who is responsible for the environmental harm caused by airports and general disagreement regarding what the environmental harm consists of or how it can be measured.[1]

There is little doubt that noise is the focal point of community opposition to new airports, and yet it is one of the most difficult environmental issues with which to deal.[2] Psychological studies verify that intrusive noise, such as would be experienced by persons living under flight paths, interrupts sleep, decreases the effectiveness with which tasks are performed, and makes conversation difficult. Yet, there is also evidence that persons can adapt to noise and perform a variety of tasks in quite intensive noise.[3]

This research was supported by the Environmental Quality Program at Texas A&M University.

[1] A survey of these issues may be found in U.S. Environmental Protection Agency [12].

[2] See National Academy of Sciences [11] for a discussion of the role of noise in the opposition to a fourth airport in the New York area, or Commission on the Third London Airport [9] for an attempt to grapple with these issues.

[3] Kryter [10] gives an able review of this research.

In terms of man's auditory system there is no distinction between sound and noise. Noise is unwanted sound. Values or tastes must, therefore, be introduced to separate noise from other sounds — one person's rock music is another's noise. This is an important point because most noise experienced by persons living near an airport is not of such intensity as to induce pain or other symptoms of physiological stress. The noise is just irritating, perhaps in and of itself, or because of what it interferes with or interrupts. Because of this, and because most opposition to noise is voiced in complaints, the research on airport noise has focused on the conflict between the airport operator and community.[4] It is almost as though the Bishop Berkeley were alive today to say, "There is no noise if no one complains about it."

Of course, to the economist, with his logical positivist point of view, there is some merit to such an operational definition of noise. This point has not been wasted on airport authorities nor the Federal Aviation Administration (FAA), both of whom spend a great deal of time and money moving people away from noise, thereby "eliminating" it.[5] On the other hand, the economist knows that the complaints reflect the underlying legal uncertainties as to who has the right to quiet or to emit noise, and that the allocation of resources to noise abatement is unlikely to be efficient if it is done to minimize complaints since the marginal cost of complaining surely is close to zero.[6]

There are three general issues taken up in this paper. First, is there a theory of noise; that is, does economic theory provide a basis for a model of behavior in the presence of noise? This is a natural question to ask since tastes and ongoing activities have been shown to shape response to noise. The answers to this question are then applied to the theory of urban land rents to establish some of the properties of the implicit noise market. The last task consists of an empirical evaluation of a model of the housing market surrounding a major jetport.

I. SCALING INDIVIDUAL REACTION TO NOISE

According to Kryter [10] noise is sound that interacts with activities, diminishing their value or impairing the ability of persons to enjoy or perform them. The characteristics of a sound that relate to its perceived noisiness are:

(1) *Spectrum content and level*. Generally, sounds with high pressure and intense high frequencies are noisier.

---

[4] On this see Berland [3], Berger [2], Clark [7], Clark and Pietrasanta [8], or the bibliography in U.S. EPA [12].

[5] DOT/FAA order 5050.2, December 7, 1970, defines noise impact in terms of the number of people residing in the impacted area and an "acceptable" level of noise.

[6] The report by the U.S. EPA [12] and Altree *et al.* [1], among others, find that the right has not been fixed.

(2) *Spectrum complexity*. Sounds having energy concentrated in narrow frequency bands, or containing pure tones are noisier than sounds having a more level distribution of energy.

(3) *Duration*. Sounds are noisier the longer their duration.

(4) *Duration of increase*. The more rapid the rise of the sound pressure from ambient to peak, the noisier the sound is. This is a startle effect.

Psychoacoustic research has established these dimensions of sound as being the characteristics that persons process in distinguishing between sounds of differing noisiness. Noisiness is a personal ranking of sounds according to their characteristics. Index numbers have been constructed that combine these characteristics to rank the noisiness of complex noise environments such as those found near airports. These indices are unique to a linear transformation and concave contoured (equal noise contours are concave over the characteristics of the sound signature). Since such properties are the general features of the utility function, this research justifies the assumption made here that households rank locations in terms of their noise exposure through some utility function.

II. THE DEMAND FOR HOUSING AND THE IMPLICIT DEMAND FOR QUIET

Let housing units be ranked according to the levels of their characteristics h_1, $i = 1, \ldots, n$. Following the usual procedure of ranking the noise exposure of sites in terms of an index number, let N_k represent the noise exposure of a housing site located k miles from the airport. Let the attenuation function

$$N_k = N(k, N_s) \tag{1}$$

relate the noise exposure of a site at distance k to the level of the noise at the airport source N_s. The function $N(k, N_s)$ is monotone decreasing and concave in h and separable in N_s and k.

Assume the airport including its surrounding commercial center is an employment center as well as a noise source. Let travel costs between the employment center and a home k miles from the airport be

$$t = t(k) \tag{2}$$

with $t(\cdot)$ an increasing function which may be concave or convex depending on the transportation system of the urban area. If m is household income to be spent on housing and $p_i(k)$ is the price of the ith household characteristic located on a circle of radius k about the airport, then the household budget constraint is

$$m - t(k) - p(k)h' = 0 \tag{3}$$

where p is the $1 \times n$ price vector and h' the $n \times 1$ characteristics vector.

The household is to maximize utility by choice of the vector h and by choice of k which implicitly determines the prices paid for characteristics and the household's noise exposure. In order to have the objective function be concave, let the negative of noise be quiet, i.e. $Q = -N$ and let the household utility function be

$$U = U[h, -N(k, N_s)].\tag{4}$$

A solution to the maximization problem exists if the budget constraint (3) is convex in h and $-N$, where $-N$ is a function of k. The constraint is convex in h for any given k. For a given h it is convex in $-N$ provided that

$$\frac{\partial^2 N}{\partial k^2} - \frac{\partial^2 t}{\partial k^2} < 0.\tag{5}$$

This condition requires that the marginal rate at which noise attenuates with distance must be greater than the rate at which marginal transportation cost attenuates with distance. Without this condition, airport noise would not attenuate to the ambient noise level within the bounds of the urban area, and the household would always be induced to move closer to the airport were the airport noise level to be increased. Because noise attenuates so rapidly with distance this problem does not present itself. For air pollution, however, with its very gradual rate of attenuation, the problem is present and hampers the interpretation of empirical work on the cost of air pollution.

Maximization of (4) subject to (3) now yields

$$\frac{\partial U}{\partial h_i} - \lambda p_i(k) = 0, \qquad i = 1, \ldots, n\tag{6}$$

$$\frac{\partial U}{\partial Q}\frac{\partial Q}{\partial k} - \lambda \sum_{i=1}^{n} \frac{\partial p_i}{\partial k} h_i = 0\tag{7}$$

since $-\partial U/\partial N = \partial U/\partial Q$ and $-\partial N/\partial k = \partial Q/\partial k$, the first term of (7) may also be written $\partial U/\partial N \, \partial N/\partial k$. Interpretation of these conditions is straightforward: The household purchases housing characteristics to the point where the marginal utility of the ith characteristic equals the marginal utility of income times price. The household optimizes its noise exposure through selection of the distance of this residence from the airport in whose commercial center the income earner is assumed to work. Greater distances bring utility in the form of reduced noise. The cost of distance is the cost of transportation plus the change in characteristics prices due to distance. The derivative of prices with distance $\partial p_i/\partial k$ may be positive or negative, but, whatever its value, is taken as given by the individual homeowner.

III. EQUILIBRIUM IN THE HOUSING MARKET

Each home buyer taking housing prices as given, purchases his home and selects its distance from the airport on this basis. At the market level, however, housing prices are not given, but must represent the solution to demand and supply forces. Likewise, the slope of housing prices as one moves away from the airport must represent a balancing of transportation costs and noise exposure that achieves equilibrium across the distance.

Assume a fixed stock of housing characteristics along each distance ring and let the city be bounded. Let

$$H_{i_k}^s = \sum_{j=1}^{Q(k)} h_{i_k}^j \tag{8}$$

be the stock of characteristic i on distance ring k where the number of housing units is $Q(k)$, a function of the radius of the ring. The demand of individual γ for h_{ik} may be written

$$h_{ik}^\gamma = h_{ik}^\gamma(p_i(k), m - t(k), N_k). \tag{9}$$

Aggregating (9) over individuals and equating demand with supply gives the solution for the equilibrium price of the i characteristic in ring k as

$$P_{ik} = G_{ik}(m - t(k), H_{ik}^s, N(k, N_s)). \tag{10}$$

In equilibrium, it must be impossible to arbitrage over the individual markets and make a gain. This requires that housing prices must be fully compensatory of transportation costs and disutility due to noise. Thus solving (7) for each $\partial P_i / \partial k$ singly gives

$$\frac{\partial P_i}{\partial k} = \frac{(\partial U / \partial N)(\partial N / \partial k) - \lambda \, \partial t / \partial k}{\lambda h} \tag{11}$$

as the solution for the property value gradient.

The economics of this condition is best understood in terms of the diagram in Figure 1. In this figure I have plotted housing value against distance from the airport. The upper curve, labeled V_t, indicates the usual value gradient obtained for any employment center. If the airport were nonpolluting, then V_t would indicate the employment benefits of the airport, and the value surface would slope away at a rate equal to marginal transportation cost until it intersects the underlying urban value surface. Since the airport is a pollution center as well, we have an additional effect to consider. The reduction in value due to the disutility of noise is labeled V_n and is drawn below the horizontal line to indicate its negative effect on value. This curve is shown starting at some point of negative intercept and increasing with k, reflecting the fact that the noise discount

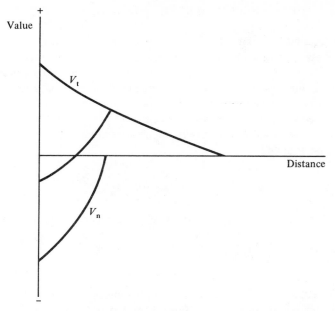

Figure 1. The equilibrium value surface centered on the airport.

diminishes as noise attenuates with further distance from the airport. The noise discount takes a "bite" out of the V_t curve; at every point where noise is above the ambient level its presence lowers the premium for proximity to the airport. The net effect of the airport is the sum of these two curves, shown as the heavy line in the figure.

The resultant net effect of the airport is a transformation of the value surface into a crater with a low center and high ridges which slope off to join the underlying urban value surface. In the very center the noise effect may so offset the proximity effect that values are depressed beyond what is normal for the urban area without the airport. This depressant effect is limited however by the price at which residential land near the airport would sell for commercial uses. Since commercial users are less affected by noise and benefit more by proximity to the airport, one would expect a commercial zone to form around the airport. The theory nicely explains this well-known pattern of land use. Somewhat surprising is the prediction that the commercial zone will be greater in extent the noisier is the airport for any given level of airport employment. The density of dwelling units near airports is also explained by the theory. In the valley of the crater and the lower portion of its slopes one expects moderate residential densities mixed with commercial land use since residential land prices are depressed in this area. The depressed prices induce low residential density and draw fringe commercial activity. Nearer the peaks of the crater, where residential land is at its highest price per acre, one expects high density. The result is the typical fringe of apartments that one finds surrounding commercial airports. The lower sensitivity of apartments to noise also contributes to this pattern.

Finally, it is apparent why appraisers often produce contradictory results when they survey land values around airports. Their findings will depend on which part of the surrounding value crater they sample. Sophisticated sampling techniques must be employed to obtain reliable estimates since the effect the appraiser is attempting to isolate is not uniform.

IV. THE EMPIRICAL MODEL

From the preceding theoretical analysis I have derived the demand function for housing characteristics and the reduced form solution for housing prices in each distance ring, Eq. (10). In addition, condition (11) relates prices across distance rings. Since the price of a characteristic cannot differ anywhere in the urban market, (11) will set the land value in each distance ring that is required for market equilibrium. The land value will be separable from the price or value of the characteristics of housing located on the land. Competitive equilibrium in the housing market suggests the following equation for the value of the jth house on a ring of radius k centered at the airport:

$$V_{jk} = \sum_{i=1}^{n} P_{ik} h_{ik}. \tag{12}$$

Using (10) this becomes

$$V_{jk} = \sum_{i=1}^{n} G_{ik}(m - t(k), H_{ik}^s, N(k, N_s)) h_i, \tag{13}$$

which competitive separability of land rent and characteristic prices allows to be written

$$V_{jk} = V_{jk}^l(k, N_s) + \sum_{i=1}^{n} P_{ik}(m, H_{ik}^s) h_i. \tag{14}$$

I estimate this reduced form solution of the model using data for Dallas, Texas. The airport involved is Love Field, which in 1970 was a busy commercial airport located close to downtown and closely surrounded by residential development.

My source for housing characteristics and prices is the 1970 Census of Housing. I use the block level data in a sample of blocks. The variables used are as follows:

> *VALUE* the average value of housing in the block as estimated by owners,
> *OWN*   the percentage of homes that are owner occupied,
> *ROOMS* the average number of rooms per house,
> *AGE*   the average age of housing,
> *STAY*   average length of stay of residents,
> *AC*   percentage of homes which are air conditioned,
> *DAP*   distance from airport,
> *DCBD*   distance from central business district.

Since income data are only available at the tract level, I have not attempted to include it in my estimation procedure which requires block level data in order to provide sufficient variation in noise exposures.

Rewriting (14) in terms of these variables and treating N_s as a parameter for the sample

$$V_j = V_j^1(DAP, DCBD) + \beta_1 OWN + \beta_2 ROOMS + \beta_3 AGE + \beta_4 STAY + \beta_5 AC. \tag{15}$$

In this model the variable *DAP* picks up both the negative noise effects and the positive location value of the airport. According to (4) the value surface should rise and then fall with distance from the airport. Because of this, using *DAP* as a continuous variable would cause a serious specification error in the model since it would require a single slope over the data. I have partitioned blocks into distances from the airport and from downtown and used a qualitative (dummy) variable procedure to indicate the presence of a block in a particular distance ring. Setting up five distance rings around the airport gives the four qualitative variables *DAP01, DAP02, DAP03, DAP04*. When each of these is zero, the block lies somewhere beyond 8 miles distance from the airport, otherwise it lies in one of the intervals $0-1, 1-2, 2-3, 3-4$ as indicated by a value of one of the respective qualitative variable. A similar procedure gives the following qualitative variables for *DCBD: DCBD01, DCBD02, DCBD03, DCBD04*.

Assuming *DAP* and *DCBD* are separable from housing characteristics, substitution into (15) gives the model

$$VAL_t = \beta_0 + \beta_1 OWN_t + \beta_2 RMS_t + \beta_3 AGE_t \, \beta_4 STAY_t$$
$$+ \beta_5 AC_t + \beta_6 DAP01_t + \beta_7 DAP02_t + \beta_8 DAP03_t + \beta_9 DAP04_t$$
$$+ \beta_{10} DCBD01_t + \beta_{11} DCBD02_t + \beta_{12} DCBD03_t + \beta_{13} DCBD04_t + \epsilon_t \tag{16}$$

where ϵ_t is assumed $N(0, \sigma^2)$.

Estimates of (16) are given in Table 1. Each of the housing characteristics, except for *STAY*, is positively associated with value at a high level of statistical

TABLE 1

Estimates of *DAP* with *DCBD*[a]

Source	β values	|T|	Prob > |T|
Intercept	−25426.66	17.68	0.0001
OWN	96.95	11.30	0.0001
RMS	6183.64	33.03	0.0001
AGE	183.56	4.26	0.0001
STAY	121.19	1.34	0.1779
AC	67.76	5.12	0.0001
DAP01	−2607.54	6.06	0.0001
DAP02	567.86	1.41	0.1571
DAP03	2668.19	6.65	0.0001
DAP04	350.85	1.00	0.3169
DCBD01	3208.54	3.79	0.0002
DCBD02	−283.71	0.72	0.4662
DCBD03	459.97	1.33	0.1815
DCBD04	−1050.89	2.72	0.0066

[a]$df = 1255$; F-value $= 437.96$; $R^2 = 0.8193$.

significance. The results for the *DAP* variables indicate that being located within 1 mile of the airport is associated with a fairly sizable reduction in value, the coefficient for *DAP*01 is also highly significant statistically. The *DAP*02 coefficient is only significant at the 16% level. This, along with the low estimated value of the *DAP*02 coefficient, suggests that a proximity of 1−2 miles to the airport exerts an inconsequential effect on value. The *DAP*03 coefficient is positive and highly significant, indicating that a location from 2 to 3 miles from the airport raises property value. Beyond 3 miles the airport exerts neither a positive nor a negative effect on value.

In my opinion, the estimates indicate that the environmental degradation due to the airport overwhelms the location advantages within 1 mile. From 1−2 miles these opposing forces are offsetting and there is no effect on value. The stationary point predicted by the model obviously must fall within this distance range at present noise levels. The distance of 2−3 miles appears to be great enough so that proximity to the airport more than offsets environmental effects. Beyond this distance values are no longer affected by the presence of the airport.

Distance to the central business district exerts a positive effect on value within 2 miles, no effect over 2−6 miles, and thereafter distance to the CBD reduces value in the usual manner. In effect, the value surface falls steeply just out of the CBD, becomes flat over a 4-mile segment, and then falls again at greater distances, although at a more moderate rate.

The overall effect of the airport on housing values is positive. Homes within 1 mile of the airport lose roughly $13 million in value in total. More than offsetting this loss is the roughly 25 million gain in value experienced by homes lying between 2 and 3 miles from the airport.

REFERENCES

1. Altree, L. R., *et al.*, "Legal Aspects of Airport Noise and Sonic Boom," Parts I and II, Stanford Univ., February 1968.
2. Berger, M. M., "Nobody Loves an Airport," *Southern California Law Review*, Fall 1970, **43**, 631–789.
3. Berland, T., *The Fight for Quiet*, Englewood Cliffs, New Jersey: Prentice-Hall, 1970.
4. Bishop, D. E., *Analysis of Community and Airport Relationships/Noise Abatement*, Vol. II: "Development of Aircraft Noise Compatibility Criteria for Varied Land Uses," FAA, December 1964.
5. Bishop, D. E., and M. A. Simpson, "Noise Exposure Forecast Contours for 1967, 1970 and 1975 Operations at Selected Airports," Bolt, Beranek and Newman, DOT/FAA-NO-70-8, September 1970.
6. Bishop, D. E., and R. D. Horonjeff, "Procedures for Developing Noise Exposure Forecast Areas for Aircraft Flight Operations," FAA Rep. DS-67-14, August 1967.
7. Clark, W. E., "Reaction to Aircraft Noise," Bolt, Beranek and Newman, ASD Tech. Rep. 61-610, November 1961.
8. Clark, W. E., and A. C. Pietrasanta, "Intrusion of Aircraft Noise into Communities Near Two USAF Air Bases," Bolt, Beranek and Newman Rep., February 1959.
9. Commission on the Third London Airport, *Papers and Proceedings*, Vol. VII, Part 1: "Proposed Research Methodology;" Part 2: "Results of Research Team's Assessment;" Part 3, London: Her Majesty's Stationery Office, 1970.
10. Kryter, K. D., *The Effects of Noise on Man*, New York: Academic Press, 1970.
11. National Academy of Sciences, *Jamaica Bay and Kennedy Airport*, Volumes I and II, 1971.
12. U.S. Environmental Protection Agency, Office of Noise Abatement and Control, "Transportation Noise and Noise from Equipment Powered by Internal Combustion Engines," December 1971.

Discussion

DAVID F. HEATHFIELD

University of Southampton, England
and
Washington University, St. Louis

The paper may be divided into two parts: the first outlines some of the difficulties of measuring the many dimensions of sound and defining those subjective criteria that identify noise, the second is an empirical study of the relationship between a measure of noise and property values around Dallas Love Field Airport. The connection between the two parts of the paper is somewhat tenuous since the only dimension of noise that varies across the sample is that of sound pressure level; frequency, suddenness, night flights, etc., are the same for all observations. Sound pressure level is transformed into noise exposure forecast (NEF). It is not quite clear what is gained by this or how sound pressure level and NEF are correlated.

It is to the second part of the paper that I wish to speak. It is puzzling that simply adding the NEF variable to the value explaining equation adds nothing to its explanatory power and yet partitioning the sample into NEF zones gives rise to significantly different parameter estimates. The reason offered by the author I find difficult to accept. Why, for example, should the market value of air-conditioning vary across the sample when the cost of installing it does not? The age of a house implies nothing about the age of the occupants, but length of stay clearly does.

NEF, distance from airport (*DAP*), and distance from central business district

(*DCBD*) are introduced into the explanatory equations as sets of dummy variables and therefore have the effect of changing the intercept. Without more information about the specifications of these dummy variables it is difficult to say what the estimated intercept means. It is everywhere large and negative; does this mean that land has negative value around Dallas? It is also difficult to say very much about the absolute values of the dummy coefficients. It is clearly possible to say that the value in *DAP* zone 03 is higher than that in *DAP* zone 01, but they could both be below the "no airport" datum. It would be interesting therefore to see the form of the dummy variables and also a variance—covariance matrix.

Even if we succeeded in estimating the value/noise gradient in the cross-section study, under what conditions would it correspond to a time series value/noise gradient as, for example, an airport were introduced into a community and gradually increased its noisiness? Specifically, how is it possible to allow for any cross-sectional value gradient that existed before the airport?

There seems to be no a priori reason for suggesting that changes in property values reflect social costs of pollution. Clearly they cannot capture consumer surplus losses or gains nor the adjustments costs as persons move or alter their life styles. In the present case it is possible for increased pollution to increase property values. Imagine a community the inhabitants of which have some location loyalty. This may be due to school zoning or familiarity with the district or whatever. If an airport were to "pollute" half the houses, would there not be increased demand for the available unpolluted (or partially polluted) housing stock? It is difficult to see why any resulting increase in value should be regarded as a social benefit. Perhaps problems such as "where to build airports" are not amenable to technical economic assessment, and we should look to political economy for improvements in social decision making processes.

Fiscal Externalities, Taxes, and Suburbanization

DONALD R. HAURIN†
University of Chicago

GEORGE S. TOLLEY
University of Chicago

I. INTRODUCTION

The continuing suburbanization of urban population has raised questions of what the optimal distribution of population is and what forces may lead the current pattern to be nonoptimal. The answers to this spatial question involve the concept of a fiscal externality. Recent discussions of externalities in a spatial context have involved public goods, congestion, pollution, and scale economies (see, e.g., Buchanan and Goetz [5], Buchanan and Wagner [6], Flatters *et al.* [11], Rothenberg [21], Smith [24], Tolley [26, 27], Tolley and Haurin [28]). The externality of interest in the present paper, a fiscal externality, results from supplying a common level of local government services to residents within the jurisdiction while financing through taxes levied that do not necessarily reflect the level of services received by taxpayers (some other studies of fiscal externalities are Bradford and Kelejian [3], Bradford and Oates [4], and Rothenberg [20, 22]). An example is financing elementary education through property taxes. The externality has spatial implications because the distribution of tax—service ratios may vary across jurisdictions within an urbanized area.

---

†Present address: Department of Economics, Ohio State University, Columbus, Ohio.

The version of the model to be developed is based upon the assumption that high income groups can form communities and exclude lower income residents. This assumption provides a theory of suburbanization as a response to the fiscal externality. (For a nonexclusionary version of the model, see Tolley and Smith [29].) The welfare and spatial effects will be estimated in empirical work in this paper for the city of Chicago. An important application will be to the question of the optimal form of urban governments. Specifically, the welfare costs of a metropolitan government that allows no "escape" will be compared to those of a city—suburban system.

In early work on this topic (Tolley and Smith [29]) a model was developed to explore the response of the relatively wealthy to incentives to migrate away from low income groups. A brief summary of the basic points follows.

Consider the decision of a high income resident living on the edge of the city choosing whether to live in the city, receiving the same level of services as other city residents and paying at the same tax rate, or forming a separate jurisdiction just outside of the city. Allow the availability of an exclusionary device such as zoning a minimum housing consumption for community residents. The marginal decision will be based on the difference in levels between taxes paid on housing (land and structure) and services received (a function of the distribution of housing in the city, the tax rate, and quantities of industrial and commercial property). If a net loss is incurred, then the incentive will favor suburbanization. Given that urban theory suggests that the most wealthy will live farthest from the center given certain parameter values, and that it is they who will have the largest tax payment, it is likely that suburbanization will occur. They will lose a subsidy from commercial and industrial property but gain a saving in cost of supplying a given level of governmentally provided services. However, there is inherent in the urban model a counterforce to suburbanization, that being the additional transportation costs incurred in travel to workplace (assumed to be to the city center). As the suburbs grow, commuting distances from the edge increase, and the advantage of moving to the suburbs falls. When the area of suburbanization has spread so that the tax savings equals the additional transportation cost from city to suburban edge, equilibrium will occur. Thus the areal size has been determined and population size may be determined with the additional consideration of the labor supply effects in the central city.

The land in the central city is temporarily vacated as suburbanization occurs. Labor in other cities now finds this land's relative price lower with reference to some initial equilibrium among cities. Immigration will occur leading to an increase in population of the urbanized area, the final equilibrium being a function of labor demand in the city possibly affected by economies of scale. This revision of the income distribution in the central city will have secondary effects upon the demand and supply of the publicly provided good, further affecting the amount of suburbanization. This iterative reaction will continue until convergence occurs.

The model just described is extended in the present paper to allow for changes in the level of public services in the central city as suburbanization occurs and to allow for changes in housing consumption. Like the earlier model, the present paper takes as its starting point the basic residential model for an urban area exposited by Alonso [1], Muth [17], Wingo [30], and Mills [15]. Whereas the earlier model focused primarily on commuting costs as suburbanization occurs, the present paper develops, in addition, estimates of welfare losses in the public service and housing sectors. Specific functional forms for demand are assumed, and a simple voting model is specified determining the level of public services for the heterogeneous population of the central city.

II. AN URBAN MODEL WITH PROPERTY TAXES

One of the conditions assumed by Tiebout [25] was that households receive their income through a means such as dividends payments and not by commuting to employment in a central business district. Households then bear no additional costs if they choose to separate themselves into homogeneous subgroupings. In reality, there are costs of complete separation. A result is that within a large city one finds a heterogeneous distribution of income groups. Implications are that the provision of public goods will not be optimal and transfers from the relatively wealthy to the poor will occur.

On the other hand, it has been hypothesized that the homogeneous suburban communities surrounding a large central city may come close to approximating a Tiebout world. One chain of reasoning (Hamilton [12]) involves the consideration of taxes levied by a homogeneous community and the benefits derived from these taxes. The analytical result is that the property tax is viewed as a head tax to live in the community (i.e., the price to enter) and receive benefits in the form of public services that are just equal in value to the tax. The implication is that there will not be a distortion in the consumption of housing even though a tax on housing is levied, thus no social welfare costs are generated.

We wish to consider what happens when a central city with distortions exists surrounded by Tiebout suburbs. A single urban public service is assumed to be supplied. Though it could be of the form of a pure public good in the Samuelsonian sense [23], more realistically, it takes the form of a private good provided through the public sector. The public sector's behavior constraint is that all recipients are offered the same amount of the good. The example we have in mind is elementary education where national external effects and local spillovers are ignored. Thus we have two distortions, the property tax in the city where full Tiebout adjustment does not occur and a constraint creating a distortion in consumption of public services.

It is assumed for simplicity that services are provided at constant costs and each family has the same number of children (when the service is education).

The equilibrium level of services in the city is derived endogenously. Overall equilibrium is determined by total taxes levied and the number of residents, total taxes being a function of housing consumed. This in turn is a function of the net tax on housing, a concept introduced in the formal model. Thus we have a simultaneous solution of the actual tax rate (δ), the net tax rates $(\Gamma_i$ where i is the ith income group), the amount of services consumed, and the number of residents in the city.

As a note on the empirical relevance of a model that considers the only revenue source to be a residential property tax and the only service publicly supplied to be education, Netzer [18] found that taxes on single family units and apartments constituted 55.5% of local real property taxes, while commercial and industrial taxes constituted 28.6% of the total. He also found that expenditures on education by local governments were 44.6% of local general expenditures, of which it was estimated that 51% was financed by the property tax. Although the assumptions restricting the model to considering residential property taxes and a public good such as education do not completely reflect reality, these are the single most important tax and expenditure elements in local government finance.

The Mathematical Model

Consider the households of an urbanized area with utility being a function of housing (x), publicly provided services (s), and a composite other good (z):

$$U_i = U_i(x_i, s_i, z_i) \tag{1}$$

where the subscript i refers to the income groups i, $i = 1, 2$. (The Appendix at the end of the paper presents all notation.) Households maximize utility subject to the following budget constraint:

$$y_i = p_x x_i + p_z z_i + p_{s_i} s^* + t_i u \tag{2}$$

where y is income, p_x the price per unit housing per year (similarly for p_z), p_{s_i} the price per unit public services for the respective income group, s^* the constrained level of public services, u the distance in miles to the CBD, and t_i the cost per mile per year for travel for income group i. In the central city, the two income groups are offered the same level of publicly provided services. Thus in the central city $s_1{}^c = s_2{}^c$ (superscript c represents central city). In the suburbs, where there is only a single income group, the level of services offered will be equal to that which is demanded, thus $(s^*)^s = s_2{}^s$ (superscript s represents suburbs).

The price per unit service differs among income groups in the city due to equal service provision to all households and financing the public service through the property tax. This difference is shown graphically in Figure 1.

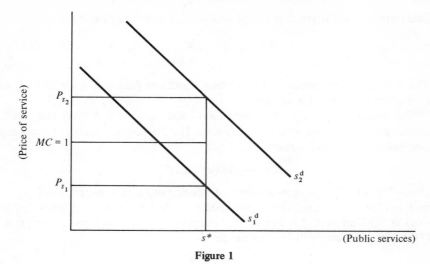

Figure 1

Letting the output of services be measured in dollar units we have a constant cost function with marginal cost 1. The demand functions are represented in Figure 1 by $s_1^{\,d}$ and $s_2^{\,d}$, the level of services provided by s^*. This may be viewed as group 2 paying p_{s_2} per unit while group 1 pays p_{s_1} per unit service.

The maximization of utility yields

$$\frac{U_{x_i}}{p_x} = \frac{U_{z_i}}{p_z} = \frac{U_s}{p_{s_i}},$$

and with respect to distance (u)

$$x_i \frac{dp_x}{du} + t_i + s^* \frac{dp_{s_i}}{du} = 0. \tag{3}$$

The unit price of services to a household is expenditure on services divided by services received. Expenditures are composed of property taxes levied at rate δ on housing expenditures $(p_x x)$. Thus, to the ith income group,

$$p_{s_i} = \frac{\delta p_x x_i}{s^*}. \tag{4}$$

Differentiating (4) with respect to distance we find

$$\frac{dp_{s_i}}{du} = \frac{\delta x_i}{s^*} \frac{dp_x}{du}. \tag{5}$$

Substituting into (3) yields the slope of the price of housing function,

$$\frac{dp_x}{du} \equiv p' = \frac{-t_i}{x_i(1+\delta)} < 0. \tag{6}$$

The only difference between this expression and one derived in a model without a property tax is the $(1+\delta)$ term.

   The model requires housing production and demand functions and public service production and demand equations. The housing production function is assumed to be Cobb–Douglas:

$$X^s(u) - AL(u)^\alpha K(u)^{1-\alpha} \tag{7}$$

where $X^s(u)$ is the aggregate amount of housing supplied at distance u, $L(u)$ the land available at u, $K(u)$ the capital used at u, and α the share of land. Define $R(u)$ as the land rent at u and $\bar{r}$ as the exogenous return to capital. Then, from (7) the marginal productivity expressions are

$$R(u) = \frac{X^s(u)\alpha p_x}{L(u)} \tag{8}$$

and

$$\bar{r} = \frac{X^s(u)(1-\alpha)p_x}{K(u)}. \tag{9}$$

Solving (8) and (9) for L and K and substituting into (7) we find

$$p_x = A^{-1} \left(\frac{\alpha}{R}\right)^{-\alpha} \left(\frac{1-\alpha}{r}\right)^{\alpha-1}. \tag{10}$$

Differentiating with respect to distance,

$$p' = A^{-1} R'(u) R(u)^{\alpha-1} \left(\frac{\bar{r}\alpha}{1-\alpha}\right)^{1-\alpha} \quad \text{where} \quad R' = \frac{dR}{du}. \tag{11}$$

The households' demand for housing is assumed to have the form

$$x_i^d(u) = By_i^{\theta_1} [p_x(1+\Gamma_i)]^{-1} \tag{12}$$

where θ_1 is the income elasticity of demand for housing, and Γ_i the net tax rate. This formulation assumes that the price elasticity is -1, corresponding to the empirical findings of Muth [16] and Reid [19] and contributing greatly to computational ease. As indicated in the introduction, the Tiebout world will not be found in a city with differing income groups. The suburban residents, denoted as income group 2, realize they are paying property taxes of $\delta p_x x_2$ as an expenditure for public services and not as a tax on housing. For them the net tax rate $\Gamma_2 = 0$, but for the city residents $\Gamma_i \neq 0$. The net tax rate in the city is not the same as the observed tax rate on housing because the city residents are receiving some services for their expenditures. The net tax rates will be determined endogenously as the solution proceeds.

Aggregate housing demand is specified by

$$X^d(u) = N_1(u)x_1{}^d(u) \qquad \text{if} \quad R_1(u) > R_2(u) \tag{13a}$$

$$X^d(u) = N_2(u)x_2{}^d(u) \qquad \text{if} \quad R_1(u) < R_2(u). \tag{13b}$$

That is, aggregate demand is the sum of household demands at a given distance. Which income lives at a specified distance is determined by land rent bids. $N_i(u)$ is the number of households of income group i at distance u.

Turning to the public services sector, in equilibrium, expenditures equal receipts for public services. Thus aggregate services provided S^* equals total tax revenues T. In the city,

$$S^* = T = \int_0^{u_0} \delta_c x_1{}^d(u) p_x(u) N_1(u)\, du + \int_{u_0}^{u_c} \delta_c x_2{}^d(u) p_x(u) N_2(u)\, du \tag{14a}$$

where δ_c is the observed tax rate in the city, u_0 the distance to the division between residents of income groups 1 and 2, and u_c the exogenously specified city limit. In the suburbs

$$S^* = T = \int_{u_c}^{\bar{u}} \delta_s x_2{}^d(u) p_x(u) N_2(u)\, du \tag{14b}$$

where δ_s is the observed tax rate in the suburbs, and $\bar{u}$ the edge of the urbanized area. Household demand for services is given by

$$s_i{}^d = C y_i^{\theta_3} p_{s_i}^{\theta_4} \tag{15}$$

where C is a constant, θ_3 the income elasticity of demand for services, and θ_4 the price elasticity of demand for services. In the suburbs, where only one income group is present, aggregate demand for services is the sum of household demands. This is represented by

$$S_2{}^d = \varphi \bar{N}_2 s_2{}^d \qquad \text{where} \quad \varphi \equiv N_2{}^s / \bar{N}_2 < 1. \tag{16}$$

That is, φ is the percentage of all of income group 2 that lives in the suburbs.

In the city, where more than one income group is present, the determination of aggregate public service demand is less obvious. The method chosen here will be to take the mean demand as representative. An alternative approach would be to take the median voter's quantity demanded as the level chosen. However, with only two income groups this would imply unrealistic results. Mean demand, moreover, allows a role for taking account of extreme demands consistent with side payment and logrolling models. The aggregate service demand in the city equals

$$S^{\mathrm{d}} = \bar{N}_1 s_1{}^{\mathrm{d}} + F_0 \bar{N}_2 s_2{}^{\mathrm{d}} \tag{17}$$

where F_0 is the percentage of all of income group 2 that resides in the city in final equilibrium.

The final equilibrium conditions of the model are

$$X^{\mathrm{s}} = X^{\mathrm{d}} \tag{18}$$

and

$$S^* = S^{\mathrm{d}} \tag{19}$$

The remaining equations complete the model by specifying land supply, agricultural rent, and total population. A circular city is assumed. Thus land supply is given by

$$L(u) = 2\pi u \, du. \tag{20}$$

The edge of the urbanized area is determined by agricultural rents $\bar{R}$:

$$R(u) = \bar{R}. \tag{21}$$

The total population of the urbanized area is $\bar{N}$, and the city–suburban boundary (u_{c}) is arbitrarily defined. Let $\bar{N}_i$ be the total number of households of income group i, $\bar{N}^{\mathrm{c}}$ the total number of households in the central city, and $\bar{N}^{\mathrm{s}}$ the total number of households in the suburbs. From the model, we have

$$\bar{N}^{\mathrm{c}} = \int_0^{u_0} N_1(u) \, du + \int_{u_0}^{u_{\mathrm{c}}} N_2(u) \, du, \tag{22}$$

$$\bar{N} = \bar{N}^{\mathrm{c}} + \int_{u_{\mathrm{c}}}^{\bar{u}} N_2(u) \, du. \tag{23}$$

For future notational convenience the following ratios are symbolized:

$$\Psi \equiv \bar{N}_1/\bar{N}_2, \tag{24}$$

$$\gamma \equiv y_1/y_2. \tag{25}$$

This completes the statement of the basic model. The method of solution will be to determine the land rent function, then demonstrate that the rich will comprise income group 2, that is, the group that lives in the suburbs and city fringe. Next, the population density function will be determined. Equilibrium conditions in the public service sector will be used to find the actual tax rates, net tax rates, and the burden to the city rich. The final step of solution involves determining the expansion of the urbanized area in response to an intraarea migration and the calculation of welfare costs.

Initially we find the gradient of the price of housing function, symbolized as p', by substituting (12) into (6):

$$p' = \frac{-t_i}{By_i^{\theta_1}[p_x(1 + \Gamma_i)]^{-1}(1 + \delta)}. \tag{26}$$

Next substitute in Eq (10) for p_x and equate (26) with (11); the result is

$$R'(u)R^{-1}(u)E_i^{-1} + t_i = 0 \tag{27}$$

where

$$E_i^{-1} = \alpha By_i^{\theta_1}\frac{(1 + \delta)}{(1 + \Gamma_i)}. \tag{28}$$

The solution of differential equation (27), using initial condition (21) and the fact that $R_1(u_0) = R_2(u_0)$, is

$$R_1(u) = \bar{R}\ \exp[t_2E_2(\bar{u} - u_0) + t_1E_1(u_0 - u)] \tag{29a}$$

$$R_2(u) = \bar{R}\ \exp[t_2E_2(\bar{u} - u)] \tag{29b}$$

where exp is the exponential function. These equations are shown graphically in Figure 2, where u_0 is the division between group 1 and 2, and it is assumed that u_c is chosen such that $u_c > u_0$, that is, initially some of each group lives in the city.

We now investigate if $y_1 \gtrless y_2$ given the rent functions in (29). At $u < u_0$, Figure 2 reveals that $R_1 > R_2$, therefore substituting in (29) and simplifying, we find $t_1E_1 > t_2E_2$.

Transportation costs may be broken down into fixed cost per mile (t_0), and a variable cost depending on income (t_yy_i). Assuming a constant marginal time cost of travel with respect to income, $t_{y_1} = t_{y_2}$, and substituting Eq. (28) for E,

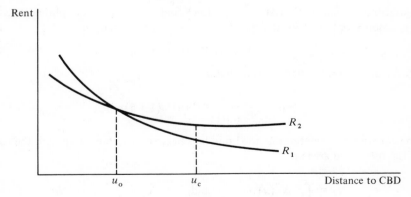

Figure 2

we have

$$\left[\frac{t_0}{y_1^{\theta_1}} + t_y\right](1 + \Gamma_1) > \left[\frac{t_0}{y_2^{\theta_1}} + t_y\right](1 + \Gamma_2).$$

If the income elasticity of demand for housing θ_1 is unity, the solution is $y_2 > y_1$. This is true because $y_2 > y_1$ implies $(1 + \Gamma_2) > (1 + \Gamma_1)$ since Γ_2 is a tax and positive while Γ_1 is a subsidy and negative. Therefore, one may drop the terms involving Γ and keep the inequality intact. The final simplification yields $y_2 > y_1$. In this case we have derived that the rich, who are group 2, will live outside of the poor. If $\theta_1 > 1$, again $y_2 > y_1$, but if $\theta_1 < 1$ the result depends upon parameters' values. With the knowledge of previous empirical estimates of $\theta_1 \geq 1$ (Muth [16], Reid [19]), we may then take it as true that the rich surround the poor in the urban area.

The equilibrium conditions in the housing market yield expressions for the spatial distribution of population and the limits of the urbanized area. From (8) and (9) we have

$$\frac{R}{r} = \frac{\alpha K}{L(1 - \alpha)}. \tag{30}$$

Solving (30) for K and substituting into (7) we derive

$$X^s(u) = AL(u)^\alpha \left[\frac{R(u)L(u)(1 - \alpha)}{r\alpha}\right]^{1-\alpha}. \tag{31}$$

On the demand side, substitute p_x from (10) into (12) and the resulting expression for x_i into (13). Thus

$$X^d(u) = N_i(u)By_i^{\theta_1} A\left(\frac{\alpha}{R}\right)^\alpha \left(\frac{1-\alpha}{r}\right)^{1-\alpha}(1 + \Gamma_i)^{-1}. \tag{32}$$

Equilibrium condition (18) equates (31) and (32). After simplification, an expression is obtained for the spatial distribution of population

$$N_i(u) = R_i(u)L(u)E_i(1 + \delta), \tag{33}$$

and by definition the density function is

$$D_i(u) = \frac{N_i(u)}{L(u)} = R_i(u)E_i(1 + \delta). \tag{34}$$

The equations that determine the boundary between income groups and the edge of the urbanized area are

$$\bar{N}_2 = \int_{u_0}^{\bar{u}} N_2(u)\, du \quad \text{and} \quad \bar{N}_1 = \int_0^{u_0} N_1(u)\, du. \tag{35}$$

These two equations along with (33), (29), and (28) form a simultaneous solution of u_0 and $\bar{u}$.

Thus far we have found the spatial distribution of the population. The solution of the model continues by considering the public service sector. In the suburbs, from (16), (15), and (4), services demanded are

$$S_2{}^d = \varphi \bar{N}_2 C y_2^{\theta_3} \left(\frac{\delta_s p_x x_2}{s^*} \right)^{\theta_4} \tag{36}$$

From (12), with price elasticity -1, housing expenditures are

$$p_x x_i = \frac{B y_i^{\theta_1}}{(1 + \Gamma_i)}. \tag{37}$$

Thus in the suburbs $p_x x_2 = B y_2^{\theta_1}$. On the supply side, from (14b) we have

$$S^* = T = \delta_s B y_2^{\theta_1} \int_{u_c}^{\bar{u}} N_2(u) \, du = \delta_s B y_2^{\theta_1} \varphi \bar{N}_2. \tag{38}$$

In equilibrium, (36) and (38) are equated, the result is an expression for the suburban tax rate:

$$\delta_s = \frac{C}{B} y_2^{\theta_3 - \theta_1}, \tag{39}$$

and a household's supply of public services:

$$s_s^* = C y_2^{\theta_3}. \tag{40}$$

Note that equation (39) implies that the tax rate will only rise as incomes rise if $\theta_3 > \theta_1$.

In the city, total taxes are the sum of those levied on the poor and the rich:

$$T = \frac{\delta_c B y_1^{\theta_1} \bar{N}_1}{(1 + \Gamma_1)} + \frac{\delta_c B y_2^{\theta_1}}{(1 + \Gamma_2)} \int_{u_0}^{u_c} N_2(u) \, du. \tag{41}$$

The number of rich initially in the city is $(1 - \varphi)\bar{N}_2$. Part of the simultaneous solution will be to specify the number of rich who move from city to suburbs. For expository convenience, this is symbolized as $\Omega \bar{N}_2$ where Ω is the variable to be determined. In equilibrium, the city will contain $(1 - \varphi - \Omega)\bar{N}_2$ residents of income group 2. Define

$$F_0 = 1 - \varphi - \Omega \tag{42}$$

$$F_1 = 1 - \varphi - \Omega + \Psi. \tag{43}$$

With the notation of (42), (43), (24) and (25), Eq (41) may be restated as

$$s_c^* = \frac{T}{\bar{N}_c} = \frac{\delta_c By_2^{\theta_1}}{F_1} \left[\frac{\gamma^{\theta_1}\Psi}{1+\Gamma_1} + \frac{F_0}{1+\Gamma_2} \right]. \tag{44}$$

On the demand side, services demanded may be expressed as

$$S^d = \bar{N}_1 s_1{}^d + F_0 \bar{N}_2 s_2{}^d.$$

Substituting Eq (15) for $s_i{}^d$ and (4) for p_{s_i} we have

$$S^d = \bar{N}_1 C y_1^{\theta_3} \left(\frac{\delta p_x x_1}{s^*} \right)^{\theta_4} + \bar{N}_2 F_0 C y_2^{\theta_3} \left(\frac{\delta p_x x_2}{s^*} \right)^{\theta_4}. \tag{45}$$

The equilibrium condition yields an expression for the city's tax rate similar to the suburban case:

$$\delta_c = \frac{C}{B} y_2^{\theta_3-\theta_1} \left[\frac{\gamma^{\theta_1}\psi}{1+\Gamma_1} + \frac{F_0}{1+\Gamma_2} \right]^{-(1+\theta_4)} \left[\frac{\psi\gamma^{\theta_3}(\gamma^{\theta_1}F_1(1+\Gamma_2))^{\theta_4} + F_0(F_1(1+\Gamma_1))^{\theta_4}}{(1+\Gamma_1)^{\theta_4}(1+\Gamma_2)^{\theta_4}} \right]. \tag{46}$$

The result is similar to (39) with the addition of a multiplicative weighting term.

The observed tax rate in the city has been determined. The net tax rates may be found as follows. The "excess cost" of services per unit public service received is symbolized τ_i and defined to be

$$\tau_i = p_{s_i} - 1. \tag{47}$$

The net tax rate is defined to be the excess cost of public services per unit of housing expenditure, thus

$$\Gamma_i = \frac{\tau_i s^*}{(p_x x_i)^c}. \tag{48}$$

The city rich will pay a price for services (p_{s_2}) that is greater than the marginal cost of services as was shown in Figure 1. Thus $\tau_2 > 0$ and $\Gamma_2 > 0$, i.e., the rich are taxed. For the poor, $p_{s_i} < 1$, therefore $\tau_1 < 0$ and $\Gamma_1 < 0$, the poor are subsidized.

Substituting (47) and the value of p_{s_i} into (48) we have

$$\Gamma_i = \delta_c - \frac{s^*}{(p_x x_i)^c}. \tag{49}$$

If $s^* = C y_2^{\theta_3} = \delta_s By_2^{\theta_1}$ as in the suburbs, then substituting this value of s^* into (49) we have $\Gamma_2 = 0$. This confirms that the model predicts there is no net tax in the suburbs and the Tiebout model holds.

We now have three equations, (46) and (49) for $i = 1, 2$ expressing the equilibrium values of δ_c, Γ_1, and Γ_2, but there is another unknown (Ω) which appears as F_0 and F_1. To get another equation we must solve for the equilibrium number of rich who migrate from the city.

To determine the final equilibrium condition, we must find the "burden" of the rich who remain in the city. Clearly, some will move out if one considers the rich on either side of the boundary u_c. On the suburban side households receive in services what they demand paying marginal cost. On the central city side, the rich households pay a price for services in excess of marginal cost and perceive a tax on housing. Thus there is an incentive for city rich to move, the offsetting cost being higher transportation costs incurred or a change in rents. We will first specify the magnitude of the burden and then develop an expression for the equilibrium condition.

The burden to the rich consists of two parts. The first is the private welfare cost of the loss in housing services due to the net tax Γ_2. The second is the loss related to the consumption and taxation of the public good. The traditional consumer surplus triangle is lost due to the housing tax since consumption is reduced. A similar statement may be made concerning a triangle loss related to the consumption of services. The major portion of the burden is created by the public service consumption constraint in the city since the rich will receive only s^* units of services but pay taxes on their total housing consumption. Algebraically, the burden may be expressed as the difference between actual taxes and services received and the welfare cost triangles of services and housing. In computing the losses the assumption was made that service supply was perfectly elastic. It was assumed that the elasticity of housing supply (ϵ) was composed of a perfectly elastic supply of capital and inelastic supply of land. With the Cobb–Douglas form of production, a standard result is that $\epsilon = (1 - \alpha)/\alpha$ where α is share of land. The forms of the welfare losses are variants of the usual $\frac{1}{2}T\,\Delta x$ in elasticity form. The burden (β) is expressed by

$$\beta = \frac{\delta_c p_x x_2}{1 + \Gamma_2} - s_c^* - \tfrac{1}{2}(\tau_2)^2 p_{s_2} s_2 \theta_4 - \tfrac{1}{2}(\Gamma_2)^2 p_x x_2 \left[\frac{\theta_2 \epsilon}{\epsilon - \theta_2} \right]. \qquad (50)$$

The final equilibrium condition depends on what assumptions are made concerning immigration to the city. There are two extremes that may be considered. The first is that no immigration will occur as the rich leave the central city for the suburbs. This implies that rents in the central city will fall and u_0 will become larger as the poor expand from the CBD. In this case the burden to the migrating rich would be offset by increased transportation costs and rent in the suburbs plus the decrease in land rent in the central city.

An alternative method is to assume there is immigration to the central city. Since this model does not specify why there is more than one income group, the proportion of rich and poor that immigrate is arbitrary. The assumption that is the easiest to work with would be to assume that only the rich immigrate. There are two implications of this assumption. The first is that in equilibrium the burden to the city rich will equal the increased transportation costs of those who migrated to the suburbs. The second is that the burden will not change in the city because the number of rich in the city is fixed by assumption. This formulation does miss the aspect of a cumulative movement of the rich out of the central city, but it will be dealt with due to its relative ease of manipulation. This assumption will lead to a higher estimate of migration and a larger welfare cost than the previously mentioned alternative. Graphically, the urbanized area expands from $\bar{u}$ to $\bar{u} + \Delta u$ (Figure 3). Equilibrium will occur when the burden of living in the city per household β is equal to the increase in transportation cost $t_2 \, \Delta u$. Thus we have

$$\beta = t_2 \, \Delta u. \tag{51}$$

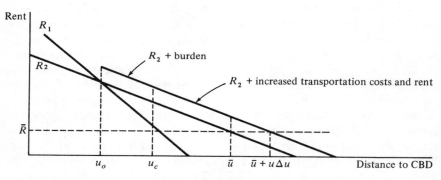

Figure 3

Two topics of interest remain to be discussed. They are the number of city residents that migrate to the suburbs and the welfare cost of the property tax in final equilibrium. The total population that migrates to the suburbs may be found as follows. The city expands by a distance of Δu past the original edge of the urbanized area $\bar{u}$. As shown in Figure 3, the land rent function, hence population density rises in the area from $\bar{u}$ to $\bar{u} + \Delta u$. Also the area of land in a ring of width Δu rises proportionately as the distance from city center increases. The total migration (M) is expressed as

$$M = \left[\int_{\bar{u}-\Delta u}^{\bar{u}} N_2(u) \, du \right] \frac{\pi[(\bar{u} + \Delta u)^2 - \bar{u}^2]}{\pi[\bar{u}^2 - (\bar{u} - \Delta u)^2]}. \tag{52}$$

From Eqs (33), (28), and (29) and the completion of the integration we find that migration is

$$M = \frac{2\pi\bar{R}(1+\delta s)}{(t_2)^2 E_2} \left[(\exp(t_2 E_2 \Delta u) \cdot (t_2 E_2(\bar{u} - \Delta u) + 1)) \right.$$

$$\left. - (t_2 E_2 \bar{u} + 1) \right] \left[\frac{(\bar{u} + \Delta u)^2 - \bar{u}^2}{\bar{u}^2 - (\bar{u} - \Delta u)^2} \right]. \tag{53}$$

The average change in distance traveled may be estimated from computation of the distance from city center in the original location within u_c and the final location outside of $\bar{u}$.

The next topic considers the measurement of social welfare costs. This involves resource allocation distortions in the provision of the public service, in the consumption of housing, and in additional transportation costs incurred in final equilibrium. The algebraic representation of the welfare cost triangles and transportation costs is

$$WC = N_2{}^c \left[-\tfrac{1}{2}(\tau_2)^2 p_{s_2} s_2 \theta_4 - \tfrac{1}{2}(\Gamma_2)^2 p_x x_2 \left(\frac{\theta_2 \epsilon}{\epsilon - \theta_2} \right) \right]$$

$$+ \bar{N}_1 \left[\tfrac{1}{2}(\tau_1)^2 p_{s_1} s_1 \theta_4 - \tfrac{1}{2}(\Gamma_1)^2 p_x s_1 \left(\frac{\theta_2 \epsilon}{\epsilon - \theta_2} \right) \right] + t_2 M \, (\Delta \text{ Distance}).$$

$$\tag{54}$$

The theoretical model has now been completed. The equations of the simultaneous solution have been derived, and welfare costs can be measured. The next section considers empirical estimates of the model's solution.

III. EMPIRICAL RESULTS

To obtain a numerical solution to the model, 1970 census data were gathered for Chicago and its suburbs (sources used were [7–10, 13, and 14]). Estimates of the income elasticity of housing and services were made using the functional forms assumed in the model. The number of suburban households in the urbanized area is $N_2{}^s = 1,020,000$. To fit an income distribution into two groups, the city population was divided equally; and the mean income of each group was chosen. The incomes and various other parameter values are as follows:

$N_2{}^c = 578,000$	$y_1{}^c = 3900$	$y_2{}^s = 15,600$
$N_1{}^c = 578,000$	$y_2{}^c = 15,600$	$F_0 = .362$
$\varphi = .638$	$\gamma = .251$	$F_1 = .724$
$\Psi = .362$	$\epsilon = 5.67.$	

The residential density function (34) may be expanded to the form

$$\log D_2(u) = [\log(\bar{R}E_2(1+\delta)) + t_2 E_2 \bar{u}] - (t_2 E_2)u \qquad (55)$$

and be used to generate estimates of travel costs.

A regression of average house values for suburban communities on income yields an estimate of the income elasticity of demand for housing. Other factors that were not considered in the model were included as independent variables, examples being median age, size of household, percent of aged heads, and age of dwelling unit. The regression form (56) is derived from Eq. (37),

$$\log(p_2 x_2) = \log B + \theta_1 \log y_2. \qquad (56)$$

From a third regression the value of the income elasticity of demand for services may be found. Equation (39) transformed into logs is

$$\log(\delta_s) = \log\left(\frac{C}{B}\right) + (\theta_3 - \theta_1)\log y_2. \qquad (57)$$

The coefficient of income will yield an estimate of θ_3 since θ_1 was found in (56). Other factors to be held constant include median age of a community, average number of years of parental education (Ed), percentage of children in private schools (Pr), household size, and the percentage of heads of households over 55 years of age (assumed to have no elementary age school children). Elementary school tax rates were used due to the closer correspondence of elementary than secondary school districts to municipal boundaries.

The best estimate of Eq. (56) was

$$\log(p_2 x_2) = -2.07 + 1.05 \log y_2$$
$$(.5)(20.2) R^2 = .83.$$

(The figures in parentheses are t-statistics.) Thus the income elasticity for housing is estimated to be 1.05. The estimate of Eq. (57) was

$$\log(\delta_s) = -3.41 + .05 \log y_2 - .34 \log(\text{age})$$
$$(-1.35)(.42)(-3.06)$$
$$ + 1.11 \log(Ed) - .06 \log(Pr)$$
$$(3.17)(-1.39) R^2 = .44.$$

Since the coefficient of y_2 ($= \theta_3 - \theta_1$) is not significantly different from 0, we find $\theta_3 = \theta_1$. From this information the undistorted values of housing consumption and the suburban tax rate may be calculated as $p_x x_1 = 745$, $p_x x_2 = 3070$, and $\delta_s = .243$. Also, the undistorted values of public service consumption are derived to be $p_s s_2 = 747$ and $p_s s_1 = 175$.

To find a numerical solution, (46) and (49) are solved simultaneously for δ_c, Γ_1, and Γ_2. Equation (44) may then be used to determine $s_c{}^*$, the level of public services in the city. From (37), housing consumption levels may be found and the tax rates on education derived from (47). The density regression indicated $t_2 E_2 = .18$, and from (28) the value of E_2^{-1} is determined. The estimate of travel costs (t_2) may then be determined. (The average value was 94 corresponding to a value of time equal to 40% of the wage rate at 30 mph and 10¢ per mile fixed cost.) The burden to the rich and the expansion of the suburbs are then determined. A slight modification is made to allow for Chicago's semicircular shape. Given the observed radius of 28.5 miles for the urbanized area, the relative expansion, migration, and welfare costs are found.

The results for a number of possible cases are presented in Tables 1 and 2. Table 1 presents results under the assumption that the price elasticity of demand for public services is -1; Table 2 presents the case where the price elasticity is $-.36$ (see Barlow [2] and Bradford and Oates [4]). Columns 1–3 present the results for the city–suburban form of government; columns 4–6 present those of the metropolitan form for comparison. The assumptions employed in deriving columns 1 and 4 are that the central city residents perceive a partial tax on housing and fully pay the tax. Columns 2 and 5 are based on the assumption that the tax on housing is passed fully to the landowner and does not distort housing consumption at any location in the urbanized area. Columns 3 and 6 assume that the full distortion based on the observed tax rate occurs.

In the comparison of metropolitan and central city–suburban governments, certain statistics best summarize the results. In row 9, the level of provision of public services to central city residents rises by at least a valuation of $100 in the metro government. The metro government lowers welfare cost per household due to the elimination of the transportation cost component, but the increased number of households subject to distortions in consumption offsets that effect to some extent. The net effect is to lower welfare cost per household (row 27) by amounts of $94–112 ($\theta_4 = -1$), or $55–60 ($\theta_4 = -.36$). The total amount of transfer payments in kind, valued at marginal cost, per receiving household increases under the metro form by $107–135. Finally, the collection cost of transfer payments (welfare cost per dollar transfer payment, row 28) falls in the metro government by at least 28% and possibly up to 90% under the various assumptions. Thus the conclusion of the empirical work is that the welfare costs associated with the fiscal externality are significantly reduced by a metropolitan form of government.

This conclusion has to be taken within the context of the assumptions of the model. For example, the welfare cost generated by incremental commuting costs was an upper limit, this biases the result in favor of the metro government. Commercial and industrial property were not included in the formulation and since the central city is relatively more industrialized, the burden to the rich would be smaller than estimated here. This would reduce the expansion of the suburbs, cut the incremental commuting costs, and again bias the result against the city–suburban form of government. As a final note concerning the general

TABLE 1
$(\theta_4 = 1)^a$

	(1)	(2)	(3)	(4)	(5)	(6)	Row
	Central city–suburban			Metropolitan government			
	Net tax	No distortion	Full distortion	Net tax	No distortion	Full distortion	
δ_s	0.243	0.243	0.243	–	–	–	1
δ_c	0.223	0.243	0.321	0.227	0.243	0.321	2
$P_x x_1$	745	745	745	745	745	745	3
$P_x x_2$	3070	3070	3070	3070	3070	3070	4
$(p_x x_1)^c$	975	745	564	1088	745	564	5
$(p_x x_2)^c$	2856	3070	2324	2986	3070	2324	6
$p_s s_1$	175	175	175	175	175	175	7
$p_s s_2$	747	747	747	747	747	747	8
s^*_c	423	460	460	561	594	594	9
Γ_1	-0.236	0	0.321	-0.315	0	0.321	10
Γ_2	0.075	0	0.321	0.028	0	0.321	11
τ_1	-0.545	-0.606	-0.606	-0.611	-0.695	-0.695	12
τ_2	0.507	0.622	0.622	0.149	0.256	0.256	13

β	318	431	565	—	—	—	14
Δu	3.3	4.2	6.8	0	0	0	15
$\Delta u/\bar{u}$	13.1%	17.3%	31.3%	0	0	0	16
M (m)	0.132	0.166	0.410	0	0	0	17
$WC(M)$ (m)	126	171	340	52	64	296	18
$WC(\Delta)$ (m)	117	102	199	52	64	296	19
Total WC (m)	243	273	539	0	0	0	20
$WC(M)/WC$	52%	63%	63%				21
TP (m)	119	161	161	181	239	239	22
CC	2.04	1.70	3.35	0.29	0.27	1.24	23
Total HH (m)	2.17	2.17	2.17	2.17	2.17	2.17	24
WC/HH	118	126	248	24	29	136	25
percentage metro better than CC–S				80%	77%	45%	26
Amount metro better than CC–S				94	97	112	27
Collection							
percentage metro better				86%	84%	63%	28
Amount metro better				1.75	1.43	2.06	29
E_2^{-1}	532	572	460				30
t_2	95.8	103	82.9				31

^{a}(m), millions; WC, welfare cost; M, migration; HH, households; TP, transfer payments; CC, collection cost.

Donald R. Haurin and George S. Tolley

TABLE 2

$(\theta_4 = -0.36)^a$

	(1)	(2)	(3)	(4)	(5)	(6)	Row
	Central city–suburban			Metropolitan government			
	Net tax	No distortion	Full distortion	Net tax	No distortion	Full distortion	
δ_s	0.243	0.243	0.243	–	–	–	1
δ_c	0.247	0.231	0.298	0.228	0.236	0.307	2
$P_x\text{-}x_1$	745	745	745	745	745	745	3
$P_x\text{-}x_2$	3070	3070	3070	3070	3070	3070	4
$(p_x x_1)^c$	968	745	575	1080	745	570	5
$(p_x x_2)^c$	2829	3070	2365	2966	3070	2349	6
$p_s s_1$	175	175	175	175	175	175	7
$p_s s_2$	747	747	747	747	747	747	8
s^{*c}	462	438	435	560	577	574	9
Γ_1	-0.231	0	0.298	-0.310	0	0.307	10
Γ_2	0.085	0	0.298	0.350	0	0.307	11
τ_1	-0.484	-0.607	-0.610	-0.598	-0.695	-0.695	12
τ_2	0.520	0.619	0.620	0.185	0.256	0.256	13

							No.
β	283	323	438	—	—	—	14
Δu	3.0	3.1	5.3	0	0	0	15
$\Delta u/\bar{u}$	11.8%	12.2%	22.5%	0	0	0	16
M (m)	0.118	0.116	0.286	0	0	0	17
$WC(M)$ (m)	112	119	237	34	23	237	18
$WC(\Delta)$ (m)	41	37	120	34	23	237	19
Total WC (m)	153	156	357	0	0	0	20
$WC(M)/WC$	73%	76%	66%				21
TP (m)	119	154	154	181	231	231	22
CC	1.28	1.01	2.32	0.19	0.10	1.03	23
Total HH (m)	2.17	2.17	2.17	2.17	2.17	2.17	24
WC/HH	71	71	164	16	11	109	25
WC/HH							
percentage metro better than CC–S				77%	85%	34%	26
amount metro better than CC–S				55	60	55	27
CC							
percentage metro better				85%	90%	52%	28
amount metro better				1.09	0.91	1.29	29
E_2^{-1}	529	572	460				30
t_2	95.2	103	82.9				31

[a] (m), millions; WC, welfare cost; M, migration; HH, households; TP, transfer payments; CC, collection cost.

equilibrium nature of the model, if the initial equilibrium among cities is nonoptimal, that is, some cities are too large or too small, then we enter a second best situation. The result is that the expansion of a city for the reasons specified in this model may be a social gain, not a social cost. This fact would alter empirical results favoring a metropolitan government and the current fragmented system could then be the social welfare cost minimizing form of government. However, in this second best world, it is possible that the relatively smaller size of urbanized area found in a metro government would lead toward the optimal city size. The empirical results derived here should be viewed as the first step in formulating a policy statement concerning the welfare costs of fiscal externalities and the effect of the form of government upon these social costs.

IV. CONCLUSION

The task posed for this study was to explore the spatial and welfare implications of a fiscal externality in an urbanized area. A model was developed with a heterogeneous central city population and homogeneous suburbs. Property taxes were found to be an efficient means of raising revenue for public services in the suburbs but not in the city. A combination of a consumption constraint on public services and raising revenues via taxation led to a distortion in housing and public service consumption in the city. These distortions in addition to the net loss to the city rich due to the difference between taxes paid and public services received create the incentive to escape the city and migrate to the suburbs. Equilibrium is inherent within the model since commuting costs rise as continued migration occurs, the empirical estimate being an 18% expansion of the urbanized area. If an alternative method of financing local public services were used, such as lump sum taxes, the social cost resulting from the distortion in housing consumption would be eliminated but there would still be an incentive for migration. The institution of a metropolitan government would eliminate the cost created by increased commutation but not that resulting from distortions in housing and public services.

The empirical work found a reduced welfare cost per household and increased transfer payments in the metropolitan form of government relative to the fragmented city—suburban form. It was noted that the estimate of the burden to the rich in the city and the amount of migration to the suburbs was biased upward, thus biasing the result in favor of a metro government. Also, the results were stated in terms of an initially optimal distribution of city sizes. If such is not the case, results may differ in the second best world. A final judgment on the socially best form of urban government must incorporate the results found here, but also consider other factors such as economies of scale and public good spillovers.

APPENDIX NOTATION

α Land's share in Cobb—Douglas housing production function

L Land in square miles

R Rental of land

$\bar{R}$ Rental at edge of urbanized area

K Capital

$\bar{r}$ Rental of capital (exogenous)

x^d Household housing demand

X^d Aggregate housing demand

X^s Aggregate housing supply

s^d Household service demand

S^* Aggregate service supply

s^* Constrained level of public service supply (household)

z Composite other good

T Aggregate taxes

p_x Unit price of housing

p_z Unit price of composite good

p_s Unit price of services = 1

δ Observed tax rate

Γ_i Perceived tax rate of income group i

τ "Tax" on services

y Income per household

t_0 Fixed transportation cost per mile

t_y Time component of transport costs per mile, a function of income

$t = t_0 + t_y y$

u Distance to CBD in miles

u_0 Boundary between rich and poor $< u_c$

u_c Edge of central city

$\bar{u}$ Edge of urbanized area

Δu Derived expansion of suburban area

D Density

WC Welfare costs

M Migration

$\bar{N}_1$ Total number of households of income group 1

$\bar{N}_2$ Total number of households of income group 2

$\bar{N}_c$ Total number of households in central city

$\bar{N}_s$ Total number of households in suburbs

$\varphi = \bar{N}_s / \bar{N}_2$

$\Psi = \bar{N}_1 / \bar{N}_2$

$\gamma = y_1 / y_2$

$F_0 = 1 - \phi - \Omega$

$F_1 = 1 - \phi - \Omega + \Psi$

$\Omega \bar{N}_2$ Number of migrant households from city to suburbs

$E_i^{-1} = \alpha B y_i^{\theta_1}(1 + \delta_i)$

β Burden to the rich if they remain in the city

θ_1 Income elasticity of demand for housing

θ_2 Price elasticity of demand for housing, -1

θ_3 Income elasticity of demand for services

θ_4 Price elasticity of demand for services

REFERENCES

1. Alonso, W., *Location and Land Use*, Cambridge, Massachusetts: Harvard Univ. Press, 1964.

2. Barlow, R., "Efficiency Aspects of Local School Finance," *Journal of Political Economy*, September–October 1970, 78, 1028–1040.

3. Bradford, D., and H. Kelejian, "An Econometric Model of Flight to the Suburbs," *Journal of Political Economy*, May–June 1973, 81, 566–589.

4. Bradford, D., and W. Oates, "Suburban Exploitation of Central Cities and Governmental Structure," *Urban Institute Conference*, "Economic Policy and the Distribution of Benefits," Washington, D.C., March 1972.

5. Buchanan, J., and C. Goetz, "Efficiency Limits of Fiscal Mobility: An Assessment of the Tiebout Model," *Journal of Public Economics*, 1972, 1, 24–34.

6. Buchanan, J., and R. Wagner, "An Efficiency Basis for Federal Fiscal Equalization," in J. Margolis, ed., *The Analysis of Public Output*, National Bureau Conference Series No. 23, New York: Columbia Univ. Press, 1970, 139–158.

7. *1970 Census of Population, Detailed Characteristics*, PC(1)-D15, Illinois, U.S. Bureau of Census, Washington, D.C.: U.S. Govt. Printing Office, October 1972.

8. *1970 Census of Population, General Social and Economic Characteristics*, PC(1)-C15, Illinois, U.S. Bureau of Census, Washington, D.C.: U.S. Govt. Printing Office, April 1972.

9. *Chicagoland's Community Guide*, Chicago: Law Bulletin Publ. Co., 1968.

10. *Fifty-fifth Biennial Report of the Superintendent of Public Instruction of the State of Illinois*, Circular Series A, No. 175, Office of the Superintendent of Public Instruction, July 1972.

11. Flatters, F., V. Henderson, and P. Miezkowski, "Public Goods, Efficiency and Regional Fiscal Equalization," *Urban Economics Report #89*, Univ. of Chicago, 1973.

12. Hamilton, B., "Zoning and Property Taxation in a System of Local Governments," *Working Paper 1207-14*, The Urban Institute, October 1972.

13. *Illinois Property Tax Statistics*, 1970, Department of Local Government Affairs, Illinois, 1970.

14. *Illinois Public Schools, 1970 Assessed Valuations and 1971 Tax Rates*, Circular Series A, Nos. 292, 293, 299, Office of the Superintendent of Public Instruction, October 1971.

15. Mills, E., *Urban Economics*, Glenview, Illinois: Scott, Foresman, 1972.

16. Muth, R., "The Demand for Non-Farm Housing," in A. Harberger, ed., *The Demand for Durable Goods*, Chicago, Illinois: Univ. of Chicago Press, 1960, 29–96.

17. Muth, R., *Cities and Housing*, Chicago, Illinois: Univ. of Chicago Press, 1969.

18. Netzer, D., *Economics of the Property Tax*, Washington, D.C.: The Brookings Inst., 1966.

19. Reid, M., *Housing and Income*, Chicago, Illinois: Univ. of Chicago Press, 1962.

20. Rothenberg, J., "Strategic Interaction and Resource Allocation in Metropolitan Intergovernmental Relations," *American Economic Review*, May 1969, 59, 495–503.

21. Rothenberg, J., "The Impact of Local Government on Intrametropolitan Location," *Papers of the Regional Science Association*, 1970, 24, 47–81.

22. Rothenberg, J., "Local Decentralization and the Theory of Optimal Government," in J. Margolis, ed., *The Analysis of Public Output*, Nat. Bur. Conf. Ser. No. 23, New York: Columbia Univ. Press, 1970, 31–64.

23. Samuelson, P., "The Pure Theory of Public Expenditures," *Review of Economics and Statistics*, November 1954, 36, 387–389.

24. Smith, B., "Some Basic Principles of Optimum City Size," *Urban Economics Report #94*, Univ. of Chicago, 1972.

25. Tiebout, C., "A Pure Theory of Local Public Expenditures," *Journal of Political Economy*, October 1956, 64, 416–424.

26. Tolley, G., "Economic Policy Toward City Bigness," *Proceedings of Conference of the Committee on Urban Economics*, Cambridge, Massachusetts, 1969.
27. Tolley, G., "National Growth Policy and the Environmental Effects of Cities," *Proceedings of Conference of Regional Economic Research*, Washington, D.C.: Economic Development Administration, 1972.
28. Tolley, G., and D. Haurin, "The Rural Town and the Scale Question," *Proceedings of Western Agricultural Economics Association*, Logan, Utah, 1972.
29. Tolley, G., and B. Smith, "Fiscal Externalities and Unemployment in a Spatial System," *Urban Economics Report #91*, Univ. of Chicago, 1973.
30. Wingo, L., *Transportation and Urban Land*, Washington, D.C.: Resources for the Future, 1961.

Discussion

HUGH O. NOURSE

University of Missouri
St. Louis

Whereas most of the papers for this conference concentrated on the control and effects of external social costs occurring in private markets, the Haurin–Tolley paper concentrates on the external costs to some families of political decisions made in a large heterogeneous city compared to the lack of those costs in a homogeneous suburb. In effect the high income families living in the city pay taxes for public services, such as schools, that they would prefer at a different level given those prices (taxes). Because the variance among preferences in the large city is so great, high income families suffer an external cost for decisions that the median voter wants, but which they do not. As a result the higher income families find it economical to move to the suburbs to avoid these costs. When they do, however, they suffer the increased transportation costs of commutation to the city center. Thus, there is a limit to their migration. The model is used to explain the migration of high income families to the suburb and as a framework for estimating welfare costs for metropolitanwide government compared to central city–suburban government.

The existence of the externality cost of political decisions in a large heterogeneous area is granted, but I question the magnitude of the estimates and whether migration to the suburbs has been caused by this particular externality.

The authors admit that their estimates of the welfare cost to the rich in the city is high, and that the amount of migration is overestimated because they have assumed that continuous migration of rich to the central city will maintain the number of higher income families in the city. The assumption has been made to simplify the empirical estimates. There may be only three cities in the United States for which such an assumption may even come close: Chicago, Philadelphia, and New York. Fortunately, they are making estimates for Chicago. But I would be more comfortable with the assumption, even for Chicago, if the authors had made some empirical study of the incomes of migrants to the city. Furthermore, the estimate is used to show that the welfare costs of a metrowide government are less than that of the central city—suburban form of government. Since the bias is in favor of the proposition supported, there is no way to know if they are right. The better research design would be to make assumptions so they are biased against the metrowide government and then see which form of government the estimates favor. The case for metrowide government would be strong if the estimates still came out in favor of metrowide government.

More importantly, however, I suspect that fiscal externalities have little to do with internal migration within the metropolitan area, although they are certainly one element. My reason for arguing this is that population data on the spatial distribution within cities have shown that the population density gradient within the central city was falling long before the development of suburban governments in the post World War II period (see Institute for Urban and Regional Studies [3] and Mills [4]). That is, people left the inner ring and shifted to the outer ring within the central city from the 1880s to the present. The main reason given for this migration has been the reduction of transportation cost from home to work and the dispersion of employment centers. Furthermore, if high income families are the only ones who can afford to buy new, then they will be the ones occupying the fringe of the urbanized area. Once this fringe has moved past the original boundary of the central city, the arguments on fiscal externality easily explain why these citizens on the fringe outside the central city established suburban governments rather than allowing themselves to be annexed to the central city.

Although the basic urban land market model used by the authors has been favored in research and has usefully explained land value and population gradients, its use for other purposes may be questioned because many of its assumptions are contrary to fact. In recent years employment has dispersed from the central city, so that the explanations utilizing the journey to work costs are unreasonable. Rees and Schultz [5] in their Chicago labor market study discussed two possible models for the city. You could have all employment in the center, as in the traditional models, with residential areas surrounding, or you could fix housing in the center and have employment places scattered around the housing. In the former and traditional model, rents bear the cost of transportation. Rents on land are different in order to equalize welfare among workers because their journeys to work cost different amounts. In the latter model wages would be higher for those workers hired to travel to work at more distant locations. In reality, of course, the city is a mixture of both models. They found that the core city model was not consistent with the labor market structure in Chicago.

In fact Bailey [1] has developed a model that can be used as a basis for externalities in the housing market between families of different income levels without resort to the single center model of the city. Imagine the city divided into two housing markets: one for high income families and one for low income families. The distinction between high and low income depends upon the income necessary to purchase a new house. High income families have sufficient income to purchase new; low income families do not. Furthermore, high income families prefer to live among other families with the same income. Low income families prefer to live adjacent to high income families, perhaps because of proximity to better public services. Prices for housing on the boundary for high income families are discounted from the price within the area surrounded by high income families, while boundary prices for low income families carry a premium over houses surrounded by low income families. The internal prices for high and low income families depend upon demand relative to supply. In fact the price for high income families must be close to construction cost. For if it were higher, new housing would be built, forcing the price down. If there should be a shortage of housing for the low income families, prices in the interior of the low income area would rise, prices plus premium on the boundary with high income families would rise, and when prices plus premium were greater than the discounted prices for high income families on the boundary, houses would be shifted from high income families to low income families. Prices in the high income area would increase with the reduced supply encouraging new construction.

Although we have only briefly sketched the possibilities of the approach, it is easy to see that it would be useful for understanding the market impact of a wide variety of variables, such as building codes, zoning, demolition of older housing for poor, and racial prejudice, without making any assumption about the location of employment centers or the price gradient of land with respect to distance from the CBD (see Bish and Nourse [2]). This model more directly incorporates the externalities prevalent in the housing market than the Haurin—Tolley traditional model.

REFERENCES

1. Bailey, M. J., "Note on the Economics of Residential Zoning and Urban Renewal," *Land Economics*, August 1959, **35**, 288–292.

2. Bish, R. L., and H. O. Nourse, *Urban Economics and Policy Analysis*, New York: McGraw-Hill, 1975.
3. Institute for Urban and Regional Studies, *Urban Decay in St. Louis*, Springfield, Virginia: Nat. Informat. Serv., No. PB-290-947, 1972.
4. Mills, E. S., *Studies in the Structure of the Urban Economy*, Baltimore, Maryland: Johns Hopkins Univ. Press, 1972.
5. Rees, A., and G. Schultz, *Workers and Wages in Urban Labor Market*, Chicago, Illinois: Univ. of Chicago Press, 1970.

Externality Production Functions

EPHRAIM F. SUDIT

The Chase Manhattan Bank

DAVID K. WHITCOMB

Rutgers University
and
New York University

This paper presents a general framework for estimating externality production functions. We adopt as the abstract model of externality production the generalized joint supply model developed by Whitcomb [41] because it avoids the highly restrictive assumptions of the traditional strict joint supply model. We then consider the problems involved in empirical specification of alternative joint product models, depending on the nature of the joint production process and the availability of data on the possibilities of input allocation among salable commodities and externalities. Alternative statistical estimation techniques for multivariate models are reviewed in terms of their relative merits with regard to taking full account of the jointness in production and the stability of the estimates they produce.

Apart from estimation techniques, the issue of specification of proper functional forms is discussed in detail. It is shown that for joint product externality models "conventional" production function forms (such as Cobb–Douglas, CES, homothetic, and CRES) may be even more restrictive than in ordinary cases. Consequently, it is recommended that highly nonrestrictive forms (e.g. additive and multiplicative nonhomogeneous types) may be used. Most of these forms do not impose convexity; hence the realism of the convexity assumption which must be invoked in deriving an externality cost function can be tested.

I. THE THEORY OF EXTERNALITIES IN PRODUCTION

Most economists have specified externalities in such a way that the external effect on the recipient firm or consumer is a direct function of the producing firm's output of its salable commodity.[1] Whitcomb [41] shows that this implicitly assumes a strict joint product production function which may be appropriate for mutton and wool or beef and hides but does not adequately describe the production possibilities facing an externality producer. In other words, the traditional model implicitly assumes that producers can only alter externality levels by altering their outputs of desirable commodities in strict proportion; they cannot alter externality levels by varying modes of production or input mixes. This may condition public thinking to the conclusion that we can reduce various forms of pollution only at the price of a serious reduction in our standard of living. This may be true, but it should not be a built-in assumption. The traditional model may also result in incorrect taxes or subsidies and in the doubtful conclusion of Buchanan [6] that a tax on an imperfectly competitive producer of pollutants likely reduces rather than increases welfare.

Whitcomb's [41] generalized joint supply model explains on the one hand why we have a positive level of the externality in laissez-faire equilibrium, and on the other hand how we can alter the externality level in the most efficient manner.[2] It provides for the optional treatment of externalities as collective (public) goods: it is often true that the amount produced equals the amount received by each affected party. The generalized joint supply production function (in implicit form) is

$$F_r^1(q_r, X_r^1, v_r^1, z_r) = 0 \qquad (r = 1, \ldots, R; \quad n = 1, \ldots, N;$$

$$F_r^k(x_{rm}, v_r^k, z_r) = 0 \qquad k = 2, \ldots, K; \quad m = k - 1) \qquad (1)$$

$$v_{rn} = \sum_{k=1}^{K} v_{rn}^k$$

---

[1] See Meade [24], Bator [4], Henderson and Quandt [18, chapter 7], Buchanan and Stubblebine [7], Davis and Whinston [13, 14], Wellisz [40], Dolbear [15], Ayres and Kneese [3], Buchanan [6], Shapley and Shubik [31], and Mishan [26]. Coase [10], Turvey [35], and Mishan [25] do not use explicit cost or production functions. Meade [24] gives a production function and Buchanan [5] a cost function which do not imply the model above.

[2] This model (as well as the efficiency conditions derived using it) is not restricted to any particular market form, such as perfect competition. It should be noted, though, that when any externalities model is applied to the case of perfect competition, we must assume some firms would earn economic rent were external diseconomies not imposed on them. Wellisz [40] has shown that without rent on resources supplied by the owners of a firm, the introduction of external diseconomies would simply result in resources switching to other uses (or locations) in long-run equilibrium. This costless transfer or resources would be socially desirable since there is always a cost to reducing the externality. With rent, laissez-faire "equilibrium" may result in Pareto inefficient externality levels.

where

$q_r = (q_{r1}, \ldots, q_{rL})$, a vector of salable outputs of firm r.

$X_r^{\ 1} = (x_{sm}^r)_{s,m}$ $(s = 1, \ldots, R, \neq r; m = 1, \ldots, M)$, an $(R - 1)$ by M matrix of externalities *received* by firm r. Externalities produced by r do not appear in $F_r^{\ 1}$. x_{sm}^r is the amount of externality type m produced by s.

x_{rm} is an externality produced by firm r. If x_{rm} has the character of a collective good, the amount received by each firm will be x_{rm} ($x_{rm}^s = x_{rm}^s \mid s = 1, \ldots, R \neq r$). If x_{rm} is a private good, the amount produced will equal the sum of the amounts received by all firms ($x_{rm} = \sum_{s=1}^{R \neq r} x_{rm}^s$).

$v_r^{\ k} = (v_{r1}^k, \ldots, v_{rN}^k)$, a vector of ordinary inputs to equation k of firm r's production set.

$z_r = (z_{r1}, \ldots, z_{rp})$, a vector of joint inputs appearing in all equations of firm r's production set.

In this model, we assume for simplicity that the production of several salable outputs can be described in a single equation.[3] Externalities received by a firm are treated as inputs ("negative inputs" if they are diseconomies) to the process that produces the salable outputs. Externalities are produced by the firm as by-products; that is, positive levels are produced in laissez-faire equilibrium where the externality "price" is zero. Ordinary inputs, which can be allocated among the K equations of the production set, cannot explain this by-product relationship; why reduce salable output levels by allocating scarce inputs to any of the equations $2, \ldots, K$ which describe production of a valueless output?[4]

Joint inputs explain the production of an externality. We require a separate equation for each externality with the same input quantity appearing in an externality equation ($k \geqslant 2$) and in a salable output equation ($k = 1$) so as to make it impossible to eliminate the externality and save money at the same time by diverting inputs from externality to salable output production. To be concrete, say joint input v_{rp} is a grade of oil with high sulfur content. It is used to produce electricity (because it is cheap) and produces smoke as a by-product. The amount used in producing electricity is automatically "allocated" to producing smoke; hence the same amount appears in both equations. If the firm wishes (or is forced) to produce less sulfurous smoke, it can substitute a different type of oil or allocate some ordinary input to clean the sulfur out of the smoke. The present notation conveys these possibilities.[5,6]

---

[3] If the salable commodities are produced in several distinct production processes, a multiple equation model would be preferred (see Danø [12, Chapter 10], for example). We are concerned here with the production of externalities and shall avoid this issue.

[4] Allocation of ordinary inputs to these equations is provided for here only because it may become efficient when the government regulates externality production by fiat or by taxes/subsidies.

[5] If the nature of the joint production process is such that none of any input, or portions thereof, can be allocated separately to any one output, a joint production function of the type $F(q_r, X_r, z_r) = 0$ would result. It may be doubted theoretically whether separate

When production function (1) is assumed to be strictly convex, the following propositions can be proved using it (see Whitcomb [41]). (a) By constrained cost minimization subject to (1) and constant input prices, a set of minimum cost input combinations can be found for each level of the salable outputs and externalities, and the cost of these efficient input combinations can be written as a function of the output and externality levels

$$C_r = C_r(q_r, X_r) \tag{2}$$

where q_r is a vector of output levels and X_r is a matrix of externalities received and or produced by r. This cost function allows externality levels to be varied independently of salable outputs by varying cost. (b) By maximizing total output of one commodity subject to constant levels of all other salable commodities and inputs, production sector Pareto efficiency conditions can be derived. When externalities have a collective good character, the marginal social cost (units of ordinary or joint inputs) of producing one more (less) unit of the external economy (diseconomy) must equal (minus) the *sum* of the marginal rates of substitution between the input and the collective good for all firms consuming both in their production process. These conditions are analogous to those derived for pure collective goods by Samuelson [30] and for externalities (using community transformation functions or traditional production functions) by Buchanan and Stubblebine [7], Buchanan [5], and Mishan [25]. (c) When externalities affect only a perfectly competitive production sector, the conventional optimization rule "maximize combined profit" satisfies the Pareto efficiency conditions.

II. FRAMEWORK FOR ESTIMATION OF EXTERNALITY PRODUCTION FUNCTION SPECIFICATION OF THE GENERALIZED JOINT PRODUCTION MODEL FOR EMPIRICAL ESTIMATION

Consider, for the sake of simplicity, a single firm producing a quantity q of a single salable output as well as a quantity x of a single externality. Input v_1 is used jointly for the production of q and x, and is not allocable between the

---

allocation can be impossible for all inputs, but it may be difficult in some cases to determine empirically the allocation possibilities, so we shall explore this function further in Section II.

[6] Many of the variables may have zero levels in particular equations or in firm r's entire production set: some salable commodity or externality types may not be produced by r; a zero amount of ordinary input n may be allocated to any one or all the equations; the level of the joint input may be zero in a particular equation (e.g., the amount of sulfurous fuel oil does not affect electrical utility noise level).

production of the salable commodity and the externality. Input v_2 *is* allocable with quantity v_{21} used in the production of q, and v_{22} used in the production of x. Assuming that the firm under consideration does not receive externalities from other firms, the generalized joint product model in (1), stated explicitly, takes the form

$$q = f_1(v_1, v_{21}), \qquad x = f_2(v_1, v_{22}). \tag{3}$$

(3) can be treated as an ordinary recursive model and estimated by applying ordinary least squares to each of the equations in (3) separately. If the firm under consideration were a strict profit maximizer in a laissez-faire economy (i.e., with no tax—subsidy provisions or societal pressure to modify behavior), we would always *observe* $v_{22} = 0$. Consequently, we would be able to estimate f_2 only by obtaining engineering estimates. However, most actual observations, particularly from recent years, will reflect the response of firms to legislative and societal pressure, enabling us to estimate f_2 from actual data.

In case *all* of the firm's inputs are applied jointly to the production of the salable commodity and the externality the generalized joint product model must take the form

$$F(q, x, v_1, v_2) = 0. \tag{4}$$

For empirical purposes, (4) should be specified in lieu of (3) only if (a) the nature of the production process is such that no significant portion of any input can be meaningfully allocated to the production of a specific output,[7] or (b) the empirical data for a meaningful allocation are not obtainable. Otherwise, empirically at least,[8] (3) is preferable to (4) in the context of the single salable commodity, single externality model since it does not call for multivariate estimation techniques. A suitable estimation method for the (4) type of multioutput joint production specification is canonical correlation originally due to Hotelling [21]. If stable estimates of the parameters are obtained by this method, they should reflect the jointness of the production process.

When the firm under consideration produces more than one output and one externality, multivariate estimation techniques have to be applied to the generalized joint product model (3). The canonical correlation technique recommended for (4) may be considered. However, the more variables are involved the greater the chance that some of them will be highly intercorrelated, particularly if time series data are tested. A high degree of multicollinearity may cause the canonical correlation estimates to be highly unstable and unreliable.

---

[7] In reality few production processes fit into this category; possibly, the case of the production of wool and mutton is an appropriate example (see Vinod [37]).

[8] Theoretically, there seem to be no a priori grounds for preferring (3) over (4). Both allow for variations in the externality levels via changes in the input mix. Likewise, both allow for positively sloped transformation curves.

To alleviate this problem, Vinod [38, 39] has recently suggested the integration of the ridge regression method due to Hoerl and Kennard [19, 20] into a "canonical ridge" model. The canonical ridge method takes full account of the jointness of the production via canonical correlation, and at the same time, reduces the ill effects of multicollinearity by the incorporation of ridge regression.

If canonical correlation estimates are not satisfactory in terms of economic plausibility and statistical quality and stability, estimation of (4) via input requirements functions may be considered.[9] For simplicity of illustration assume a Cobb—Douglas specification of (4) of the type

$$a_1 \ln v_1 + a_2 \ln v_2 = b_1 \ln q + b_2 \ln x. \tag{5}$$

Consequently, the input requirements functions are

$$
\begin{aligned}
v_1 &= \frac{b_1}{a_1} \ln q + \frac{b_2}{a_1} \ln x - \frac{a_2}{a_1} \ln v_2 \\
v_2 &= \frac{b_1}{a_2} \ln q + \frac{b_2}{a_2} \ln x - \frac{a_1}{a_2} \ln v_1.
\end{aligned}
\tag{6}
$$

Two stage or three stage least squares can be applied to (6). The estimate of the coefficient of $\ln v_1$ should not significantly differ from the inverse of the estimate of the coefficient of $\ln v_2$. Statistical tests of the significance of the difference between the two provide an important check on the stability of the results. Given the estimates in (6), the parameter equations can be solved for the parameters in (5). Although the results produced by the estimation via input requirements functions may at times be more stable than canonical correlation findings, it should be remembered that the latter estimation method takes full account of the jointness in production whereas the former does not.

In the present framework the traditional model, stated explicitly, takes the form

$$q = k_1(v_1, v_{21} + v_{22}), \qquad x = k_2(q). \tag{7}$$

System (7) can be estimated by application of two stage least squares. The restrictiveness of (7) in not allowing for the possibility of varying x through changes in production techniques — the v_1, v_2 mix — should be reflected in the economic and statistical quality of the findings.

Specification of the Appropriate Production Function Forms

When externalities are among the outputs of the production processes, some of the conventional properties and restrictions on the functional form do not necessarily apply on a priori theoretical grounds. This should be taken into account in the specification. To illustrate this point, consider a firm operating in

---

[9] For a similar approach in the estimation of ordinary production systems, see Mantell [23].

a laissez-faire economy and producing externality x. The marginal product of a certain input in producing x, say $\partial x/\partial v_1$, can be negative with the firm still operating in the economic region. This will be true because of the absence of a profit incentive to change the level of v_1. Numerous examples of such occurrences can be cited. For example, if the firm under consideration is emitting chemical wastes into a nearby stream, then v_1 may be a chemical that has a certain purifying side effect on the wastes. Increase in v_1 will thereby decrease the quantity of generated pollution x causing $\partial x/\partial v_1 < 0$. However, if the firm has reached the optimal level of v_1 input in the production of its salable commodity q, in the absence of a tax on x or some payment offer for the reduction of x, there will be no incentive for the firm to continue to increase v_1 so as to further decrease pollution. Thus $\partial x/\partial v_1$, being negative throughout, will remain negative in the economic region of production. By the same logic $\partial x/\partial v_1$, whether positive or negative, may exhibit increasing rather than diminishing returns, with the laissez-faire firm still in the economic region of production.

The above considerations will of course apply regardless of whether x is a negative or a positive externality, and are important to bear in mind in specification. Obviously, any functional specifications that a priori restrict the marginal products of inputs in producing externalities to nonnegative values or diminishing returns are unduly restrictive. Such specifications should be avoided by proper empirical analysis of externalities, unless justified by specific prior knowledge of the production processes involved. Likewise, it is doubtful whether it is proper to assume homogeneity of the production processes on a priori grounds. Homogeneity gives rise to disturbing implications concerning long-run equilibria with regard to ordinary products (see Sudit [33, 34]). In addition, it has been established empirically that production processes in industries where externalities are rampant such as electric utilities, paper, pulp, primary metals, and petrochemicals diverge from the homogeneous pattern (see Haldi and Whitcomb [17]). Thus, it is preferable, in the absence of additional information about the production process, to specify nonhomogeneous production functions, thereby also providing the estimates to test the degree of homogeneity of the process empirically.[10]

In view of the preceding considerations, one should be very cautious in specifying such common homogeneous forms as the Cobb—Douglas or the CES in the process of estimating externalities.

By the same rationale, assuming constant pairwise ratios between partial elasticities of factor substitution (CRES) is equally dubious (see Mukerji [27]).[11]

---

[10] See Vinod [36] and Sudit [33, 34]. Vinod's form, for example, permits testing the adequacy of the Cobb—Douglas form.

[11] Nonhomogeneous forms of the types proposed by Vinod [36] and Sudit [33, 34] can produce estimates of partial elasticity of factor substitutions for each observation. The degree of constancy of such series or their ratios can be examined by simple tests of significance.

It is therefore preferable in initial specification of joint product externality models to allow for nonconstrained variability in the elasticity of factor substitution. Once series of variable elasticities of factor substitution are empirically estimated, their degree of constancy or the degree of constancy in their ratios can be tested statistically.

Homothetic production forms (see Clemhout [9], Zelner and Revanker [42]) may also be considered undesirable for initial specification of the joint product externality models presented in this paper. The homothetic form imposes independence of the impact of variations in the scale of operations from the impact of variations in the input combinations. This precludes the possibility that greater ease in the substitution between certain inputs may decelerate the magnitude of returns to scale in the production of a negative externality or accelerate the magnitude of returns to scale in the production of a positive externality.

Several nonrestrictive production formulations have been recently proposed in production function literature. For example, Christensen, Jorgensen, and Lau's translog form [8], Vinod's [36] multiplicative nonhomogeneous form, and Sudit's [33, 34] additive nonhomogeneous form are bound neither by homogeneity nor by homotheticity and allow for variability of elasticities of factor substitution, negative marginal products, and increasing returns. To illustrate the point, application of the translog form to (4) gives

$$
\begin{aligned}
\ln(F + 1) = a_1 &+ a_2 \ln q + a_3 \ln x + a_4 \ln v_1 + a_5 \ln v_2 \\
&+ \ln q(\tfrac{1}{2}a_6 \ln q + a_7 \ln x + a_8 \ln v_1 + a_9 \ln v_2) \\
&+ \ln x(\tfrac{1}{2}a_8 \ln x + a_9 \ln v_1 + a_{10} \ln v_2) \\
&+ \ln v_1(\tfrac{1}{2}a_{11} \ln v_1 + a_{12} \ln v_2) \\
&+ \ln v_2(\tfrac{1}{2}a_{13} \ln v_2).
\end{aligned}
\tag{8}
$$

The advantages of (8) are that it can be shown to be a second order approximation to any arbitrary function, and that F-tests can be applied to test for more restrictive properties, such as homogeneity and constant elasticity of substitution. Estimation difficulties may however be encountered. Because of the large number of regressors, the data may not support statistically second order approximations.

Specifying Sudit's form to model (3) we obtain

$$
\begin{aligned}
q &= a_1 v_1 + a_2 v_{21} + a_3 v_1 \ln v_{21} + a_4 v_{21} \ln v_1 \\
x &= b_1 v_1 + v_2 v_{22} + b_3 v_1 \ln v_{22} + b_4 v_{22} \ln v_1.
\end{aligned}
\tag{9}
$$

Substituting v_1 in the x function into v_1 in the q function in (9), we get

$$q = a_1 \frac{(x - b_2 v_{22} - b_4 v_{22} \ln v_1)}{(b_1 + b_3 \ln v_{22})} + a_2 v_{21}$$

$$+ \frac{a_3 \ln v_{21}(x - b_2 v_{22} - b_4 v_{22} \ln v_1)}{(b_1 + b_3 \ln v_{22})} + a_4 v_{21} \ln v_1. \qquad (10)$$

Given a certain input mix $(\bar{v}_1, \bar{v}_{21}, \bar{v}_{22})$, the marginal rate of substitution between q and x is

$$\frac{\partial q}{\partial x_{(\bar{v}_1)}} = \frac{a_1 + a_3 \ln \bar{v}_{21}}{b_1 + b_3 \ln \bar{v}_{22}}. \qquad (11)$$

In conclusion, it seems to us that a generalized joint supply model offers a promising and theoretically sound empirical approach to the measurement of externality production. In the specification of the model and the choice of the functional forms, the analyst should be aware that the presence of externalities makes the need for less-restrictive formulations even greater than in the empirical analysis of ordinary production.

REFERENCES

1. Arrow, K. J., "The Organization of Economic Activity," in Joint Economic Committee, *Analysis and Evaluation of Public Expenditures: The PPB System*, Washington, D.C.: U.S. Govt. Printing Office, 1969, 47–64.
2, Arrow, K., H. B. Chenery, B. Minhas, and R. M. Solow, "Capital Labor Substitution and Economic Efficiency," *The Review of Economics and Statistics*, August 1961, **43**, 225–250.
3. Ayres, R. V., and A. V. Kneese, "Production, Consumption, and Externalities," *American Economic Review*, June 1969, **59**, 282–297.
4. Bator, F. M., "The Anatomy of Market Failure," *The Quarterly Journal of Economics*, August 1958, **72**, 351–379.
5. Buchanan, J. M., "Joint Supply, Externality, and Optimality," *Economica*, N.S., November 1966, **33**, 404–415.
6. Buchanan, J. M., "External Diseconomies, Corrective Taxes, and Market Structure," *American Economic Review*, March 1969, **59**, 174–177.
7. Buchanan, J. M., and W. C. Stubblebine, "Externality," *Economica N.S.*, November 1962, **29**, 371–384.
8. Christensen, L. R., D. W. Jorgensen, and L. J. Lau, "Transcendental Logarithmic Production Frontiers," *Review of Economics and Statistics*, February 1973, **55**, 28–45.
9. Clemhout, S., "The Class of Homothetic Isoquant Production Functions," *Review of Economic Studies*, January 1968, **35**, 91–104.
10. Coase, R. H., "The Problem of Social Cost," *Journal of Law and Economics*, October 1960, **3**, 1–44.
11. Cobb, C., and H. Douglas, "A Theory of Production," *American Economic Review*, March 1928, **18**, 139–165.

12. Danø, S., *Industrial Production Models – A Theoretical Study*, Vienna–New York: Kobenhavns Univ. Okonomiske Inst., Springer-Verlag, 1966.
13. Davis, O. A., and A. B. Whinston, "Externalities, Welfare, and the Theory of Games," *Journal of Political Economy*, June 1962, 70, 241–262.
14. Davis, O. A., and A. B. Whinston, "On Externalities, Information and the Government-Assisted Invisible Hand," *Economica N.S.*, August 1966, 33, 303–318.
15. Dolbear, F. T. Jr., "On the Theory of Optimum Externality," *American Economic Review*, March 1967, 57, 90–103.
16. Frisch, R., *Theory of Production*, Dordrecht: Reidel, 1965.
17. Haldi, J., and D. K. Whitcomb, "Economies of Scale in Industrial Plants," *Journal of Political Economy*, August 1967, 75, 373–385.
18. Henderson, J. M., and R. E. Quandt, *Microeconomic Theory – A Mathematical Approach*, New York: McGraw-Hill, 1958, 2nd ed., 1971.
19. Hoerl, A. E., and R. W. Kennard, "Ridge Regression: Biased Estimation for Non-orthogonal Problems," *Technometrics*, February 1970, 12, 55–67.
20. Hoerl, A. E., and R. W. Kennard, "Ridge Regression: Application to Nonorthogonal Problems," *Technometrics*, February 1970, 12, 69–82.
21. Hotteling, H., "Relations Between Two Sets of Variables," *Biometrika*, 1936, 28, 321–377.
22. Lange, O., "The Foundations of Welfare Economics," *Econometrica*, July–October 1942, 10, 215–228.
23. Mantell, L. H., *Returns to Scale in Bell System Long Lines*, Office of Telecommunications Policy, 1974.
24. Meade, J. E., "External Economies and Diseconomies in a Competitive Situation," *Economic Journal*, March 1952, 62, 54–67.
25. Mishan, E. J., "The Relationship Between Joint Products, Collective Goods, and External Effects," *Journal of Political Economy*, May–June 1969, 72, 329–348.
26. Mishan, E. J., "The Postwar Literature on Externalities: An Interpretative Essay," *Journal of Economic Literature*, March 1971, 9, 1–28.
27. Mukerji, J., "Generalized SMAC Function with Constant Ratios of Elasticities of Substitution," *Review of Economic Studies*, October 1963, 30, 233–236.
28. Pigou, A. C., *The Economics of Welfare*, New York: Macmillan, 4th ed., 1932, reprinted, 1952.
29. Ridker, R. G., *Economic Costs of Pollution: Studies in Measurement*, New York: Praeger, 1967.
30. Samuelson, P. A., "The Pure Theory of Public Expenditure," *Review of Economics and Statistics*, November 1954, 36, 387–389.
31. Shapley, L. S., and M. Shubik, "On the Core of an Economic System with Externalities," *American Economic Review*, September 1969, 59, 678–684.
32. Starrett, D. A., "Fundamental Nonconvexities in the Theory of Externalities," *Journal of Economic Theory*, April 1972, 4, 180–199.
33. Sudit, E. F., "Additive Non-homogeneous Production Functions in Telecommunications," *The Bell Journal of Economics and Management Science*, Autumn 1973, 4, 499–514.
34. Sudit, E. F., *New Types of Non-homogeneous Production Functions*, unpublished dissertation, New York Univ., October 1973.
35. Turvey, R., "On Divergences Between Social Cost and Private Cost," *Economica*, August 1963, 30, 309–313.
36. Vinod, H. D., "Nonhomogeneous Production Functions and Applications to Telecommunications," *The Bell Journal of Economics and Management Science*, Autumn 1972, 3, 531–543.

37. Vinod, H. D., "Econometrics of Joint Production," *Econometrica*, April 1968, **36**, 322–336.
38. Vinod, H. D., "Canonical Ridge and Econometrics of Joint Production," *Journal of Econometrics*, 4, 1976.
39. Vinod, H. D., "Application of New Ridge Regression Methods to A Study of Bell System Scale Economies," unpublished paper, 1974.
40. Wellisz, S., "On External Diseconomies and the Government-Assisted Invisible Hand," *Economica N.S.*, November 1974, **31**, 345–362.
41. Whitcomb, D. K., *Externalities and Welfare*, New York: Columbia Univ. Press, 1972.
42. Zelner, A., and N. S. Revankar, "Generalized Production Functions," *Review of Economic Studies*, April 1969, **36**, 241–250.

Discussion

CHARLES G. STALON
Southern Illinois University
Carbondale

Passing over the mind-boggling problem of defining and classifying "externalities" in favor of the simple assumption that whatever they are "externalities," or at least a subset of them, can be represented as objectively measurable, continuous variables generated via production functions that are twice differentiable, the authors present an externality production function that is capable of representing a much broader range of alternatives than production function concepts usually employed in economic analysis. The cost paid for this advance is the increased complexity of the new concept over the old.

The gains in analytical relevance seem to justify this cost for that subset of problems usually grouped under the heading "technological externalities." On the other hand, for that broad class of externalities which impinge on peoples' senses, such as beauty, ugliness, and malodors, which are presently nonquantifiable, the gains seem insignificant. Since those nonhuman conceptual entities we call "firms" do not have senses, the application to interfirm analysis seems to be the principal area of analytical application for the production function. Even here, however, there are important nonquantifiable externalities, such as worker discipline, morale, honesty, and education, which escape even this broad externalities production function.

Still, the authors have fairly stated their objectives and their assumptions and have competently displayed their results. My qualification and doubts should not detract from their contribution.

Index